Carl H

Carl Hubbell

A Biography of the Screwball King

LOWELL L. BLAISDELL

McFarland & Company, Inc., Publishers

Jefferson, North Carolina, and London

All photographs are courtesy of National Baseball Hall of Fame
Library, Cooperstown, N.Y.

LIBRARY OF CONGRESS CATALOGUING-IN-PUBLICATION DATA

Blaisdell, Lowell L.
    Carl Hubbell : a biography of the screwball king /
Lowell L. Blaisdell.
        p.   cm.
    Includes bibliographical references and index.

    ISBN 978-0-7864-4465-6
    softcover : 50# alkaline paper ∞

    1. Hubbell, Carl, 1903–1988.   2. Pitchers (Baseball)—
United States — Biography.   3. Baseball players — United
States — Biography.   4. New York Giants (Baseball team)—
History — 20th century.   I. Title.
GV865.H83B53   2011
796.357092 — dc22   [B]   2010023651

British Library cataloguing data are available

Front Cover: Carl Hubbell, 1929 © 2011 Arthur K. Miller,
www.artofthegame.com; background © 2011 Shutterstock

Manufactured in the United States of America

McFarland & Company, Inc., Publishers
  Box 611, Jefferson, North Carolina 28640
    www.mcfarlandpub.com

This book is in memory of my father, Lowell S. Blaisdell. He served in World War I as a front-line infantryman. Injured quite seriously in battle on July 4 and October 8, 1918, he received the Purple Heart. Throughout his service, he maintained an extensive diary. With the war's centennial not many years away, any scholar who might be interested in its contents can find it at the War Department's Carlyle, Pennsylvania, archives.

Some years later, my father had much to do with his son's turning, at mid-childhood, into a lifelong Chicago Cubs fan. In his youth, my father had developed just such an attachment at a time when the Cubs had won four pennants and two World Series. Thereafter, the team accomplished another six pennants, but lost in the World Series every time. All this transpired in the first forty-five years of its twentieth century existence. In the sixty-five years that followed, not once did another pennant, not to mention a World Series, ever come its way.

Acknowledgments

The author extends his deepest appreciation to those instrumental in enabling him to present Carl Hubbell's career and life to interested readers. In the publishing world, publishers' expectations and specifications have an importance comparable to the merits of a writer's submission. He needed a great deal of help to succeed in this realm.

In alphabetical order, the indispensables were Doris A. Blaisdell, Nancy Gorman, the late James Harper, Peggy Leeck, and Carol Wheeler-Liston. All were highly competent. One combined both a high level of typing skill with a thorough knowledge of publishing firms' procedures.

On a smaller scale, others also aided. Friendly next-door neighbors provided brief but direct help. At the Denton (Texas) primary museum, a fellow greeting partner offered timely advice. So, too, did a close friend, Paul Young of Norman, Oklahoma. Further, numerous academic and non-academic friends proffered their good wishes.

To each and every one of you, the best wishes always.

Lowell L. Blaisdell

Table of Contents

Preface

The following pages offer a biography of the late, great New York Giants hurler Carl Hubbell. Because Hubbell's most exciting accomplishments were what propelled him to fame, they receive the primary emphasis. Nonetheless, his overall career is explored. Hubbell's long life after his pitching career ended also is presented, but much more briefly.

Biographies of famous baseball twirlers are no rarity. However, none to date have had Hubbell as its subject. Why did this writer choose to focus upon him?

To begin to answer that question I must go back to my earliest years of adolescence. As a Chicago native, at the age of ten, I became a Cub loyalist, partly because my father also was. By the age of eleven, I had taken up box score perusal as a pastime.

July 3, 1933, being a Monday, I looked with alacrity at the box scores of the Sunday games. One absolutely astonished me. In the opener of a Polo Grounds double-header, the New York Giants had outlasted the St. Louis Cardinals in eighteen innings. Astonishment turned to disbelief when the box score showed the Giants had used a single pitcher, Carl Hubbell. How, I asked myself, could a team ask its hurler to last out the equivalent of two regular-length games?

When by the next day I learned there had been no misprint, it increased my interest in the New York southpaw. Before long, it went up further when I attended two games in which Hubbell pitched.

Each season unfailingly I would survey the Cubs' box score first, then turn to the Giants' one to see if Hubbell had pitched. By the close of the 1936 season, I, like many others, had decided the Giants lefty was a great hurler. Someone ought to do a biography of him, and soon.

To write the biography of a once-famous athlete involves the collection of a large amount of information. To start, I turned to the National Baseball Hall of Fame, Cooperstown, New York. The NBHF representatives provided Xeroxed copies of its Carl Hubbell data. It added up to enough material to offer an encouraging beginning. Next, a Google search of NBHF, Hall of Fame, Carl Hubbell, produced a long list of leads.

Thenceforth, I moved about to various mostly regional research-minded institutions. In Oklahoma, Hubbell's home state, were the Oklahoma State Historical Society, Oklahoma City, and the University of Oklahoma–Norman. Both were extremely helpful for their newspaper collections, the first state, the second national.

In Texas, the University of North Texas–Denton helped considerably as, on a lesser scale, did the University of Texas–Dallas and Southern Methodist University–Dallas.

In Washington, D.C., the Library of Congress newspaper collection was very helpful concerning one startling aspect of the Hubbell's minor league years, and in St. Louis, the primary public library aided via the availability of the city's two major newspapers.

Secondary sources also were combed. Biographies of players who were Hubbell's contemporaries contained references to him that often could be fitted in. Journal articles varied in merit. The better ones provided supplemental details as well. Ones in which the reporter had had an interview with the principal offered the most.

Since record books are not uniform, a number were used. Hubbell's season-long performances needed citation, as did his positions as a record qualifier on some aspects of hurling.

One aspect of my efforts brought me a smaller return than I orginally had hoped. Though Hubbell's remarkable pitching career could draw readers by itself, I felt that a focus broader than his pitching would add to its appeal. If Carl's personal side were included and developed, but kept as a minor chord, it would provide the additional breadth to add to the story.

Aware of Meeker's place in the Hubbell story, I drove to the town. The Hubbell Museum is *the* feature for any visitor. While there, I had in mind making contact with Hubbell descendants. However, the young people with whom I conversed, while aware, of course, of the name of Meeker's only celebrity, had no acquaintance with surviving relatives. A little later, I addressed a letter in which my aims were summarized to a museum representative, but it drew no response.

Another time, I visited the Lincoln County Historical Society at Chandler, north of Meeker. It houses the Carl Hubbell Collection. The Society provided me with no more than a copy of the service honoring Hubbell after his decease.

In Hubbell's day, a reporter, unless a player got caught up in a scandal, had little time in an interview or print space to learn much about a player's private life. This writer, coming along much later, too easily convinced himself that with time available and arduous efforts to expend, he could gather more about Hubbell than they had. With regard to one quite important matter alone, through sheer needle-in-a-haystack searching, I did succeed in nailing down some data I did not find anywhere else. Otherwise, however, I found only what the press had reported at the time in bits and pieces.

Chapter 1

Varieties of Farming

One of the most famous names in Oklahoma sports history is that of Carl Hubbell. Most Oklahomans', as well as many others', continued familiarity with the name stems entirely from his fame as a great baseball pitcher. Since he was inclined to be quite private about his personal life, aspects of Hubbell's life unrelated to his hurling have largely passed unnoticed or are difficult to trace.

In the pages that follow, the primary aim is to present the subject as fully and fairly as circumstances permit. The second objective is to provide insights into the nature of baseball in the 1920s and 1930s. The differences between the game in that day and the modern day are quite significant. The contrast can help enlighten a contemporary fan on how the National Pastime played out in the long ago.

Over the roughly 135 years of major league professional baseball, a great many outstanding pitchers have come and gone. Wherein lies Hubbell's claim to hurling greatness?

First, Hubbell achieved baseball's National Hall of Fame status in 1947. This was only four years after his retirement as a tosser. Because 87 percent of the voters cast ballots in favor of his election so soon after his career ended, most observers felt it sufficient to entitle him to greatness.

Many baseball addicts add another criterion. One of the sport's dozens of volumes compiling and measuring players' performances and achievements is *Total Baseball*. In this hefty volume, Hubbell is ranked among the twenty greatest moundsmen ever to cast baseballs. Further, Oklahoma, his adopted home state, inaugurated its Sports Hall of Fame in 1986. The organization chose Hubbell as one of the initial sportsmen to be included.

On a small farm near Carthage in southwestern Missouri, Carl Hubbell entered this world on June 22, 1903. His parents were George and Margaret Hubbell. He was one of the younger sons in a large family. There were seven children altogether. Older brothers included Jay, Kern, John and Edwin. Younger than he were Merritt and a sister, Mildred. Though born in the "Show Me" state, Carl lived in it only in his earliest childhood.

In 1907, when Carl was four years old, the Oklahoma Territory achieved statehood as the forty-sixth state. At the time of statehood, the areas of central Oklahoma, both east and west of Oklahoma City, were thinly populated. Back in the Great Land Rush of the 1890s, the northern and southern portions of Oklahoma had been quickly settled by "Sooners" from Kansas and Missouri. In the south, settlers also came from Texas and Arkansas. Oklahoma as a new state offered potential settlers fresh opportunities.

Carl Hubbell's father moved his family to land a little southeast of the Lincoln County village of Meeker. This was an area of woods and rolling hills. Meeker was forty to fifty miles northeast of Oklahoma City. The senior Hubbell was a tenant farmer who raised cotton and pecans and also had a herd of cattle. Growing up, the Hubbell sons learned to work long hours doing hard but invigorating farm tasks.

Much of the information concerning Carl's early years is anecdotal — essential for its reconstruction, but subject to the frailties of such sources. The primary difficulty is that the longer the time from the originating events, the greater the recounter tends to drift into overstatement or even slip into factual errors. In Hubbell's case, much of the data comes from recollections long after the incidents recalled. In fact, Hubbell's own recollections were sometimes inaccurate in details while largely correct with regard to the overall picture.

Carl became a baseball enthusiast in childhood. As he described it long afterwards, "I was just so crazy about playing baseball. I wanted to be a pro because I knew they played every day. I had no thought of making a lot of money or being a big leaguer."[1] Carl followed the box scores of the Oklahoma City Professionals. He hoped that some day he could pitch for that organization.

How Carl learned baseball essentials in his early years seems to have been a combination of overcoming adverse farm conditions amidst a favorable environment. The farm was what it was intended to be. There was neither a playing field, nor even a baseball. With the help of family members and boys from neighboring farms, the baseball deficiency was overcome through saving twine. The saved twine was wrapped tightly, thus creating a "twine ball."

Also, it must have surely been helpful to him to be a member of a family in which others liked to play the game. Several of his brothers played baseball. As a pastime, his father played as a left-handed catcher — a long-since extinct phenomenon.

By the time Carl reached high school age, he had apparently become a pretty fair country ball player. He wanted to become a pitcher, nothing else. In the junior year of high school, the volunteer coach, Jeff Hampton, chose him as a team member. At six feet, Carl was the tallest member of the team.

Also, he was the only left-handed participant. The young Carl became the team's pitcher while one of his brothers, Jay, handled the shortstop post.

A batting opponent from another small town was Lloyd Waner during some of the games Carl's high school team played. Waner was a batter whom Hubbell was to face many times in the National League a few years later. In 1922 or 1923 — but more likely the former — the Meeker Redbirds won the Class C high school baseball championship. The "C" classification indicated the category of a small town.

On Sunday afternoons, the apprentice pitcher hurled for semi-pro teams in neighboring villages. He especially remembered when, at sixteen, he rode on muleback nine miles to Sparks. There he won, 1–0. His reward totaled exactly one dollar.

Ponca City, large for the vicinity, featured its Maryland Refining Company team called the All Stars. They traveled about Oklahoma and the neighboring states challenging semi-pro aggregations to take them on. They rarely lost. One year, the cocky All Stars invited tiny, rural Ralston, reputedly having a good team, to Ponca City for a clash. So confident did the All Stars feel that they paid the Ralston's players' expenses just to appear. Upon arrival, the Ralstonites looked ridiculous — "sodbusters, some of them wearing bib overalls ... and work shoes."[2] To the mild surprise of the All Stars, a stranger appeared to do the visitors' pitching, but they readily approved of him. The stranger was Hubbell, who was in town to visit his high school sweetheart.

Hubbell squelched the All Stars in short order with an 8–0 no hitter. About a decade later, when Hubbell was making headlines as a great pitcher, the Ponca City players realized who the pitching unknown had been. Previously, they had been scratching their heads to figure out how they could have been flummoxed by a "nobody" that day. Thereafter, they were able to brag that it had taken the great Carl Hubbell to obliterate the All Stars.

After high school, it took Carl some time to obtain a tryout with a professional team. Fortunately, a Meeker acquaintance intervened on his behalf. Hubbell's fellow villager convinced Ned Pettigrew, manager of the Cushing team in the Class D Oklahoma State League, to give the youngster a tryout. He did well enough to land his first professional job.

Little information has survived concerning the lowly Oklahoma State League. Its eight teams came mostly from small towns and attracted little interest. In the latter part of the 1923 season, Hubbell, according to his own recollection, won about seven out of ten games. The league collapsed in 1924 halfway through the season. With the collapse of the league, the secretary simply discarded the records; thus, it is not possible to verify or correct his recollection. However, the probability of its accuracy is fairly high because a newspaper report shows that Cushing won the league title in 1923.

In 1924, after the league folded around the Fourth of July holiday period, a reshuffling of franchises occurred. Carl, with his pitching aspirations, was transferred to Ardmore, Oklahoma. It was in the Western Association, a better classification. A couple of box scores from the Ardmore paper have survived. These records are perhaps the earliest ones that can be found in games in which he pitched. For Ardmore, Hubbell won and lost one game each.

Then another aggregation, the Oklahoma City Indians of the Western League, acquired Hubbell's contract. This represented another step up the classification ladder. It appears as if Ned Pettigrew had much to do with his ascent to Oklahoma City. In 1925, Ned became manager of the Indians. Clearly he had been communicating with them prior to becoming manager. Probably impressed with the youth's showing in Cushing, he urged the Oklahoma City owner to acquire Carl, which he did.

In 1924, Carl pitched only briefly, in two games, for the Indians. Of the two games he pitched in 1924, he lost one. Then Carl contracted a case of typhoid fever. Fortunately, in the 1924-25 off-season, he managed to make a full recovery. This allowed Hubbell an entire season of hurling for the Indians.

In 1925 — as he had now and then in 1924 — the young Hubbell began to experiment with a new pitch. A little doubtful as to whether his fast ball was really swift enough, he looked for an offbeat pitch that would be something of a novelty. During the season, he observed at Des Moines, one of the Indians' opponents, a well-worn higher minor league pitcher, Claude (Lefty) Thomas. Thomas would throw a sinker that often would induce right-handed batters to ground into double plays. In spring training, Carl had tinkered with something similar. Observing Thomas's skill a little later, he decided that this pitch definitely was what he needed. When spring training arrived in 1925, Hubbell worked hard on it.

Before long, Carl became aware that the pitch put a strain on his arm. He decided to lift weights and to squeeze a rubber ball, over and over, to strengthen his arm. As his wrist, elbow and lower arm grew stronger, the discomfort gradually disappeared, and Hubbell became more confident of the pitch's efficacy.

Better yet, he improved the pitch. As it was originally, it was a "sinker." In making his pitch, at the last instant, Carl would give his wrist a twist, releasing the ball between the middle and ring fingers. This way, the pitch not only broke down, but also away. It flummoxed his right-hand batters, always a menace to left-handed pitchers. The risk, of course, consisted in the strain it put on his arm if he threw it very often in this manner. To some degree, Hubbell's physique diminished this danger. He was six feet in height and weighed about 175 pounds. Carl was careful not to add any poundage.

His arms were longer than most people his height. But of greatest advantage to Hubbell was the fact that his wrists were very supple. Therefore, the strain on his arms and wrists was less than it appeared.

Hubbell practiced the pitch at every opportunity. Through this practice, he gradually learned that throwing it directly overhand created the widest break and deepest sinkage. The final step in creating his "odd" pitch was practice to control it. Carl achieved this control only on the verge of reaching the major leagues.

In the spring of 1925, John Holland, the Oklahoma City Indians' owner, observed Hubbell in practice and took a shine to him. The club's top official was a typical example of a once-familiar minor league operator prior to the advent of major league-owned farm teams. Holland made his living, or at least some of it, by developing promising youthful baseball players, then selling them to higher-category minor league teams, or better yet, to major league teams. He acquired the reputation of being an especially shrewd detector of pitching potential. The *Daily Oklahoman* described Holland as "famed throughout baseball for his ability to develop pitchers."[3] In particular, he had advanced the careers of Jim Scott, a White Sox hurler of some years before; of Ed Willett, Detroit contemporary of Scott; and of Emil Yde, a Pittsburgh pitcher at the time of Hubbell. Most notably, Holland seized upon and took under his wing Dazzy Vance, by then a star hurler with the Brooklyn Dodgers.

The Western League's 1925 season got underway. Hubbell started and won the Indians' second game. He obtained the fans' liking when he hung in to the end despite receiving a hard line drive that struck him in the foot. After a few wins and losses, Carl began to enjoy success with his new pitch.

On the first day of the Memorial Day weekend, Hubbell hurled a game that impressed observers. The opposing manager, like a very modern one, put together a lineup of nearly all right-hand hitters. Against Hubbell, this brought poor returns. In a twelve-inning struggle, the Oklahoma City southpaw won, 3–2. He allowed only six hits. Both the opposition runs were unearned.

A few days later, this time against a left-hander like himself (who was regarded as something special), he won a brilliant duel 4–1. Later in June came another 3–2 win. Then, pitching on July Fourth, Hubbell stopped archrival Tulsa, allowing only three hits. The *Daily Oklahoman*'s scribe called him "the brilliant Oklahoma southpaw."[4]

That so much attention was given Hubbell in the city newspaper may have partly been Holland's influence. He wanted to encourage Carl, but also desired to improve his own prospects for selling Hubbell. At this stage, Holland's new find stood at an impressive 10–3 win-loss record. The day after

Hubbell defeated Tulsa, a Sunday, the sports section offered a prophetic headline: "Oklahoma Ace Faces Great Future."

The accompanying piece referred to Holland directly. After mentioning the four earlier hurlers he had helped to advance, the article quoted Holland as saying, "Hubbell is a much better prospect than any of the others were when they were sent to the major leagues."[5] Eventually, Hubbell fully realized Holland's assessment, even to the extent of outdoing Dazzy Vance as a memorable hurler. (After Carl reached the majors, the Oklahoman soon had reason to remember Vance.) Holland was hinting that Carl could have been advanced to a major league club right then and there. In a much later day, that surely would have been the case. It took Hubbell another three years to reach the top.

When Hubbell first arrived with the Oklahoma City club, he had fulfilled his youthful ambition to do more than pitch for the aggregation. Surely through all of the "to-do" over him by the Fourth of July weekend, if not well before, Carl had begun to aim for the majors. Perhaps he had even started to aim for stardom.

Quite soon, the second half of the season turned into a disappointment for the Indians' star, and to some extent, for his sponsor. A few weeks after July 4, Carl's record showed 13–6. This was still very good, but indicated a 3–3 pace after the high point. Nevertheless, the *Daily Oklahoman*'s writer informed his readers that "Lefty Hubbell is the best pitcher in the league...."[6] He did emphasize what he considered a shortcoming in the pitcher's armor: loss of stamina.

Hubbell had just lost a 6–5 game to Omaha, pitching rather ineffectively. This had followed a start in which the pitcher had gone eleven innings to win. Earlier, there had been an instance or two after an extra-inning game when Carl had not been as good in the following start. To the correspondent, this showed a need for Hubbell to gain greater stamina. Actually, especially for a young pitcher early in his professional career, it is not at all surprising that weariness should appear after long performances. This was the first year in which Hubbell was pitching from early spring through early fall.

Also, much of this slippage was due to a run of bad luck interspersed with an inadequate defense. The latter was a common ailment in minor league ball. For instance, in early September, Hubbell lost a game 7–0. This could indicate that the pitcher had a very poor day. In fact, every single one of the opposing team's (Omaha) runs was unearned. Another game Carl lost 7–6, but again, errors cost him the game. Finally, on September 21, the last day of the season, Hubbell lost the second game of a closing double-header, 4–3. Again, it was errors that marred his effort.

Oklahoma City closed with an 88–76 record, good for third place. Due to his second half fall-off, Hubbell ended up with 17–13 W–L. This meant a winning percentage better than his team, but not noticeably so: 56.6 percent to 53.6 percent. Rather than ending up the season as the league's best pitcher, his performance compared to that of the other leading moundsmen showed him to be only among the best half dozen.

It is possible the raw statistics were not as reliable as they appeared. Extraneous factors entered in — notably the errors quotient. Further, figures did not pinpoint sufficiently two failings that Hubbell had exhibited. First, he had shown a weakness on defense, especially through errant throws to second and potential double plays. Second, for the 284 innings pitched, Hubbell's base-on-ball total was high: 108. This is an average of four per game. This high number of balls may have been due to the difficulty Carl had in controlling the screwball. Nonetheless, clearly here was a dimension of pitching which he needed to improve.

After the season ended, the young twirler's second half did not seem to diminish his attraction for higher-level clubs. Reports had it that Holland was able to peddle Hubbell for $20,000, a very high figure for a minor leaguer emerging from a Class B circuit. Acquired by the Detroit Tigers, Carl Hubbell spent 2¼ years with that organization. The Detroit management finally seems to have concluded he was not, after all, a top prospect, and sold him in mid–July, 1928, to another major league team. From there, Hubbell went on to fame and fortune.

Since this is one of the most glaring instances of a club fumbling away a future star, numerous commentators have expressed amazement at Detroit's blunder. Why were the Detroit officials so myopic in their handling of Carl Hubbell?

First, it is likely that of all the sports who try to estimate a youthful player's prospects to succeed at the highest level, baseball is the most difficult. This is doubly true of pitchers, where there are so many variables to enter in. Many other teams, not only Detroit, have made the mistake of letting a great prospect get away.

Nonetheless, the popular impression that Detroit officials behaved like somnambulists in their handling of the Hubbell case is essentially correct. To a reader of the details, the thought that emerges is that Hubbell's best pitch, his screwball, was a handicap whether he used it or not. If he did, Detroit's management forbade it. If he did not, observers felt that he did not have quite enough stuff to succeed in the majors. In this, they may have been mistaken. Without the screwball, Carl would not have become a great star. However, with experience and cunning, even without the screwball, he might have become an Eddie Lopat or a Jamie Moyer — both contemporary stars of a later day: the 1940s and 1950s.

In the early stages of the relationship, the Detroiters treated Carl well. He made it to the 1926 training camp. The manager, however, was Ty Cobb. Cobb was great as a player, but nearly the opposite as a manager. Often his way with the rookies was simply to ignore them until they had proved themselves. Hubbell could not recall a single instance in which Cobb spoke directly to him.

Since this was his first time with a major league team, Hubbell recalled several incidents that occurred. While warming up one day with Johnny Bassler, one of the Detroit catchers, he threw his odd pitch. Bassler exclaimed, "That's the screwiest pitch I've ever seen." Then and there Bassler and Hubbell decided to call the pitch a "screwball."

In an intrasquad game, an amusing incident occurred. The batter was Lu Blue. He was a switch hitter, adept at drawing walks and hard to strike out. On a three-and-one count, Hubbell threw his screwball. Blue swung, missed. On three-two, Carl threw it again. Blue swung and missed again, returning to the dugout talking to himself.

Then came a disappointment for Hubbell. Cobb employed as his chief coach that year George McBride, once a Washington Senators second baseman. One day, McBride informed Carl that he must drop his screwball. It was unduly hard on the arm. McBride cited as an example Hub Pruett, a St. Louis Browns pitcher who briefly achieved headlines by repeatedly striking out Babe Ruth. However, using Hubbell's type of pitch, Pruitt soon hurt his arm. Being a newcomer, a rookie, and desiring to be cooperative, Carl complied. Neither Cobb nor McBride seems to have observed Hubbell closely to ascertain whether the young left-hander, with his supple arms and wrists, might be an exception to the widely held belief that his type of pitch created an enormous strain on a pitcher's arm. Of course, in the long run, Cobb and McBride could be considered to be proven right. A dozen years later, Hubbell's arm gave out; however, most pitchers' arms were done for in that length of time anyway, even though they did not throw screwballs.

Near the end of spring training, the Tigers dispatched the Oklahoma hopeful to Toronto for more seasoning. Despite Holland's optimism that his find might be able to pitch in the majors then and there, most teams would have done the same. Toronto, in the Class AA International League, meant a two-level jump for Hubbell, and thus a considerable vote of confidence. However, except for one seemingly favorable journal reference that summer, the aspirant's relations with Detroit went steadily downhill thereafter.

Arriving in Toronto, Hubbell quietly received another setback. Detroit had notified Dan Howley, the Maple Leafs' manager — and later a major league one — that the new farm hand should forego using his screwball. In addition, Toronto felt that it had a good chance at last of replacing Baltimore as league champion. They had enough starting pitchers, so Hubbell worked as a reliever, a function with which he had no previous experience. Toronto went on to win the International League title. Howley's starters, Wally Stewart, Owen Carroll, Vic Sorrell, Jim Faulkner, and Clarence Fisher did well.

All of these pitchers reached the major league in advance of Hubbell. Their careers, however, illustrate the uncertainties of pitcher evaluation. Stewart was the most successful. In the major leagues, he won 100 games while losing considerably fewer. He had two outstanding seasons. Sorrell, hurling for Detroit's then-chronic "also rans," won 92 games, but lost over 100, thereby becoming an "also ran" himself. Carroll drifted in and out of the majors for almost a decade. He pitched for three teams, but won only 65 games while losing almost 90. Faulkner pitched for a brief time with the New York Giants, where he met Hubbell again, but won only ten games. Fisher won none. By contrast, Hubbell won more than 2½ times as many as Stewart, the best among the others.

Sheer chance is not, however, the only criterion for major league success. In Hubbell's case, though his employment in 1926 largely as a reliever made his season appear that he was only a mediocrity, there are some important clues at hand that should have caught the Detroit supervisors' attention. Apparently Detroit's owner and observers noticed only the young hurler's 3.72 ERA and 42 walks in 93 innings, suggesting mediocrity.

The Toronto relief pitcher revealed his potential via the team's exhibition schedule. Major league teams in those days would often use an off day in their schedule to play a minor league club. On June 3, 1926, the Washington Senators arrived to play the Maple Leafs. They were a strong team, having won the 1924 World Series and lost the 1925 Series only in the seventh game, playing in rainy conditions. Howley decided that he did not want to use one of his regular starters, turning to Hubbell instead. Warming up on the sidelines, Carl threw in a screwball now and then. One of the Toronto coaches, Steve O'Neill, sometimes served as a bullpen catcher. (O'Neill earlier had been the Cleveland Indians' first-string catcher for years and later became a successful major manager.) Hubbell asked O'Neill if he could try his screwball against the Senators and O'Neill did not disapprove.

The Senators, with their lineup of solid hitters, found themselves completely unable to compete with the local nobody's odd pitch. To the pleasure of the Maple Leaf fans, their team squelched the big leaguers 6–1. The Senators managed only five hits, and their three best hitters, Sam Rice, Goose Goslin (a prominent power hitter), and Joe Judge, collectively went for 2 and 11. Each struck out once. The Senators' only runs were unearned. Hubbell's main flaw was in allowing five walks.

This exhibition made no deep impression on Howley, who returned Hubbell to infrequent relief appearances. A month passed and who should arrive but Hubbell's sponsors, the Detroit Tigers! Howley decided to give his reliever another try. The Tigers' fate was similar to the Senators'. As the *Toronto Globe* put it over its box score, "Twist Tigers' Tails," 5–4. The four Detroit runs were misleading because they were unearned. They collected a mere three hits. Lu Blue went 0 for 3 with two walks; Charlie Gehringer, 0–2; Harry Heilman, once a .400 hitter, 0–2. Hubbell struck out six. As before, his major failing showed up in six walks. Manager Cobb, who chose not to play, sat fuming in the dugout. Soon after this, *The Sporting News'* Detroit correspondent reported, "The chief consolation Cobb drew from the exhibition was that Hubbell is still Detroit property. Hubbell seems to be developing rapidly. It is reasonably certain he will be in the Tiger camp next season."[7]

In September, the New York Yankees, with Babe Ruth and other stars, arrived en route to the 1926 pennant. Of course this drew a large crowd. Howell sent out Hubbell as starter for a third time. This time the results were different. The Yankees won 8–2, although until the late innings, Hubbell kept the score low and close. Eventually fatigue or nervousness got the better of him, and Carl gave up a final total of a dozen hits while surrendering six walks and committing two errors of his own. Ruth went 2–4 with a walk, both hits singles; Lou Gehrig 1–2; and Bob Meusel 1–5, a single. No Yankee struck a home run. That the game was played carelessly might be indicated through the eight errors committed by the combined clubs.

Despite Hubbell's poor showing against the Yankees, Howley, with the International League race virtually won, gave his left-hander another chance as a starter. Hubbell defeated Buffalo easily, pitching an "excellent game" and winning 8–3. The walks diminished to two. In a few fill-in starts, Carl had performed equally effectively.

Toronto played Louisville in the Little World Series that year, trouncing the American Association winner in five straight games. So easy was the Maple Leafs' triumph that Hubbell did not have a chance to pitch either as a starter or reliever.

Hubbell was returning to Oklahoma for the winter and his train passed through St. Louis. The World Series was on. Hubbell detrained, headed for Sportsman Park, and fell in line with hundreds of other "bleacherites" scrambling to get cheap tickets. Carl succeeded in getting in and saw one of the three games played in St. Louis that year. Anyone would wonder whether he mentioned his occupation to fellow bleacher fans or the fact that only a few weeks before he had pitched against Babe Ruth.

That off-season plunged the Detroit management into turmoil. For the public's sake and his own prestige, Ty Cobb announced his resignation. Actually he had been fired. The firing was not only for the obvious reasons, but for very hush-hush ones as well. The Cobb headache pursued the Detroit management all winter. Detroit's greatest player departed in a huff, privately raining countless imprecations on Tiger owner Frank Navin. Because Cobb's expectations of his players were so unrelentingly demanding, the widespread opinion that he was a failure as a manager has been confirmed by time.

In Hubbell's situation, Cobb's dismissal may have been injurious. Cobb had witnessed the Toronto exhibition and might have seen the potential in Carl. Otherwise Detroit's botching of the handling of its left-handed prospect in 1926 and 1928 seems entirely inexplicable. *The Sporting News'* writer's comment in mid-summer 1926 indicated that Cobb might have been willing to give Hubbell a full shot at spring training in 1927. As it turned out, this was far from the case.

Over the winter of 1926-27, Frank Navin chose a new manager. Feeling that it would be wise to select a person familiar to Detroit's fans, he chose George Moriarty. It was a poor selection. Also available were Eddie Collins, recently released as White Sox manager, where he had done reasonably well with mediocre players. Bill McKechnie, well known for his skills in developing pitchers, was available as well. In 1927, McKechnie managed in the International League.

Moriarty was devoid of managerial experience. He had been the Detroit third baseman in pennant-winning years twenty years previously. Then he became an American league umpire until the close of the 1926 season. Arguing with pitchers over his ball and strike calls provided Moriarty with the opposite of a desirable experience in handling hurlers' needs.

Given the circumstances of Cobb's departure, it is unlikely he informed his successor to keep an eye on Hubbell. At any rate, unlike 1926, Carl did not receive an invitation to the 1927 Detroit spring training camp. Instead, his assignment was to report to the Fort Worth Cats in the Texas League — a step down. Hubbell pitched only three games there, two in relief and one a start, which he lost. This was nowhere near time enough to assess Hubbell's wares. He was sent packing again.

Carl was sent to Decatur in the Three Eye (Illinois-Indiana-Iowa) League — wherever that was. This was a step below the Texas League. Thus, the ambitious young pitcher's reward for winning two out of three games against major league opponents while with Toronto was to be demoted two levels. So much did this rankle Hubbell that in an interview he gave in his old age, he expressed his resentment.

Little is known concerning Hubbell's year in the Three Eye League. In his various recollections, he did not ever refer to it directly. The Decatur, Illinois, team did fairly well for a while, but then faded into fifth-place losers. Carl was restored as a starting pitcher, and his box scores from *The Sporting*

News for the league's games indicate that he pitched well for the Decaturs. One game he pitched would have gained the attention of observers had he been at a higher level.

On August 15, 1927, Hubbell lost an astonishing seventeen-inning game, 3–2, pitching the entire way. That a young pitcher, whose arm might not yet be fully mature, should throw as many pitches such a long game required, defies common sense. However, baseball lives by its customs, superstitions, and assumptions, which come and go with time. In that day, managers simply took for granted that the pitcher, unless he pitched very poorly or had to be replaced with a pinch hitter, would stay the route — nine innings or longer.

At the season's end, Hubbell, hurling for a sub-.500 second division team, won fourteen, lost only seven, while pitching 185 innings in only 23 games, and a nice 2.52 ERA. He ranked as one of the league's five best hurlers. Clearly he was better than his company.

Doing so well earned the southwesterner another invitation to Detroit during the 1928 spring training at San Antonio. It was for naught, however. Before it was over, he was optioned out once again, this time to Beaumont in the Texas League.

This move by Detroit soon brought Hubbell's relations with the Bengals to a close. Major league regulations specified that a team farming out a prospect for the third time forfeited its right to control his contract. Within a reasonable time, the team was expected to make the player available to any interested major league potential buyers. Later that summer, another club gobbled up Hubbell, and in a short time, he became a winner for them. The Detroit management, both then and later, had a great deal of explaining to do.

At the time, a tale was evolved concerning the Tigers' final demotion of Hubbell. This tale began with a reasonable, probable basis in fact. Then it turned into a means by which the blunder could be explained away. The yarn has it that, a moment too late, the Tigers realized that they had a fine prospect in their midst. The reason Carl got away wasn't that they did not recognize his talent, but that a slip-up in the front office caused the third option to go into effect without realizing this was the "close-out" one. Though Detroit was a major loser, no matter what the reason, from a public relations standpoint it seemed easier to make the fans believe in this explanation than to allow them to suspect that sheer on-field ineptitude was the truth.

A key figure in the evolution of the tale was Frank Shaughnessy, long a power in the International League. In 1928, he served as a Tiger coach. Moriarty, like many managers, split his spring training players into squads: one, the regular players; the other, the hopefuls or "Yanigens." Hubbell pitched for the latter. Long after the events, Shaughnessy recalled that the second stringers played a game in Austin against the University of Texas. In that game, Hubbell pitched, and did outstandingly well. Shaughnessy promptly notified Moriarty, who was looking for another starting pitcher, that he had exactly the right fit in the person of Carl Hubbell. Moriarty was duly grateful. Unfortunately, he learned almost simultaneously that the third option had gone into effect and Hubbell had slipped away. Thus, the cause of the mistake was the carelessness of some anonymous office worker rather than a stunning failure in observation by the spring training staff.

How much truth underlies this version? That there was a mistake somewhere in letting the third option take effect is probably correct, but not because the Tigers had finally realized Hubbell had solid ability. It is more likely that Detroit intended only to shop him out in the same aimless fashion as before. Meantime, they would make up their minds what, if anything, they would want with Hubbell, and then recall him. That the farm-out spoiled their belated recognition of his skills is not born out by the evidence.

For instance, on March 18, 1928, the *San Antonio Express* reported that what the Tigers most needed was "two more winning pitchers."[8] Clearly at that stage, the Detroit observers had not detected anything special in Hubbell.

On March 21, Hubbell made his only appearance with the "regulars." It was in the last innings of a Detroit game against Minneapolis that had already been sewed up, 10–1. This appearance did not make an impression, and it hardly could, as he pitched in a meaningless situation.

On March 25, 1928, Hubbell was farmed out to Beaumont. That this was viewed as nothing special is demonstrated by the fact that Hubbell's name simply was listed with three other "nonentities" who were farmed to various other minor league clubs.

What about Shaughnessy's recollection of a game that the prospects played against the University of Texas in Austin? This did indeed take place on March 24, the day before Hubbell was sent out. Therefore, Shaughnessy's recall was correct to this extent. However, his version has an important erroneous twist to it.

The pitcher in that game against the "university boys" was not Hubbell. It was a long-forgotten figure, Haskell Billings. He did pitch very well against the Texas undergraduates. Thus, as is so easily the case, with the passage of the years, Shaughnessy's memory had lapses. The pitcher he had so strongly recommended to Moriarty was Billings, not Hubbell.

Haskell Billings is an interesting case. The Tigers that spring were quite high on this pitcher, who was several years younger than Hubbell. In 1927, the year that Hubbell labored obscurely for Decatur, Billings pitched in several major league games for Detroit. In 1928, he pitched quite often for them, and in 1929, he briefly received a final chance. Hubbell, meantime, received none. In his major league career, Billings won ten games, Hubbell 253. In assessing the comparative skills of pitching prospects, the Detroit on-field staff thus displayed its acumen!

That the Tigers at last spotted Hubbell's potential a moment too late seems highly improbable. What remains a mystery is why the overseers, who seemed unable to figure out what to do with this candidate, simply did not let him throw his screwball. Carl could have shown them what he could do with it.

In Beaumont, Hubbell felt discouraged at first. It was possible he, like most minor league pitchers, might never reach the majors. Soon, however, Carl learned that his Detroit connections had ended. This heartened him. No longer subject to their orders, and feeling he had nothing to lose, he resurrected his screwball.

In a few weeks, Texas League hitters — like their predecessors three years before in the Western League — found themselves tied in knots by Hubbell's freakish pitch. His team, the Beaumont Exporters, amounted to very little. They quickly shrank into a dismal last-place outfit, winning only four of their first twenty games. Unavoidably, Carl made a slow start. By mid–May, however, he started to click, in spite of the fact that once or twice he had to hurl in 100-degree temperatures. Steady use of the screwball enabled Hubbell to learn to control it at last. His base-on-ball ratio dropped sharply.

On June 8, 1928, Hubbell defeated Waco, the league's best team thus far that year, 5–3. Four days later, down went the Houston Buffs, 1928's first-place club, 7–0. A Cardinal farm unit, the team featured three pitchers whom Hubbell encountered later in the majors. These were Bill Hallahan, Tex Carleton and Jim Lindsey. They also had several good hitters. Yet the Buffs "were helpless ... before the quick-breaking slants of Hubbell."[9] He gave up only five hits, fanned seven, and walked two. Then on June 16, pitching "masterful ball," he stopped Waco again, 4–0, striking out seven.

The *Dallas Morning News* had a column by George White, a sports reporter for the sports section. White commented that "another big league prospect ... is Carl Hubbell of Meeker, Oklahoma. A few days ago he hurled a masterful ball to beat the hard-hitting Houstonians."[10] He added that if Hubbell had been pitching for any other club, he would have been "nigh unbeatable."[11]

In Dallas on June 20, the Exporters arrived to play the local Spurs. Down went the Spurs, 9–2. Ten hitters fanned. One was Hack Miller, only three years previously a twenty-home-run hitter for the Chicago Cubs. Miller struck out four times, including once with the bases loaded in the ninth. This incident has interest as an early example of what could happen to slugger types who could not resist flailing mightily at Hubbell's twister. On June

24, the *Dallas Morning News* noted that Hubbell offered the "finest 'slabbing' of the season."[12] By then, he had completed fifteen of sixteen starts and, despite being on a poor baseball team, was leading the league in innings pitched.

The hitters' discomfiture continued. On June 24, down went Wichita Falls, 19–4. Mostly due to Hubbell, the Exporters actually had won six in a row! Eventually Carl reached nine straight wins. On July 1, he went twelve innings to defeat San Antonio, striking out ten batters.

By this time, major league clubs began to take notice of Hubbell, especially once they realized Detroit had lost him. It is possible Navin's realization of what he had lost sank in only when he began to receive phone calls asking to purchase him. If Hubbell's recollection from long afterward was true, he received a telegram asking — or was it begging? — him to sign with the Detroit Tigers. At any rate, Cleveland and the New York Yankees were interested in the Beaumont moundsman.

It was on July 5 that Carl pitched the game that almost certified he would be a big leaguer. The Exporters were to play Houston at home. Beaten by Hubbell once, this time they had home field advantage. But the Exporter pitcher did them in again, allowing only three hits and winning 2–1. His opponent was Tex Carleton, against whom he was to pitch numerous times in the major leagues, on one memorable occasion in particular. According to the wire reports, Hubbell once again made the Houston diamond observers wonder why the Detroit Tigers had sent him to Beaumont.

In the National League, one team that was interested in Hubbell's service was the New York Giants. Out of their attention, one of baseball's best-known tales arose. The key figure in the story was Dick Kinsella, the favorite scout for John McGraw, the manager of the Giants. Skillful at spotting talents on the hoof, Kinsella's greatest find turned out to be Hubbell.

In its full dimensions, the tale is a fine example of a baseball legend. The sole purveyor at first had to be Kinsella himself. Before long, it was repeated time and again, sometimes even including the (supposed) exact words that Kinsella spoke to McGraw over the phone. The scout attended the 1928 Democratic National Convention, held in Houston. The story goes that during an afternoon of a dull session, Kinsella departed to take in a Buffs game. They were playing the Exporters. Quite by chance, Hubbell took the mound for Beaumont. Observing him, Kinsella was amazed by his skill. The scout hurried to a telephone after the game. He called McGraw, saying excitedly, "I've found you another Art Nehf, Mac. Grab him fast."[13] Nehf had been McGraw's star left-hander in the early 20s. So informed, the manager quickly contacted Detroit and landed the Texas League pitcher.

How much is true in this yarn? As with the Detroit one, fully true is only the initiating fact. The rest consists of exaggerations, typical of legend development. There is no doubt that the scout called McGraw, telling him that Hubbell was pitching at a major league level and that he should obtain him immediately. At the time, New York was in a close pennant race with the St. Louis Cardinals. However, two of their starters had come to grief, so McGraw was in an acute need of at least one more hurler, preferably a left-hander.

The dramatic quality shrinks when the reader learns that Kinsella had been "trailing ... the ... young southpaw from Beaumont ... with ... whom the old talent picker had become enamored."[14] McGraw had sent the scout to the Texas League earlier, although at exactly what date is unknown. Thus, Kinsella, already having observed Hubbell, surely also would have been following any items in the sports sections of the state's papers concerning Carl.

Therefore, it is probable that the sequence of events in Kinsella's tale is reversed. It was not while the convention was on that he decided to see the Houston/Beaumont game as a break from boredom, but because he was already on Hubbell's trail. The convention ended June 30. Why was Kinsella lingering around Houston to watch a game played on July 5 when the Democrats had gone home four days earlier? It was because he wanted to observe how the pitcher he was trailing would do against the league's first-place team at home.

Further, Kinsella's call to McGraw did not settle the matter then and there. The Giants were on a road trip and had reached St. Louis. McGraw directed Kinsella to "entrain" to the city for a conference. It was at this confab that the manager decided he would go after Hubbell immediately. The Giants paid Navin what they considered a large amount ($50,000), suggesting there were other would-be buyers.

It is not unlikely that Kinsella inflated his tale due to an understandable desire, once his protégé achieved prominence, to obtain as much credit for his find as he could garner. Actually, by July 1928, it was saying too much to claim Hubbell as an unknown. Prior to the farm system's management of scouting, it was possible, once in a while, for a sleuth to locate a true find. Scouts usually did not receive as much credit as they deserved. Who could blame Kinsella for claiming he had found a gold nugget?

In the Hubbell situation, Detroit president Navin had another possible embarrassment before him. If he had allowed another American League team to acquire Hubbell, and the pitcher turned out well, including defeating Detroit sometimes, Navin would be made to look worse than he already appeared. Therefore, Navin determined to rid himself of the Hubbell headache by allowing only a National League team to acquire him. This was one reason why the Giants had the chance to obtain Carl. Since this decision meant that the American League half of Navin's potential market was closed to him, this vexed him a great deal. Actually the $50,000 he received for the Giants' acquisition of Hubbell's service was regarded at the time a large sum for a Class A minor league hurler. In this peculiar fashion, Hubbell's tour through the lesser leagues — the farms — finally drew to a close.

Chapter 2

Pitching for
"Little Napoleon"

On the morning of July 18, 1928, Carl Hubbell embarked upon his career with the New York Giants. They were at Chicago on their road trip and the team had an off day. At that time, they trailed the St. Louis Cardinals by 5½ games. The new arrival encountered the road secretary at the hotel. The latter invited the newcomer to "hie himself to the suite of the manager, John McGraw, and identify himself."[1]

Of course, Hubbell had heard of McGraw. Here was a field boss more famous than his players. A winner of ten pennants and three World Series, his name is among the most familiar of the Hall of Fame members. He had earned the honor largely through his thirty or so years of managerial success, and to a lesser extent, for his skill as a player back in the 1890s.

Though most players disliked their crusty manager, he extracted every ounce of effort from them. Laggards soon found themselves en route elsewhere. However, unlike Hubbell's experience with Ty Cobb, who could only turn out hitters, McGraw succeeded with all types of players. Among Hubbell's brethren, McGraw helped Christy Mathewson and Rube Marquard to reach Hall of Fame levels of skill.

With position players likewise, McGraw knew how to develop native talent when he observed it. Only a few years before Hubbell's arrival, he supervised the development of third baseman Freddy Lindstrom, shortstop Travis Jackson, and right fielder Mel Ott. Also, to some extent, McGraw had pushed Bill Terry, the Giants' fourth star, toward prominence. Another of the manager's traits was that, despite his harshness, he (unlike Cobb) realized that young players needed to be handled a little more leniently than regulars.

"Little Napoleon," as many privately called McGraw, enjoyed the complete confidence of the owner, Charles Stoneham. This enabled him to handle playing personnel and in-game tactics as he saw fit. Further, he enjoyed virtual

This photograph was apparently taken early in Hubbell's career, with the rising young pitching star leaning back, the first step toward throwing a practice pitch at a cooperative teammate batter.

immunity from reportorial criticism. Along with Babe Ruth over at the Yankees, McGraw was figuratively "co-monarch" of New York City baseball.

Unfortunately, by the time of Hubbell's arrival, the kingpin's best days were behind him. Although each year McGraw's teams finished in the first division, no longer did he win pennants. Resistance to the changing times made him too inflexible to achieve top results any longer. In the Jazz Age, symbolic of the aftereffects of World War I, the younger generation was becoming more independent, more insistent upon acting on its own terms. With extra comforts, a multiplicity of amusements and new gadgetry available, their outlook departed from that of the prewar generation.

McGraw's later 1920s players exemplified the new mood. Increasingly they resisted his tyrannical ways. They detested his shouting at them in public and his dictation of every aspect of their in-game actions. Bob O'Farrell, a first-string catcher and a common-sense person, said of McGraw, "You couldn't do anything right for him, ever. If something went wrong, it was always your fault, not his. Maybe [it was] because he was getting older and was a sick man, but he was never any fun to play for. He was always so grouchy."[2] Behind his back, many players called him what were then unprintable names. However, to his face, they were careful to address him as "Mr. McGraw."

Always angered by signs of insubordination and what was at times outright resistance, the famous manager made several damaging trades in the years immediately prior to Hubbell's coming. One year he obtained Burleigh Grimes, one of the league's very best hurlers. Grimes was just as irascible as the manager. Though Grimes pitched very well for the Giants, McGraw evidently could stand him no longer and traded him for another pitcher far inferior in skill. The same happened with Rogers Hornsby, the National League's most famous player. Another, Hack Wilson, notorious for his intemperance, McGraw banished to the minors. Soon the Chicago Cubs grabbed him in the minor league draft, leaving the Giants with nothing to show for him.

Against this background, the new pitcher entered the manager's room a little uneasily. To his mild surprise, McGraw greeted him more affably than he had anticipated. The high price the New Yorkers had paid to acquire Hubbell probably helped. Carl, aware that living in New York City was likely to cost considerably more than it had in Beaumont, wanted to ask for a salary increase. He hesitated to say so. In a second surprise, McGraw proceeded to *volunteer* a salary that exceeded what he had intended to ask. The visitor did not mention that his most effective pitch was a rarely used one.

The interview concluded, Hubbell spent the rest of the day with his new teammates. He spent time with Jim Faulkner, reviving their Toronto acquaintance. In addition, Carl encountered a *New York Times* reporter, Richards

Vidmer. The scribe reported his age and quoted Hubbell as saying that "he doesn't use any freak deliveries to fool the batters."[3] Since that was *exactly* what the Oklahoman did do, his reluctance to tell the truth probably arose from his worry that he might again be told he should not use his screwball. Carl soon learned that McGraw did not object to the screwball, and even encouraged him to rely on it.

For quite a while after his career ended, Hubbell credited his second major league manager with helping him in several ways when he needed assistance. McGraw did not sour on him, after an initial setback. On the contrary, McGraw reassured Carl that he would receive more chances. Unlike when he was a Detroit farm hand, Hubbell was not denied opportunities. Instead, he was offered them.

However, in his old age, Hubbell's view of his first Giants superior became much more critical. Like the other players of his time, he felt that McGraw was unreasonably authoritarian. He insisted on signaling to the catcher every pitch a hurler threw. Decades later, it became common practice for the manager or pitching coach to do this, but among Giants pitchers in the late 1920s, it was greatly resented. Thinking back on it, the retiree felt that the steady diet of screwballs, curves and change-ups McGraw decreed could easily have led to arm trouble.

Though McGraw could no longer manage effectively, his skill in developing talent stayed with him. Kinsella's recommendation and his own observations enabled him to perceive, or intuit, that in Hubbell he had the potential of a *great* hurler, not just a good prospect. In two years, the maladroit Detroiters had found nothing in Carl worthy of serious attention. McGraw took only a little over a month to turn Hubbell into a winning major league pitcher.

An advantage in having a despotic manager lay in his freedom to take chances and to devise tactical moves several days ahead. By contrast, a field boss three quarters of a century later had pitch counts, reportorial pressure, and fan expectation to circumscribe him considerably. It became harder for a manager to make a move recognizably different from any other one.

When Hubbell began to pitch against National League teams, three clubs dominated the scene: the St. Louis Cardinals, the Chicago Cubs, and his own. The Pittsburgh Pirates often constituted a quite serious fourth contender, with the Brooklyn Dodgers occasionally replacing them in this position. The other three — Boston Braves, Cincinnati Reds, and Philadelphia Phillies — were too poor to be anything more than "also-rans."

The Cardinals had some of the best players in the league. These included Jim Bottomley, first baseman; Frank Frisch, second baseman; and Chick Hafey, left fielder. The Cardinals' pitching staff centered on the aging but famous

Grover Cleveland Alexander; Jesse Haines, also a star; and Willie Sherdel, a skillful left-hander.

The Cubs were made strong by Hack Wilson and Kiki Cuyler, both outfielders, as well as Gabby Hartnett, catcher. In 1929, they added the formidable Rogers Hornsby, second baseman and batting powerhouse, to make the team's hitting even stronger. The Cubs' pitchers were Charley Root, Pat Malone, and Guy Bush, a strong trio of right-handers.

The Giants' strength could be found in Mel Ott in the outfield, Travis Jackson at shortstop, Bill Terry at first base, and Freddy Lindstrom at third base. In 1928, the club's best pitcher was Larry Benton, with Fred Fitzsimmons a close second. Their pitching staff was otherwise shaky at best until Hubbell arrived.

Pittsburgh had two outstanding hitters in third baseman Pie Traynor and outfielder Paul Waner. They also had several other better-than-average ones. Their perennial shortcoming was a pitching deficiency.

McGraw's freedom to plan ahead worked to maximum advantage in Hubbell's case, in spite of a poor start. The Giants returned home and played a series against the Pirates. On the closing day of the series, July 26, McGraw launched his new southpaw's career. Usually a manager would try to ease in a freshman hurler by starting him against the opposition's third or fourth starter or a rookie like his own. But McGraw had Hubbell challenge "Grouch" Grimes, the Giants' own best pitcher of the year before.

As one of the two remaining spitball pitchers left in the National League, the veteran hurler had been pitching very well for Pittsburgh. He had beaten the Giants four times. Whether Hubbell realized it or not, McGraw's belief that on Carl's very first try he could match the "Burly One"[4] amounted to a vote of confidence in him.

In short order, the Pirates fell upon Hubbell, winning 7–5. This was Grimes's fifth win against the Giants. It was a stinging setback to the Giants' pitcher and manager. In the Associated Press account, "The kid southpaw was hit hard and supported weakly when three New York errors accounted for all but two of Pittsburg runs." Vidner confirmed the AP report, stating that Hubbell was "battered from the box ... after the infield had collapsed behind him."[5]

Long afterward, Hubbell recalled that McGraw directed one of his sarcastic remarks at him when the game began to go bad. Before the game the manager had directed Carl to work Paul Waner high and away. Waner lashed a hard double off the top of the fence. McGraw yelled, "I didn't tell you to throw high and outside the park, Hubbell."[6]

Called in for an after-game assessment, Hubbell faced McGraw in a state of trepidation, fearing that the manager would send him back to the minors then and there. To his surprise, "Mr. Sarcasm" treated him mildly. While noting that Hubbell had pitched poorly, he blamed the Giants' poor defense for the loss as much as he did his pitcher. He observed that at least Hubbell had granted no walks. McGraw emphasized that to win in the majors, a pitcher must stay ahead of the hitters, advice that Hubbell always remembered and applied. McGraw concluded with the reassurance that after a few relief appearances, Hubbell would be given a chance to start again.

McGraw used Hubbell in relief four times: thrice against the Cubs, who followed the Pirates, and once against their successors, the Cardinals. On July 29, he pitched a scoreless inning against the Bruins. On July 31, the teams went at it in a double-header. In the first encounter, he again held the Chicagoans scoreless for an inning. In their half of this round, the home team rallied to take the lead, and held it for the rest of the action. Hubbell benefited in that this made him the winning pitcher. Returning again as reliever in the second encounter, he hurled three innings, but gave up a pair of runs.

In his fourth relief stint, Sunday, August 5, Hubbell pitched so well that he dispelled any doubts the manager might have entertained after his initial setback. It was a hot, humid day with the Cardinals on hand. About 35,000 fans were present, hopeful that the home boys could cut a game off the Redbirds' lead.

McGraw chose Faulkner as his starter. By the third inning, the visitors were four ahead, with runners on first and third and only one out. There was a strong possibility the Cardinals would break the game open. The manager pulled Faulkner in favor of Hubbell. Most accounts have it that this was the moment Carl used his first screwball. Chick Hafey was the batter. With the count three and one, Hubbell threw him successive screwballs. On the second, Hafey bounced into a double play, ending the inning.

From then until the ninth inning, Hubbell pitched hitless ball and the Giants gradually caught up. The *New York Herald-Tribune* reporter mentioned that he "hogtied the Cardinals with a tricky curve.... He would throw it at the batters anywhere from the waist to the knees."[7] For several years, columnists would refer to the left-hander's "odd" or "tricky" curve. It would have helped an avid fan to add that it broke in the *reverse* direction from what the batter expected, but no reporter did so. Neither did any call it a "screwball."

In the first of the ninth, the Redbirds threatened again by creating a one-out first and third situation. To the fans' delight, Hubbell scraped through a second time without the Cardinals' scoring. The game went on into the twelfth. This time, Hubbell's fielding weakness cast him into a deep jam. Bill McKechnie, the Cardinals manager, had three straight hitters starting the inning with bunts. Hubbell botched the first two, but he finally obtained an out on the third. With the fans standing up in their excitement, Carl squeaked out of it without the opponents garnering a run.

The game went on. Hubbell hung on through the thirteenth and fourteenth innings. Richards Vidmer, *New York Times* writer, speculated that Hubbell might have muttered, "What do I have to do to win a game in this league?"[8]

In the fifteenth inning Carl weakened. He had pitched 12⅔ innings. The Cardinals chalked up a pair on two doubles and a single. The Giants lost 6–4. In those 12⅔ relief innings, Hubbell gave up six hits, two runs, fanned three and walked four — two were intentional. The *New York Times* writer described him as leaving the field "battered and beaten after a brilliant performance."[9]

Most likely it was this game that convinced McGraw that Hubbell had both stamina and *sang-froid*. The manager rewarded him with five full days off. Then Carl was given his second start. This time McGraw was more cautious. He started him in a home game again, but to maximize his chance of success, arranged for the start to be against the hapless Philadelphia Phillies, the league's weakest team. In the 1920s and '30s, the Phillies in tiny Baker Bowl were looked upon as a "good hit, no field, no pitch team."[10] But in 1928, they lacked hitting and would manage to lose an eyebrow-raising 109 games. Making matters even easier for Hubbell, the Philadelphia starting pitcher was Jack Milligan. He was fresh from the New York–Pennsylvania League and was making his major league debut.

Hubbell seized the opportunity, throwing a four-hit shutout. He struck out five and walked none. Travis Jackson supplied the offense, driving in all four runs. Hubbell was backed by splendid defense from third baseman Fred Lindstrom, shortstop Jackson, and first baseman Bill Terry. The only threat the Phillies made came in the seventh, when they put runners on second and third. As teams far better than the feeble Phillies were to learn, to have Hubbell on the ropes in the late innings could turn into a very frustrating experience.

After a series with the Boston Braves, the Giants departed for a trip throughout the Midwest to play Chicago, St. Louis, Cincinnati, and Pittsburgh. The first two teams were considered to be tough customers, especially in their own parks. Planning ahead, McGraw for the second time decided to test Hubbell by placing Carl up against a famous pitcher — Grover Cleveland Alexander.

At the time, nearly all managers relied on a four-person starting staff of pitchers. Thus each starter had three days off to regain arm strength. Every day the national newspapers printed the box scores of all major league teams from the preceding day. The managers, and usually the players, particularly the hurlers, perused the previous day's boxes.

Since Hubbell had defeated Philadelphia on Saturday, August 11, his next start seemingly would have been on Wednesday the 15th, four days out. If there had been a rainout or a day off, then he would have started the following day. On these days, the Giants were playing the Cubs and the manager did not use Hubbell on either of them. Nor did McGraw use him on Friday, the first game of the St. Louis series.

In the meantime, on Tuesday, August 14, the "Great Alex" beat the Boston Braves, 6–1. Thus McGraw could foresee the high probability that Alexander's next start for the Cardinals would be Saturday, August 16, against his team. By 1928, Alexander's greatest days as a pitcher were behind him due to a combination of alcoholism and age. Nonetheless, Grover could still pitch extremely well when sober.

Once the Giants reached St. Louis from Chicago, McGraw held a locker-room meeting to lecture his players on the importance of this series. For the Friday game, immediately at hand, he chose Fred Fitzsimmons as his hurler. Bill McKechnie, the manager of the Cardinals, used Clarence Mitchell, the only active left-handed spitball pitcher in the majors. Fitzimmons, helped by Larry Benton near the end, did a good job. The Giants won 3–2. The narrow win diminished the Redbirds' lead to only a game and a half.

With Alexander, McKechnie's likely choice for the next day, McGraw immediately let it be known that Hubbell would be his starter for Saturday. Since he had pitched so well against the Cardinals when they were in New York, this increased the likelihood that McKechnie would select Alexander as his hurler.

McKechnie, however, said that he would wait until near game time to announce his pitcher. He mentioned Alexander *and* Haines, his two best, along with a couple of other pitchers who were used only infrequently as starters. However, since Haines had pitched only the day before, his selection was extremely unlikely. With his team's lead shrunk to a narrow margin, it was unlikely the Cardinals' manager would turn to a second-string starter for so important a clash. Despite McKechnie's vague statement, McGraw very probably anticipated that St. Louis's actual choice was bound to be Alexander. What a coup it would be if his protégé should succeed in getting the better of a great hurling opponent!

The Saturday crowd reached only 17,000 and rain held up the start of the game by a half hour. When the pitchers began to warm up, out came Alexander for the home team and Hubbell for the visitors. At that moment, the "Great Alex" stood 13–6, win-loss; Hubbell, 2–2, a noticeable contrast. Up to that point in his career, the St. Louis great had won over 360 games, the newcomer, as noted, just 2.

Once underway, the struggle turned into a contest of a fading master versus an ambitious future one. Through eight innings, the two fought evenly to a pair of runs. On Hubbell's showing, he allowed runners fairly frequently, but restricted the Cardinals' scoring. In the *St. Louis Globe-Democrat,* the newspaper's Cardinal scribe, Martin Haley, lamented that Hubbell held their three top players, Bottomley, Frisch, and Hafey, to no hits. The only batter that troubled Carl was Ernie Orsatti, a recent Redbird import from Minneapolis, who stroked a double and a home run.

In the ninth, the Giants managed to add a third run against Alexander. In the Cardinals' ninth, with two outs, the potential tying run stood at third, the winner at first. Remarkably, McGraw stuck with his starter. Hubbell got the final batter on a liner to third. The Giants won again, 3–2, and Hubbell had defeated "Alexander the Great."

Afterward, in the Giants' dressing room, Hubbell received an unexpected caller. McGraw entered, walked directly to him — and presumably with other players nearby — shook Carl's hand. McGraw said to him, "You pitched a great game today,"[11] then walked away. Given the rarity of verbal compliments from this source, it surely represented a considerable boost to the Oklahoman's confidence. The next day, with Benton the pitcher, the New Yorkers garnered their third straight, a 3–2 win. This put the Giants in first place momentarily, a few percentage points ahead of St. Louis.

It was the season's peak for the Giants. They had been winning at a furious pace since their loss to the Cardinals on August 5. Sheer weariness, lucky breaks running out, and a general letdown created a drop-off that lasted well into September. The Cardinals returned to first place. The Polo Grounders slipped into a close second, alternating with the Cubs. Road defeats in Pittsburgh and Brooklyn, followed by another to the Dodgers at home, were especially damaging.

In the aftermath of his eye-catching day against Alexander, Hubbell's setbacks illustrate the Giants' downturn. At Pittsburgh, in his next start after St. Louis, he pitched very poorly and was hit hard. Carl lasted less than five innings in a game the Giants lost 13–3 on August 23.

Because Hubbell had pitched only half a game on the 23rd, McGraw started him again on August 26 in Brooklyn after just two days off. In this, his first try against the Flatbushers, Carl pitched ten innings but lost again, 4–3. The manager gave him four full days off this time. On the last day of the month at the Polo Grounds, McGraw started Hubbell for the second time against the Dodgers. His pitching opponent was Dazzy Vance. The visitors won, 4–2. In the middle innings, Carl gave up a single run four times, causing McGraw to withdraw him after seven rounds. It was the second of what was, unfortunately, to become many defeats at the hands of the Dodgers. It was also his first loss to Vance. In one close game after another over the next several years, the "Dazzler," as Vance was known, was to defeat Hubbell repeatedly.

Hubbell's three straight losses did not shake McGraw's confidence in him. Early in September, a Giants reporter McGraw liked, Frank Graham, had an interview with him. "In many respects, Hubbell is one of the most remarkable pitchers I ever saw. I had my doubts as to whether a pitcher coming out of the Texas League was capable of winning in the National League right off the reel, but Hubbell soon cleared up my doubts. The number of pitchers who have equaled his performance could hide behind a bass drum."[12]

Regaining their poise in September, once again the New Yorkers slowly began to draw close to the Cardinals. Simultaneously, Hubbell resumed winning with a six-game streak of success. This run was composed of four complete wins and one incomplete win, along with a relief one. Intermixed with the six-game run was a one-out relief effort to close out a one-run win over Boston.

The feeble Phillies helped the Giants to the revival. Hubbell won one against them, an easy 9–4 victory, ending his three-game losing streak. Next, having lost twice to the Dodgers, on the third try Carl pitched a fine game, defeating them 3–2. He followed this with another one-run win against Boston. This one he did not finish because the Beantowners tallied late, falling only one run short of tying the score. This led the manager to withdraw his favorite prospect. Even though he had lost twice to Pittsburgh, McGraw had Hubbell in for a third time against the Pirates. With his teammates again scoring heavily, he won 9–2, pitching very well in the process.

On September 20, the Giants played an important mid-week doubleheader against the Cardinals before a crowd of 20,000. Had they won both games, they would have tied St. Louis for the lead. However, the Cardinals took the opener. In the nightcap, Hubbell faced Alexander for the second time, defeating him again, 7–4. A loss in this second game would have put the Giants four games back, all but out of the race.

Actually, though Hubbell won, Alexander outpitched him. A disastrous Cardinal infield error with two outs enabled the Giants to rack up five runs in the eighth inning. Three of the runs came on a Shanty Hogan home run. Though Hubbell had allowed a run in the seventh and another in the eighth, McGraw stuck with him in the ninth. The Cardinals did not score in that inning.

Still playing St. Louis two days later, Fitzsimmons was withdrawn after only four innings. Though only a day had elapsed since his win over Alexander, McGraw inserted Hubbell in the fifth. He pitched five scoreless innings for a relief win when the Giants prevailed, 8–5. AP writer Alan J. Gould referred to Hubbell the next day as "The 'Young Lochinvar' from out of the West."[13]

With the season due to end on September 30, the decisive moment in the National League battle had actually come three days earlier, September 27. At the beginning of that day, the Giants had narrowed the St. Louis lead to half a game. While the Cardinals were to play a singleton, the Polo Grounders had a double-header with the Cubs. Hubbell pitched and lost the first one, a game that brought repercussions for several years.

The Chicago hurler was Art Nehf, Hubbell's predecessor as McGraw's favorite left-hander. The Cubs led 3–2 until the Giants' half of the sixth. It looked as if they were about to tie the game. With runners on first and third, the batter tapped to Nehf. The pitcher threw to third to try to trap the Giants' runner off the base. He fled for home simultaneous with the Cub third baseman's throwing the ball to catcher Gabby Hartnett. Hartnett had moved up to the baseline from home plate. Trying to evade the oncoming catcher, who did not yet firmly hold the third baseman's throw, the base runner fell on his hands and knees. Hartnett gripped the ball firmly after juggling it momentarily then tagged him out. Plate umpire Bill Klem called the runner out. The inning ended with the Giants failing to score. Neither did they score in the remaining innings, losing 3–2. The Cardinals had won their game. The day ended with the Giants only one game behind, since they did win their second game. With only three games left, however, the Cardinals retained their lead and won the pennant.

McGraw and his players were livid with rage at Klem's call. They argued that Hartnett had both blocked the base runner and lacked full possession of the ball when he tagged the runner. Therefore, the runner should have been allowed to score on the grounds of catcher interference and an incomplete tag out. League president John Heydler was present at the game. Heydler upheld Klem the next day.

While at home plate, the catcher is permitted to block the plate. The baselines are supposed to be the runner's possession. Therefore, it does not seem as if he is entitled to block a play on the third base line as well. In the *New York Times*, James Harrison, who covered the game, agreed with Klem's decision. McGraw felt that Klem's verdict cost the Giants the pennant. Nonetheless, at most, that day they would not have gained more than a tie. McGraw remained bitter about this game to the end of his managerial days.

On September 29, the Cardinals clinched the pennant with the Giants a close second. After only two days off, Hubbell pitched and won their finale, 4–2, against the Redbirds in a makeup game.

As the Sooner graduate returned to Meeker for the winter, he had much about which to feel proud. Hubbell had earned a major league starting pitching slot and gained an exacting manager's confidence. Carl had compiled a solid initial season record in the midst of a pennant race. Hubbell's 10–6 W-L came to a .625 winning percentage. This was significantly better than his team's 6.02 percentage. His ERA at 2.83 was nearly a run better than the club's ERA and a full 1.2 runs per game below the league average. Altogether, Carl had eight complete games and 124 innings pitched. He struck out 37 while walking only 21.

Chapter 3

Stardom Imminent

In Giants history, the years from 1929 through 1932, Hubbell's settle-in seasons, have importance for bringing the John McGraw era to a close. His insistence on staying on deprived him of leaving with honors in the summer of 1927, when a grandiose ceremony for the Giants and McGraw took place. The ceremony was presided over by New York Mayor Jimmy Walker. It also included McGraw's theatrical friend George M. Cohan, as well as other entertainers.

The next obvious opportunity to retire on a positive note came after the near-miss at the pennant in 1928. McGraw's health had been steadily declining. He was in pain, heightening his habitual impatience and shortness of temper. With the players increasingly rebellious, managing surely could no longer have given him much pleasure. Yet on he trudged. The ambition to win just one more pennant, combined with the general reluctance (displayed by many conspicuous public figures) to leave the limelight, probably explain McGraw's refusal to retire.

The internal turmoil that beset the team in these years undoubtedly diminished its effectiveness. The club stayed in the first division until 1932, but only in 1930 did McGraw come even close to winning another flag. The manager's deteriorating health forced him to miss particular games. Sometimes, when the team was on a road trip, he would miss the journey completely. "Interim managers" filled in. Since they lacked his authority and prestige, the assistants did not obtain the same grudging obedience the players usually gave McGraw. When the manager would return, the team would disappoint him and, usually, the next season a different assistant manager would be on hand.

At the same time, probably due to increasing discomfort and pain, McGraw's outbursts became worse than ever. He climbed all over the players when the team hit a slump, blaming them for everything; he took no blame for himself. Once in St. Louis, encountering League president John Heydler just before a game, McGraw threw a tantrum. He berated Heydler for the incompetent umpires he hired. He especially berated Heydler for backing Umpire Bill Klem in the 1928 disputed rundown play. McGraw had convinced himself that the episode with Klem had, by itself, cost the Giants the 1928 pennant. It may have been a coincidence or solely due to the depression that two or three of the newer umpires whose decisions against the Giants had aroused McGraw's wrath lost their jobs in 1931.

In 1929, the Giants' spring training took place in San Antonio, a city to which the manager had long been partial. For Hubbell, this location had some merits. It was not an intolerably long train ride to reach it from Meeker, Oklahoma. Also, he had some acquaintance with it from his Texas League days.

Upon arrival at spring training, Hubbell found himself paired with Bill Walker, his road roommate from the year before. The two became good friends. They were both six feet tall and 175 pounds. They were both left-handers, although Walker offered the standard fare composed of a fastball better than Carl's, a wide breaking curve to handle left-handed hitters, and a good change-up. In 1928, McGraw had used Walker sparingly, but in 1929, Walker became a regular and offered a performance almost equal to Hubbell's.

In addition to the usual exacting workouts, the manager required his Oklahoma left-hander to take special instructions in fielding his position. Hubbell's managers in the minor league days had not insisted on this requirement. In the heat of the 1928 pennant race, there had not been time for it. Now there was. The emphasis was on throwing accurately to second on force plays and on fielding bunts nimbly. Presumably, Carl also received training in a pitcher's other defensive duties.

A Giants spring surprise came when McGraw offered a job to seemingly all but washed-up Carl Mays. That baseball's most unloved player could possibly take orders from the game's most authoritarian manager struck observers as incompatibility incarnate. Yet McGraw managed to extract from Mays, long a starting pitcher, a reliever performance second in effectiveness only to Pittsburgh's Johnny Morrison, who was considered to be the best. For example, in a mid-season game when the Giants were in a five-game losing streak and badly needing a win, Hubbell provided it against the Cardinals, 3–2, helped by a wind-up two scoreless innings from "closer" relief pitching by Mays.

The Giants' season opened with the Phillies at Baker Bowl. In this year the Phils, helped by improved hitting, climbed to fifth place. Signs of their improvement showed up in their 11–9 loss to the Giants. Hubbell started, pitched seven shaky innings, but won the game. After Carl was relieved, the Phils scored five belated runs.

In assessing Hubbell's skills in the 1928–32 interlude, the league statistical figures and his performance against the other first division teams offer useful data. How the teams fell into place in these early years of Hubbell's tenure resembled, on a limited scale, the usual pattern that prevailed among the contestants in the eleven years 1928–1938. Only three teams won pennants. At three-year intervals each, the Cubs won four; the Giants and Cardinals won the other three in the interludes when the Bruins did not. Between 1929 and 1932, with the exception of the last year when New York and St. Louis temporarily fell into the second division, the accustomed trio each year gobbled up three of the four first division spots. If one or more had an off year, the first division replacement usually was either Pittsburgh or Brooklyn.

Thus in '29, a typical year, Hubbell showed 2–3 against the pennant-winning Cubs, 4–0 against the Pirates with a "no decision," and 3–0 against the Cardinals with three "no decisions." This adds up to an impressive 9–3. However, the raw figures require elaboration for a full understanding of Carl's pitching at that point in time.

In his Cub encounters, Hubbell actually did better than the 2–3 suggests. In addition to the W-L total, he pitched in a 6–6 tie and relieved briefly once. In two of the losses, he was defeated 2–0 and 1–0. Against the Cardinals and Pirates, his performances in games he won were good to very good. However, in the "no decision" games, Carl pitched poorly. This suggests that luck favored him in appearances against these two. Separately, however, what gives pause emerges from his striking ineffectiveness against that year's sub-.500 fifth-place Dodgers. Hubbell went 1–5 against them. Throughout his career, Hubbell was plagued by the Brooklyn Dodgers; his difficulties with them in '29 need special attention.

Occasionally puzzlement has been expressed as to why the Dodgers troubled Hubbell so much. The Dodger problem seems especially inexplicable since before long, he was beating everybody else, including World Series foes Washington and — halfway — the mighty New York Yankees.

Actually, the reasons are not hard to unearth. For one, the Dodgers always loved to beat their much more celebrated inter-city competitors and therefore the players would exert every ounce of energy each time the teams met. Secondly, the Dodgers team included two pitchers, Dazzy Vance and Watson Clark, who defeated Carl again and again when they encountered each other. Sometimes, his losses to Vance and Clark were because Hubbell had an off day. However, more often than usual, bad luck pursued Hubbell. Third, the Dodgers had several good hitters. One of these was Babe Herman who hit Carl often — at just the wrong time. Finally, while reporters often remarked on how imperturbably Hubbell performed in game-deciding moments, once against the Dodgers he showed signs of coming unglued when a disturbing incident occurred.

In 1929, Hubbell, like all pitchers, varied in his pitching. Overall, however, it can be summed up as far more favorable than unfavorable. There are six games during his season that illustrate this variability. Two games Carl pitched in the early part of the season illustrate him at his best. Two other games, simply through hits and errors, show him at his worst. Two other games, both against the Dodgers, demonstrate how an unsettling incident led directly to his losing one game and how, despite pitching well against them, bad luck contributed to his losing the second game.

The two games in which Hubbell absolutely scintillated occurred on May 8 and June 3. The first, at the Polo Grounds before mid-week attendees of about 8,000, is memorable as Hubbell's only no-hitter. Had he been present, McGraw would have obtained silent delight out of seeing his latest prodigy pitch a no-hitter so early in his career. Unfortunately, he was ill and could not be on hand. That year, McGraw's "interim manager" of choice was Ray Schalk, who was present that day.

In most no-hitters, at least one outstanding defensive play is needed to sustain the feat. In this game, an 11–0 victory over the Pirates, not a single difficult out appeared. Only two of the hit balls even reached the outfielders. Until the ninth, the only batters to reach first base came from the pitcher's only pass and an error by shortstop Travis Jackson.

The last inning, through no fault of Hubbell's, brought the only excitement. The first batter hit a routine fly directly at Chick Fullis, McGraw's right-hand-hitting left fielder against a left-hand starter, and he muffed it. The next batter hit a simple grounder to Jackson, who in his anxiety to turn a double play, fumbled the catch. Up came Lloyd Waner, Hubbell's high school opponent. Lloyd Waner was Paul's younger brother. Carl got Waner out on a called third strike.

The following batter was Paul Waner, always a problem for Hubbell. This time, Paul topped a roller toward Carl, who fielded it cleanly, then threw accurately to second base for the force out. The double play to end the game followed immediately. The spring training drills had paid off. Terry tossed the ball to Hubbell, who left the field "amidst the crowd's cheers."[1] Since one of the teams made no hits at all, the game came and went in an hour and twenty-seven minutes.

The second time Hubbell dazzled occurred on June 3, a dreary, chilly day in Chicago at Wrigley Field. Over the previous winter, the Cubs had acquired Rogers Hornsby from the Boston Braves. This gave them a very powerful right-handed hitting lineup comprising Hornsby, Kiki Cuyler, Hack Wilson, and Riggs Stephenson. The latter was not a home run hitter, but had a very good batting average. This hitting quartet, plus solid pitching, made the Cubs' players and fans confident that this was the year they would win the pennant. Despite the unpleasant weather, those dreams produced a fair attendance.

Another reason for this fair attendance on a bad-weather day was that some White Sox fans showed up at Wrigley Field to pay tribute to Ray Schalk. McGraw had always admired Schalk in his playing days as a hard-driving catcher. When the unpopular White Sox owner, Charles Comiskey, fired Schalk in mid-season the year before, McGraw took him on as his replacement on sick days. Even though his playing days were well behind him, Schalk caught for Hubbell for three innings.

Hubbell then proceeded to draw the hoopla by his pitching. It was an occasion on which the Cub power hitters could not restrain themselves from going after Hubbell in exactly the wrong way by swinging mightily at his screwball. Hornsby fanned twice, Cuyler and Wilson once each. As the game went on, the crowd grew restive as one batter after another grounded out or, once in a while, hit a ground single. In the ninth with a large lead, Hubbell eased up to allow a run on two more ground singles, but ended up winning easily 8–1. As Ed Burns, for many years a Cubs–White Sox games reporter for the *Chicago Tribune*, put it, "The team that day played 'lambkins' for the visiting pitcher."[2]

As it turned out, the game proved to be truly exceptional. The Giants outfield did not record a single putout. The last time this happened in the National League was August 8, 1899. Hubbell's feat was, therefore, much more extraordinary than a no-hitter.

On the other hand, Hubbell, like all first-rate pitchers, also had his off days. Two of his efforts against the Pirates are illustrative. On August 5, he lasted only 6⅓ innings, getting rapped for five runs, coughing up ten hits and, troubled by a control lapse, four walks. Yet because the Giants piled up runs early, Carl garnered a cheap win from an 11–10 victory. Again, on August 24, against one of his leading foes — ever-battling Burleigh Grimes — Carl won cheaply again, 7–6. This time he allowed six runs (five earned, one not) and thirteen hits. Nonetheless, Hubbell managed to stagger through to the end.

Illustrative of his Dodgers jinx were two losses: one to Clark, the other to Vance. On June 24, he lost the first, 5–2, before a Polo Grounds crowd of about 10,000. About half the fans were for the Dodgers, not the Giants. Brooklyn scored a couple of runs immediately. But in the second game, the Giants came rallying back. They probably would have moved ahead but for a foolish mistake by Hubbell that brought McGraw's wrath down on him. Hubbell was on first. A Giants batter hit a single. Hubbell set forth for third, but in his hurry, he overlooked touching second base. The Dodgers spotted the mistake and the inning ended with the score only tied. The Dodger fans jeered him as he returned to the dugout. McGraw yelled at him, "I can't have my ballplayers running all over the base lines. Just so you'll remember it in the future, that'll cost you $50, Hubbell."[3]

That Carl was bothered by his running lapse and the manager's outburst was shown by the Dodgers' immediately scoring a run in their next half inning. Instead of the Giants leading 3–2, the Dodgers did. They went on to score a couple of more runs a little later, after which Hubbell was through for the day.

Incidentally, there were at least two other instances in which he received a managerial tongue lashing. On potential double steal situations with runners on first and third, McGraw had his pitchers intercept the catcher's throw to second, hoping that the runner could be trapped off third. One day Hubbell forgot the sign, the catcher's throw sailed into centerfield, the runner trotted home from third, and the other one made second unchallenged. This brought a "McGrawian" lecture and another $50 fine. His feelings hurt, Hubbell complained to his catcher, Shanty Hogan, about it. Hogan told Carl, "Think nothing of it. We all get it, and if we didn't, we'd feel neglected."[4]

The loss to Vance on August 30 at Ebbetts Field, on the other hand, need not have ended as it did with a 4–3 loss, but for a teammate's error. On an unpleasant afternoon with sprinkles, Hubbell fought Vance to a 3–3 tie at the end of nine innings, slightly outpitching him much of the way. In the first half of the tenth, the Giants could not score. Then, to start the last half, the somewhat error-prone shortstop booted an easy grounder. In this type of situation against the other teams, Hubbell had often escaped via careful pitching. However, against the Dodgers, a bad break did him in. After a sacrifice, Hank DeBerry, Vance's catcher — and never much of a hitter — doubled just inside the left field line, ending the game.

To summarize 1929's season for Hubbell, he won 18, lost 11, for a .621 winning percentage, much better than the Giants' equivalent statistics: 84–67, a .556 winning percentage. Carl pitched 268 innings, struck out 106, walked 67, and had an ERA of 3.69. Bill Walker, Hubbell's roommate, won the latter category with a 3.09 ERA. It was in this year that Hubbell's name began to appear regularly among the top five in various pitching categories. Surprisingly, he finished tied for third for wins, fifth in strikeouts, and fifth in innings pitched. Of his eleven losses, five were inflicted by the Brooklyn Dodgers, a second-division outfit.

In this season, both runs scored and home runs shot up over the totals for the earlier 1920s. The 1929 league batting average stayed about the same as the previous year. However, three National League teams had batting averages over .300.

For his fine pitching in 1928–29, Hubbell received a nice raise from McGraw, who decided everything, even the players' salaries. The salary Carl received in 1930 remained the same through the next three seasons. One reason his salary did not increase again in these three years was the prolonged downturn in the economy from the fall of 1929 onward.

Early in 1930, Carl and his inamorata, Lucille Harrington, usually called "Sue," decided to venture upon matrimony. Born May 7, 1905, at Meeker, Oklahoma, she was one of three daughters of John and Amelia Herrington. Mr. John Herrington owned the only hotel in the village of Meeker. Carl and Sue had known each other since high school days. They married when he was twenty-six and she was twenty-four. Sue's good looks were palpable.

A few of Meeker's neighboring small towns provided weeklies covering local news. Surely they would have been delighted to trumpet the marriage ceremony of Lincoln County's nationally known sports figure to one of Meeker's belles. However, the marriage did not take place in Meeker in spite of the fact that one of the affianced had been born in Meeker and the other grew up not far off. The wedding took place on Sunday, January 26, 1930, in McAlester, Oklahoma, some 100 or more miles to the southeast. Not only did the weeklies in and around Meeker miss the wedding news, but the state's major dailies did, as well. The location of the newlyweds' honeymoon also did not make the news. As noted in the first chapter, Hubbell was a very private person and said little throughout his life about his personal affairs.[5]

Hubbell reported for spring training in San Antonio a few weeks after his wedding. There he met Dave Bancroft, a Giants player of a decade before. McGraw had turned to Bancroft as the latest "fill-in" manager and coach. He had been the Giants' shortstop during the three years of the Giants' four consecutive pennant streaks in the early 1920s. Remarkably, Dave managed to hold onto his position until McGraw's resignation early in the 1932 season.

In 1930, McGraw's newest reclamation project in pitchers — Carl Mays having retired — turned up in the person of Hub Pruett. Pruett was the very screwball twirler whom Cobb and McBride had warned Hubbell not to emulate four years earlier. Perhaps Hubbell's success with the pitch convinced McGraw that he might strike gold twice in this sphere. If so, in the end McGraw was disappointed. Pruett did barely passable work, mostly as a relief pitcher along with others. Twice Pruett appeared in games in which Hubbell pitched. He did not do well enough to be retained for the following year.

Hubbell's initial start in the season, again against the Phillies, brought him a 2–1 win. He allowed only four hits. For the third time, he defeated Grover Cleveland Alexander, who — in his last hurrah — had obtained a job based on immediate performance with his original club, the Phillies. In this game, Alex offered a credible showing, the last of his career. Sadly, immediately after this game against Carl, Alexander succumbed completely to alcoholism and was soon released.

What makes the 1930 season worth recapturing is that in the National League, this season offered fans the rare treat of a four-way race all the way to the wire among the Cardinals, Cubs, Giants and Dodgers. Even though by summer the early signs of the Great Depression had begun to appear, the National League pennant race produced attendance records. The American League, through the performance of Connie Mack's stellar Philadelphia Athletics team, also had a record attendance in its circuit.

The National League race closely resembled the 1928 one, but with the Dodgers as a fourth runner. The Giants' promising start probably made McGraw feel that at last this would be the year he would reach El Dorado one more time. In the early spring, he was all wrapped up in the team and stayed so until summer. Unfortunately, due to health problems, he had to leave the team in charge of the interim manager during a long road trip in the later summer.

As for Hubbell, if at the end of the season he gave thought to how he had done, he may have felt a little disappointed in himself. He pitched numerous games that a mediocre pitcher would have been glad to have as part of his record, but no game was an attention-getter comparable to the 1929 specials. More important, the Dodgers — unlike the previous year, an essential ingredient this time — gave him as much trouble as before. Finally, his pitching in heavy-breathing games did not come up to his 1928 accomplishments.

With the Giants the lead horse in the early going, they played a series in Chicago in May. The Giants swept it, perhaps even bringing a McGrawian smile. However, an incidental aspect of the games stirred the manager's ire. The following winter, a major change occurred in the style of play. McGraw was influential in the league and his displeasure at what he observed in the series, as well as his harping on it later, may have had a bearing on the winter change. Hubbell played a small part in the cause of McGraw's ire because he happened to be the starting pitcher in the second game of the foursome.

McGraw had been bothered for some time by the steadily increasing number of high-scoring games and mounting home run totals. In this particular series, these reached what to him were travesty levels. The game in which Hubbell was involved only irritated him, but it set the stage for his outburst the next day. Hubbell seemed to be on his way to an easy win, the Giants having scored heavily early in the May 11 game. Carl allowed only two runs through the seventh. Suddenly, in the Cubs' eighth, a rain of hits culminating in a home run forced the starter's removal. This illustrated McGraw's argument that hits, runs and home runs came too easily. The Giants won, 9 to 7.

The May 12 game completely exceeded the bounds of high quality major league baseball, in the mind of McGraw. The Giants did win 14–12, but almost blew a fourteen-run lead. Worst of all to him was that nine home runs were hit, a record for a two-team total at Wrigley Field in a single game. While Hack Wilson and Mel Ott might be expected to hit home runs, such non–home run hitters on the Cubs' team as infielder Clyde Beck, and reserve outfielder Cliff Heathcote, had two apiece. Charley Grimm, first baseman, had one. For the Giants, in addition to the ones by Ott, Fred Leach, not much of a long ball hitter, got a home run. What seemed most ridiculous was the starting pitcher, Larry Benton, swatted one. Benton hit just two home runs in his career.

At Wrigley Field, especially in May, the southwest wind makes baseballs soar toward and over the fences. This factor in Wrigley Field home runs appears not to have struck reporters at the time, for they seldom made reference to it. McGraw described the home run hitting as "burlesque slugging."[6] Further, McGraw emphasized that this and others like it should not be seen in the big leagues.

The Giants' lead lasted until May 29. On that day, the Dodgers tied them for first. Both teams were 23–14 W-L. Hubbell lost 4–1 to Watson Clark, the Dodgers' left-hander, and one of the two Brooklyn persecutors. Back on April 30, the right-hand equivalent had triumphed 9–4. This was the worst thumping Hubbell received since his first game in the majors. In only three innings, he had given up six runs, nine hits, and two walks.

On May 29 at Ebbets Field, Carl was much better. Until the sixth, Hubbell and Clark fought it out. Then in the Dodgers' half, Babe Herman clouted a home run with one on. Later, against a reliever, he swatted another. At this stage, about the season's quarter mile, it was not a costly loss. However, it was symptomatic of the screwballer's woes in facing the Dodgers that year.

For a while, the Flatbushers did well. By July 24, the Giants had fallen to third, 4½ back of their cross-town competitors. The Cubs were only a half game behind the Dodgers. The Cardinals continued to tag along in fourth, which appeared to be their fate for this season.

As if Clark and Vance had not already done enough to Hubbell, on August 3, a Sunday, with a crowd of 25,000 at Ebbets Field to watch, he ran into Vance again. This time the Oklahoma southpaw ate up the Dodgers, inning after inning, but so did Vance with the Giants. In the visitors' ninth, the Giants once again did not score. Up came the Dodgers. Babe Herman led off. Hubbell had him fooled on a pitch, but he got his bat on it and just barely looped a pop-up over Lindstrom's head for a lucky double. After a sacrifice, McGraw ordered intentional walks to the next two. Up came Jake Flowers.

Even years later, Hubbell remembered what followed. For the only time in his pitching career, minors or majors, he walked in the winning run — and on only four pitches. The Dodgers won 1–0. The *Times* reporter described Carl as walking "dejectedly off the mound."[7]

The finish had McGraw and his players screaming at the home plate umpire, Lou Jorda, for his calls during Flowers's at bat. Though Hubbell's last pitch plainly had been too low, the first three were corner skimmers. On each of these, Jorda gave Flowers the benefit of the doubt. After ball four, he rushed off, thereby preventing the Giants players from surrounding him to complain further. It is striking that a year later, Jorda lost his job as a National League umpire.

By late in the same month, the Giants had moved up to second place. The Cubs led by four, the Dodgers had slipped to third, and the Cardinals continued in their accustomed fourth position. At this point, the Giants faced three strenuous series against the first-divisioners, two on the road. McGraw's health having declined again, Bancroft led the team on the western trip.

In each series, Hubbell pitched one of the games. In St. Louis, the Cardinals were showing signs of pennant ambitions themselves. On August 19, Hubbell seemingly jammed a spoke in their wheels by pitching well to defeat Jim Lindsey, a Texas League opponent two years previously.

From there, the Giants moved to Chicago to confront the first-place Cubs in their own lair. On August 23, with 45,000 rabid Cubs fans on hand, Carl and Pat Malone faced off. It was a thrilling game. The two went at it 2–2 until the eighth. Twice Hubbell was saved by his own outfield when Mel Ott and center fielder Wally Roettger threw out Cub base runners at the plate. In the last of the eighth, with two outs and two runners in scoring positions, up came Hack Wilson. In his top Cub years, Wilson was an excellent clutch hitter. Sure enough, he hit a single; two runs scored. Hubbell and the Giants lost 4–2. Instead of closing only two back, they fell to four behind.

Weary after the long western trip, the Giants returned to the Polo Grounds to play the Dodgers. As if Vance were deliberately tracking him, on August 28 Hubbell had to deal with him yet again. This time, however, the Giants scored a few runs on him. Then suddenly Hubbell fell apart in the sixth. First, there was a home run, then two singles. The lead was shrinking, but the inning was still manageable. Up came Babe Herman. He lashed a triple, two runners scored, and Hubbell had to be relieved. The Dodgers won 9–7. Since the Giants had for once tapped Vance for a seven spot, the game was winnable; unfortunately, this was the moment when Hubbell had nothing.

The Cardinals gained fast in September while the other three obligingly killed each other off. The pennant race reached its decisive day on September 16. That afternoon, the Cardinals, having overtaken the Cubs, were closing in on the Dodgers. They faced them at Ebbets Field. At the same time, the Cubs played the Giants at the Polo Grounds. In Brooklyn, Wild Bill Hallahan beat Vance in a 1–0 ten-inning thriller. Simultaneously, Hubbell throttled the Cubs, allowing only three hits. He struck out ten, walked only one, and won

7–0. This did the Cardinals a big favor, advancing them to first place by a fraction. In the remaining days of the season, the Cardinals managed to end up two ahead of the Cubs, five up on the Giants, and six over the Dodgers.

Due to Brooklyn's joining the first division, Hubbell's 4–8 W–L against the three others shrank by a wide margin compared to the 9–3 W–L in 1929. Otherwise, his statistics for 1930 showed a 17–12 W–L total and a 3.87 ERA. His winning percentage was better than the team's but not by as much as in 1929. The wins were only one less than the previous year's and he had one greater loss. Carl pitched 242 innings, struck out 117, and walked 58. Again Hubbell finished fifth in strikeouts. He tied for second in shutouts and was an impressive second in ERA. However, it was more than a run higher than Vance's for a rather undistinguished second. That year six teams had batting averages over .300 and home runs reached a new high of 892.

In the winter of 1930–31, the sport's owners took a step that produced a major change in pitcher-hitter relations. In baseball's upper circles, there was a feeling that the high batting averages and enormous increase in the number of home runs during the 1929–30 seasons had shown that batting had gotten completely out of hand. At the managers' level, this reaction was most clearly expressed by McGraw's remarks early in the 1930 season.

Although the owners informed the public of their deliberations, they did not provide details as to their discussions. They limited their announcement to the news that the ball would be slowed up. One consideration had to be that the fans obviously loved the high scoring and home run barrage. Could the moguls afford to take a step to diminish the velocity of the ball? In that period, baseball had a huge advantage in popularity over the other professional sports; therefore, the fan factor did not carry as much weight as it did at a later time. The moguls were able to decide pretty much on the basis of their own assessment of the condition of their sport. They plumped for the excessive hitting argument.

The manufacturers of baseballs were instructed to slow up the flight of the balls somewhat. The two leagues were then using different baseballs. Therefore, the National League owners specified that their ball would be a little slower than the American League one. The expectation was that the benefit this would bring to pitchers would help create a hitting-pitching balance. The reduction of the ball's aerodynamics was accomplished through thickening the horsehide and raising the stitches.

When spring training arrived in 1931, it ran its course uneventfully for the pitcher from Oklahoma. With McGraw anticipating a batting reeducation, he put greater stress on offense and defense tailored to the change. In San Antonio, players brushed up on their defense and hitting tactics shaped to lower scoring games.

Once the season began, the quality of the National League teams was almost identical with that of the prior year. In the early going, the Giants occupied first briefly, but the Cardinals soon overtook and passed them. The Redbirds steadily increased their lead, winding up with a huge 13½ game lead over the Giants. The latter did manage to advance to a very unimpressive second. This left "Little Napoleon" in a huff. McGraw was complaining as early as mid-season that his players, merely because they had fallen back a little, had lost their winning drive.

As for Hubbell, despite his team's runner-up status in the final standings, three less wins than the year before came his way along with the same number of losses. Though this could be attributed to a typical seasonal variation in a starting pitcher's wins and losses, there were two indications that he had a moderately unsuccessful season. First, on several occasions there were signs that, unlike in previous years, disagreeable game developments disturbed Carl's equilibrium. After this season, given Hubbell's years as a headliner, reporters often complimented him on his imperturbability in a crisis, but in this particular year, some shakiness appeared in his demeanor. Second, in his collisions with the Dodgers, Hubbell came out the loser as before.

On May 3 at Ebbets Field, with a crowd of 36,000 present, he ran up against Vance, as usual. Hubbell pitched a respectable game until the seventh. A runner was on first and Carl either made one of his foolish mistakes or the base runner's jockeying disturbed him. He started a full windup, allowing the runner to move to second. Hogan was not even able to make a throw. Next there was a hard bouncer deep off first. Terry grabbed it. Hubbell hustled over to take the throw. In the meantime, the runner on second raced all the way home. The Dodgers had scored a run without an error and Vance beat Carl again. This time the final score was 4–3.

Whatever Hubbell's misdeed, one would think this would surely have brought a dressing down from McGraw. However, in Hubbell's reminiscences in later life, he did not mention the incident as he did other mistakes and dressing-downs. Perhaps he was lucky and McGraw was sick that day.

On May 9, the Giants won a 5–4 game against the Cubs. However, the Oklahoma left-hander departed the game sooner than expected. In each of the first three innings, the Cubs' hitters nicked Hubbell for a home run. Runs two and three were lucky loopers that barely made it into the short Polo Grounds lower deck just inside the foul line. The third home run by the Cubs really seemed to upset Carl. He walked the next three batters on three-two counts, resulting in his removal.

Hubbell's next start was May 16 against the Cardinals and something else went wrong. Even though the Giants won 7–5, Hubbell lasted only three innings. This time during the second inning, in a reversion to his old fielding mishaps, he fumbled a roller the opposing pitcher tapped, and then flung the ball over Terry's head trying to get him. Meanwhile, a run was scored by another player. In just three innings, the Giants fell five behind due to Carl's "nervous pitching."[8] He gave up five hits to go along with the runs and error. McGraw had had enough and took Hubbell out.

After a start in which Hubbell did much better, along came Memorial Day and the Dodgers. At the Polo Grounds, more than 60,000 crowded in, with standees four and five deep, for the holiday double-header. Since Hubbell's foe in the first game of the double-header was not Vance, it had to be Watty Clark. The Giants' portsider pitched a beautiful game, going into the Dodgers' ninth with a 2–1 lead. With two outs in the ninth and a runner on second, up came Rube Bressler as a pinch hitter. He was a pretty reliable pinch hitter, well known for the difficulty pitchers had in striking him out. Hubbell got two strikes on him. On the bench, McGraw signaled the catcher to have the pitcher throw a screwball on the next two pitches, both of which Bressler fouled off. McGraw ordered another screwball on the upcoming pitch. Hubbell shook off the catcher's sign. This amounted to a challenge to his Lordship's order, meaning the pitcher had better be right. On Hubbell's next pitch, Bressler hit a single to left, allowing the runner from second to score. The game was tied at two.

When the Giants did not score in their half of the ninth, McGraw sent Hubbell back out to pitch in the tenth. The Dodgers got two runners on and Del Bisonnete came up to bat. He had two strikes and then hit a three-run homer. The Oklahoma southpaw had lost another tough game to Clark and the Dodgers. In the clubhouse between games, McGraw caught up with Hubbell and berated him for "disobedience to orders."[9] When the Giants also lost the second game, it knocked them out of first place.

As if these confidence-shaking setbacks were not enough, on the Fourth of July, with the usual full house at Ebbets Field, McGraw sent Hubbell out against Dazzy Vance again. This time, Hubbell was not even in the game, losing 4–0, and pitching only mediocre ball at best.

These constant losses to the Dodgers were not altogether Hubbell's fault. Game after game, the Giants scored only a few runs for him. The Giants relied chiefly on Ott and Terry for their power. Clark, a left-hander, lowered their effectiveness a great deal.

In this fashion, the inept side of Hubbell's hurling presented itself. However, skillful days occurred more frequently than inept ones. The problem was that Carl's off days came when the team could least afford them, while the bright ones came when the opposition had little. Three of Carl's four shutouts in 1931 were against second-division clubs. His most embarrassing outing came on his last appearance of the season, against the Cubs in Chicago.

Though neither squad had more than a faint chance of winning the pennant, the second-place chase remained undecided. The Giants lost 16–6, ending Hubbell's season. Even though there was a week to go, Carl did not appear again in 1931.

When the season finished and the full statistics became available, they showed that the dead ball had indeed diminished scoring significantly. From six teams having season-long batting averages of .300 or better in 1930, there were none with that average in 1931. Home runs took a precipitous drop of 400, going from 892 in 1930 to 492 in 1931. The league batting shrank from .303 to .276, a 27 percent drop.

As applied to Hubbell, the lessened hitting helped him lower his ERA from 3.87 clear down to 2.66. Again this placed him second among pitchers. His roommate, Walker, also had his best season, winning three more and losing three fewer than Hubbell. In other categories the Oklahoman came out as follows:

- Strikeouts: second.
- Complete games: fourth.
- Shutouts: second.

Anomalous best describes this season for Hubbell.

By spring training of 1932, a change at the league level was about to take place that affected play in a significant way. A second change took place, affecting the Giants, in a way that largely ruined their season. Also, the Depression was affecting baseball in general.

The major league powers-that-be decided they had to reduce player rosters and salaries. From mid–May on, the teams could carry only twenty-three players. The diminution remained in effect for several years. This meant that a field boss had to decide how he would parcel out his diminished pool. Often at turning points in a game, he would sorely lack another pinch hitter or relief pitcher. Since some managers chose to diminish the pitching staffs, a greater burden was placed on the starters in particular. Every now and then a team would use one or more hurlers with only two days' rest when three days off had hardly been sufficient.

The second change, pleasing to the Giants' players — and in some quarters to baseball at large — came as a surprise: John McGraw resigned as the club's manager at the beginning of June. In the spring he felt confident that he had a promising team at the ready. However, at the forty-game mark, the Giants stood at 17–23, in last place. McGraw's doctor told him he could no longer go on long road trips. So resistant had the players become to his Captain Bligh–like orders and punishment that even he seemed to have recognized that he could no longer handle them. Bill Terry, the team's star first sacker, whom the retiring manager named as his successor, could not, in the three quarters of the season that remained, "repair the rips in the fabric."[10] The Giants dropped to the second division.

The third development concerned attendance. In 1931, managers, players and owners had already observed that as the Depression worsened, fan attendance for weekday games declined noticeably, especially for the weaker teams. Yet fans would continue to show up in sizeable numbers for double-headers on Sunday. This led to some increase in the commodity in 1931. From 1932 until the end of the Depression — even after — there was a plethora of double-headers, especially on Sunday if at all feasible. Baseball's double bills were an outdoor equivalent of the movies' double features. Frequent spring rainouts made so many double-headers possible. With attendance down, "rainouts" and "wet ground" cancellations went up. Later in the season, a club, instead of playing on an off day, would double up with a Sunday or Saturday game.

This double-header "rainout" and "wet field" cancellation was a factor in a 1930s phenomenon: the large number of extended winning streaks. Due to the earlier rainouts, a club might have a prolonged home stand. Meanwhile, a close rival could be undergoing an exhausting fifteen- or twenty-game road excursion. Arriving at a contender's home where they had been hot for a long spell, the travelers could sometimes get wiped out in a four- or five-game series.

In 1932, for spring training, McGraw decided that Los Angeles would be the place to be. He was anticipating solid fan turnout to watch the New York Giants. Moreover, he thought exhibition games along the West Coast would provide solid attendance. Probably due to the worsening depression, he thought wrong. Crowds were *not* good. Further, the players disliked the setting, partly because of local inconveniences and partly because of their continued restlessness at being subjected to McGraw's heavy hand. In addition, the long trek back east for exhibition games did not sit well with the players. This did not bode well for the coming season.

Though he never referred to it, Hubbell, from a farm near the obscure village of Meeker, Oklahoma, found the novelty of the Western trip may have made it worthwhile. Judging by the season that immediately followed — for him but not for the team — this trip west for spring training served him well.

Bill Terry was not able to instill a sense of direction into the team in the two-thirds of a season remaining after he succeeded McGraw as manager. The preceding turmoil and unrest doubtless were important reasons why. The club drifted into a ten-below-.500 aimless aggregation that ended up tied for sixth or seventh place. For Hubbell this was the only second-division squad for whom he pitched until after his arm injury in 1938. However, Carl did very well — far better than his team.

Had Hubbell been with a first-division unit, he would likely have won twenty games and come close to attaining the stardom that awaited him a year hence. The trouble was that the team, in addition to not hitting particularly well, suffered from a poor defense. They finished next to last in fielding. The two shortstops committed 49 errors between them. Behind the plate, Shanty Hogan had become a liability due to overweight and alcohol consumption. For Hubbell the only serious disappointment must have been his failure, despite a promising start, to break his Brooklyn jinx.

Several features of the Oklahoman's pitching in this season deserve brief elaboration. For example, early in the season he seemed to catch up with Clark and Vance. In both of his wins, the Giants' batters hit solidly for him. On April 24, he bested Watty Clark, 7–2. Hubbell allowed only five hits, with one of the runs unearned. The next month, on May 24, he defeated Dazzy Vance, who in this season encountered arm trouble and faded relatively fast, 9–4. Carl scattered eleven hits with a Hack Wilson home run, the only impressive one.

In 1932, Hubbell usually enjoyed success against an old victim, the Cardinals, winning four and losing two. One of the losses was as a relief pitcher. On June 9, he beat the Redbirds, 4–1. During this game, Carl encountered a familiar face from his Texas League days in the person of Tex Carleton. In the next several years they went head to head numerous times, with Hubbell usually the winner.

The single best game the screwballing portsider hurled came against the Redbirds on June 22. His opponent was "Wild Bill" Hallahan, who had also been a Texas League pitcher at the same time as Hubbell. However, they had not happened to be matched in that interlude. In this game, Hallahan lost 9–1. Hubbell gave up only two hits, provided his opposing batsmen with no free transportation, and "whiffed" six.

In several other games, the Meeker maestro pitched equally well, but lost. For instance, on June 16, he encountered a familiar antagonist, Burleigh Grimes. In the exertion attendant upon winning two of the four Cardinal triumphs in the World Series the previous fall, Grimes, a rare spitball practitioner, had just about pitched himself out. He was traded to the Cubs. Grimes showed very little in most of his games for them. However, on this day he pitched one last fine game, outdoing Hubbell, 2–1. The *Tribune* reporter noted that even in losing, Hubbell was an "amazing pitcher."[11]

There is a novelty interest in another game Carl lost to the Cardinals on August 26. It was the first time that he and Dizzy Dean had a mound meeting. The Dizzy won, 4–2. Some observers mistook Dean as mostly a cheap headline seeker, so the crowd was small compared to a few years later when their clashes drew headlines. One other novelty in this game was that Hubbell hit a home run against Dean. Though it went relatively unnoticed, the left-hander was a fair hitter for a pitcher.

What makes Hubbell's 1932 season distinctive is not so much his wins as his losses and "no decisions" to the Dodgers. As before, he lost more than he won, but by no means was it due to poor pitching. In that year, the Flatbushers improved markedly, in the person of Van Lingle Mungo, a promising new hurler. Also, Hack Wilson, after his gigantic 1931 flop with the Cubs, made a fairly impressive one-year comeback with the Dodgers. Moreover, after years of Wilbert Robinson, the Dodgers had a new manager in the person of Max Carey, the speedy Pittsburgh outfielder for many years.

Hubbell faced the Dodgers seven times in the rivals' eight home-and-home series that year. Only in the early wins over Clark and Vance did he prevail. He pitched poorly, and then only moderately so in only one start. All in all, Carl came out with two wins, three losses and two no-decisions.

Hubbell's ultimate in his Flatbush misfortunes came on May 26 in one of his duels with Clark. The game turned into a fierce struggle through nine, ten, eleven, and finally twelve innings before Clark prevailed. Never did Hubbell have better stuff, whiffing fifteen Dodgers, his absolute peak. From the sixth through the eleventh, the Dodgers made one hit. But in the last of the twelfth, a single, a sacrifice and a single by outfielder Johnny Frederick beat him 3–2.

On August 14 came another heartbreaker. With 45,000 at the Polo Grounds for a double-header, Hubbell faced Van Lingle Mungo in the first game. With two outs in the ninth, he led 1–0. Then Frederick, his newest Dodger nemesis, hit a pinch home run to tie the game. In the tenth, a Hack Wilson double and a single by second sacker Tony Cuccinello beat him 2–1. Carl's third loss to them was a 5–2 game. Hubbell did not pitch well in this game, but neither was he so bad as to have to be lifted mid-game. In the two "no decision" games, he could have easily won either or both. As usual, unfortunately, the Giants scored only very lightly for him.

That year the Dodgers averaged a little over four runs a game. In his seven tries, Hubbell allowed fewer than three to them, yet could win only twice. Manifestly, his troubles with the Brooklynites in this season were not due to any defect in his pitching, but to the Giants hitters' inability to score and hit consistently well behind him. Had they done so, in either of the two tough Brooklyn losses or the two "no decision" games, Hubbell would have won twenty games for a losing team.

In the 1932 statistics, Hubbell finished fifth in winning percentage, second in ERA, second in strikeouts, second in innings pitched, and third in complete games. That is the performance of a star pitcher. Moreover, in his first four complete seasons, he pitched the greatest number of innings, 1,041.

He also had the lowest accumulated ERA at 3.15. Even before 1933, he had reached the level of one of the half dozen best pitchers in the National League.

Oddly, in 1932, Hubbell's friend Bill Walker fell upon dismal pitching days, winning only eight, losing twelve and running into arm trouble. Traded over the winter to the Cardinals, Walker did not regain his early Giants pitching skills. In the 1934 World Series, pitching ineffectively in relief, Bill suffered two of the Cardinals' three losses. Walker pitched with a seemingly easy, smooth, orthodox three-quarters overhand left-hander's delivery, and yet this was his fate. Clark, another orthodox delivery left-hander, ran into arm soreness the next year. For the remainder of his career, Clark barely hung on as a major leaguer. Meantime, Hubbell, with his arm-twisting delivery, was about to embark on the five best years of his career. These three cases point up the difficulty in estimating the arm risk factor in major league pitchers' durability.

Chapter 4

The Meeker Marvel

Over the winter of 1931-32, baseball's owners made no further announcement concerning the potency of the baseball. Thus, presumably, the one each league used was the same as in 1931. However, in 1932 there appeared to be an increase in batting, especially in the National League. Home run totals went up. This led some to wonder whether perhaps the ball had to some extent been accelerated for the 1932 season.

On the whole, the speculation seems not to be borne out. The National League hitting for 1932 was almost identical with the figure for 1931. The total number of runs scored increased, but only marginally (from 5,537 to 5,680). As to why the home run total for the league went up, it seems to be a mystery.

In 1933, there was a very decided drop in hitting for the season. This led to suggestions that the ball had been decelerated once again. In the 1932-33 winter, no such announcement had been made, though back in the 1930-31 winter, the owners had so acted despite the fans' preference for hitting. By the 1932-33 winter off-season, the Depression had worsened. It therefore seems unlikely that the majordomos would have dared it again and further upset the fans. After all, attendance had taken an alarming drop in 1932. The Cubs, the pennant winners, were the attendance leaders, but still only had about 950,000. Several clubs suffered major drops in attendance. Economic discretion worked against further slowing the ball.

What was done, however, may have had a similar effect. The seams on the ball were raised. This helped pitchers, who were better able to throw their curve off heightened seams. The heightened seams gave Hubbell, with his long and flexible wrist, greater leverage on the ball as he twisted it inward, thus adding to the effectiveness of his screwball.

When 1933 spring training arrived, Manager Bill Terry had justification for feeling fairly optimistic. Despite the 1932 flop, McGraw had created the nucleus of a sound team. Four of the regulars had served the Giants in 1932. A fifth, Travis Jackson, surely would have been included had he not been injured most of the season. Even better, the pitching core comprised a sextet of holdovers. They were the four openers:

- Hubbell, clearly the ace;
- Freddie Fitzsimmons, a near one;
- Hal Schumacher, fully nurtured by 1933, and
- Roy Parmelee, the in-and-out fastballer.

As an indication of the tightened rosters, there were just two frequently used relievers:

- Dolph Luque, and
- Herman Bell, an ex–Cardinal.

The Giants were lucky that year in that none of the pitchers suffered a disabling injury.

Over the 1932-33 winter, Terry brought off a couple of trades. On the whole, partly because the breaks went the Giants' way during the season, they helped the team defensively. To obtain clever, maturing catcher Gus Mancuso, who was good defensively, the Giants' manager gave up a parcel of players to the Cardinals: Hubbell's friend, Bill Walker; another left-hander who had never developed, Jim Mooney; second string catcher, Bob O'Farrell; and reserve outfielder Ethan Allen. Shanty Hogan went to Boston, whence he had come.

In another "three-cornered deal," the Giants acquired George ("Kiddo") Davis to cover the Polo Grounds deep center field. Also, Fred Lindstrom, a very solid hitter, had to be surrendered to Pittsburgh. Lindstrom had cherished ambitions that he, not Terry, would be McGraw's successor, so dispatching him seemed necessary.

The risk involved with the trades became apparent due to injuries to Jackson, leaving the team weak from the left side. Davis did a good job defensively, but hit barely adequately and did not have much power. Jackson was mostly on the sidelines. The new shortstop, Blondy Ryan, suffered from

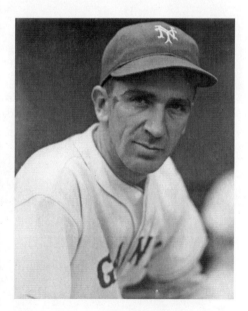

Carl in his uniform preceding pre-game practice, appearing with a rare trace of a smile.

being weak with the stick and, like Jackson, had an error tendency. At the same time, Ryan sometimes fielded spectacularly and had an upbeat, winning personality. The previous year they had lacked such a player. As catcher, Mancuso caught well, and hit passably, but did not have Hogan's line-drive strength. Such right-hand power as there was came from Johnny Vergez, the sophomore third base occupant. In the season, the portside weakness plainly hurt.

At bottom, the Giants' 1933 success stemmed from their pitching. The starters featured consistency, steadiness and, quite often, brilliance. Relievers Luque and Bell helped a great deal. Luque filled in now and then as a fifth starter. What made the Giants into surprise winners at the season's end was Hubbell's amazing hurling. Charley Dressen, former infielder, coach and itinerant manager, tagged Hubbell as Terry's "meal ticket"[1]— much to the annoyance of the Giants' boss.

Walker having departed, Hubbell needed a new roommate. Management paired him with Mel Ott. This panned out perfectly. The two became fast friends. They combined as a "roomie twosome" for seven years until Ott succeeded Terry as manager in 1941.

As the season shaped up, the Giants' chief foes figured to be the Cubs and Pirates. At the season's end, the latter grabbed place while Chicago settled for show. The Dodgers, despite their 1932 success, sank into the second division. The over-age Vance departed. By mid-season, Hack Wilson drifted back to his 1931 semi-alcoholic state. Worse yet, Watty Clark collapsed. The Giants picked him up in mid-season. Hubbell must have been relieved. Otherwise the Cardinals improved, but lacking starting and relief depth in pitching, they spent the year dodging between fourth and fifth place. Finally, the upstart Boston Braves, with their canny manager Bill McKechnie, nosed them out; the Braves obtained the bottom rung of the first-division ladder at the end of the season.

In Hubbell's situation, portents suggested he might be in for a banner season. His 1932 performance for a sub-.500 club indicated he was on the edge of stardom. A further sign was his ending up second in low ERA for the third consecutive year. Finally, there was the little matter of the raised seams on the ball.

Early signs of what he might do became apparent immediately. A couple of rainouts led to the Giants' opener taking place on April 16 at Ebbets Field. As so often happened, Hubbell pitched well enough to beat the Dodgers, but did not. However, Carl did avoid losing to them. In a fourteen-inning game that ended with a 1–1 tie, Hubbell and his opponent, Joe Shaute, an American League discard, pitched well before both were lifted after eleven.

After a day off, Carl served as a "closer" in a 3–2 Giants win over the

Phillies. Eventually Hubbell received credit for this then non-existent "save" statistic. Another couple of days passed and the Polo Grounders engaged in their belated home opener. The Boston Braves were the opponent. A small crowd of only about 10,000 was present, due in part to the chilliness of the day in spite of plenty of sunshine. Terry chose Hubbell to pitch the game. On hand to march to the flagpole for the flag raising was the mayor, John O'Brien. At his side was John McGraw, back from Florida and betting on the ponies. McGraw received hearty applause for his accomplishments as manager in earlier times.

To oppose Terry's best, McKechnie pitched Fred Frankhouse. He served as a better-than-average right-hander whose misfortune it was to toil mostly for second-division clubs. On this day, he hurled a first-rate game, but lost because Hubbell threw a brilliant one, winning 1–0. The Braves made only four hits; Carl's screwball completely baffled their hitters. He struck out thirteen, his highest for a regulation-length game.

After the standard three days' rest, Hubbell faced Brooklyn and Joe Shaute again. He shut out the Flatbushers, 4–0. After only two days off, Carl pitched three innings of relief against the Phillies as replacement for Schumacher, thereby obtaining a short-service win. After another two days of rest, Hubbell hurled the first game of a double-header against the Braves, this time at Boston. A surprising 35,000 comprised the attendance. When the home team scored two off Carl in the third, it ended a run of 28⅔ inning shutouts. He lost 3–0.

The game has mild interest as an oddity, in that Hubbell's foe was Ed Fallenstein. Fallenstein won only two games in his major league career. This was one of them. It is yet another example of how risky it is to bet on an individual game of baseball. For the month, Hubbell pitched six games, totaling 40⅔ innings, and allowed only four runs. He won three, lost one and had an ERA slightly under 1.00.

Since no pitcher, not even a deadball one, could maintain a sub-1.00 ERA, the months of May and June revealed Hubbell as human as any other pitcher. In the sixty-one-day stretch, he appeared fifteen times. Four times he served in relief. One of these garnered him a win, another a save.

Out of the eleven starts, he won six, lost four, and had one no decision. There was a noticeable slip in quality, perhaps a sign he was being overused. Subsequent events, however, did not bear out this supposition. Carl's best start during this period was a 1–0 win on May 7 at the Polo Grounds over Bob Smith of the lowly Cincinnati Reds. Hubbell gave up only five hits in a game that lasted a mere hour and twenty-seven minutes.

Four of the wins were undistinguished: 4–1 over the Cubs; 7–2 over the Dodgers; 6–3 to top the Braves again; and a 4–0 shutout of the pushover

Cincinnatis. The other two, both over the Phillies, were a little out of the ordinary. One was an 11–3 win, but he allowed an eyebrow-raising fourteen hits. In the other, a relief win, he pitched for four innings and allowed only one hit.

Of the four losses during this period, only one could be deemed an excellent showing in defeat: a 2–1 loss to the Cardinals and Bill Hallahan. The second of these losses was to the Dodgers, 5–2. They were back to their winning ways against Carl. The other two losses were to Pittsburgh. Since they emerged as serious contenders, these two hurt. One was a 7–6 loss, and the other, on June 28, ended the months of May and June with a 5–4 loss.

With the Giants holding onto first place, the western clubs — Chicago, St. Louis, Cincinnati, and Pittsburgh, where the chief opposition resided — expressed skepticism over their staying power. Conceding that the team had obtained excellent pitching up to then, the three midwestern hopefuls felt confident it would not last because the Giants' weak hitting eventually would wear out the pitching through too many low score games.

Overshadowing these self-interested expressions of doubt, a rare new phenomenon made its appearance on the baseball scene. The *Chicago Tribune*'s sports editor, Arch Ward, suggested the idea of an All-Star Game between outstanding players of the two major leagues. He succeeded in selling his concept to the usually staid, resistance-prone club owners. The game would amount to a sports supplement of the Chicago World's Fair, going strong as a Windy City diversion from the depression. In view of Ward's role, Chicago received the nod as host city. Comiskey Park exceeded Wrigley Field in capacity, so the White Sox Park became the game site. July 6, a Thursday, was the most convenient date for the game. Both leagues put off games that day so the stars could gather in Chicago.

The upcoming contest between the rival stars from the two leagues caught the public's imagination. The decision to let the fans vote to determine the players helped to increase their interest. There was an eighteen-player limit for each squad. This made it easier then than it was in later years for the voters to reach general agreement on who were the best players. Everything pointed toward July 6, 1933, as a candidate for becoming an epic day in baseball.

However, four days before the All Star experiment, an event intervened that in retrospect seems by far the greater spectacle. On the mid-summer afternoon of July 2, 1933, Carl Hubbell pitched one of the greatest games in the history of baseball. That day, the Giants played a typical Depression-inspired double-header. With the team in first place and the Cardinals their opponent, a crowd of over 40,000 awaited play. The fortunate fans who were present were destined to see a game that they could recount for the rest of their lives.

Hubbell hurled the first game. It lasted an astonishing eighteen innings. The Giants' star held the Cardinals scoreless from the first inning through the eighteenth. The home team finally won 1–0 in the last of the eighteenth. Put another way, Hubbell pitched two regulation-length games crowded into one. As the decades have gone their way, there have been several dozen no-hitters that have attracted the usual attention. There have been thirteen perfect games that have brought headlines. But not once in the three quarters of a century that has elapsed since has any other pitcher hurled eighteen consecutive scoreless innings, allowed only six hits and, most amazing of all, surrendered not a single base on balls.

What were the leading features of this titanic battle? How did the sportswriters and fans react? A factor that drew no attention at the time but was essential to make Hubbell's and his pitching opponent's feat possible was the weather that day. Rather than serving up a typical July scorcher, the temperature that afternoon reached no higher than the upper 70s. Had it been in the mid-80s, or worse, in the 90s, neither Hubbell nor his opponent, Tex Carleton, could possibly have lasted through a prolonged game. Carleton did almost as well as his rival, lasting sixteen innings.

Given such a low score, 1–0, were the Cardinals an especially light-hitting team? On the contrary, their team's season batting average placed them in second place, while their total of runs scored placed them in first. The Cardinals' lineup presented four batters who hit over .300 and a fifth who reached .298. The quintet occupied the first five slots in the lineup. An amazing feature is that each batted not four, nor five, nor six times, but seven. However, in their thirty-five tries, they made only four hits, for a sparkling .142 batting average that game.

In extreme form, this illustrates a characteristic of baseball in those days. Unlike decades later, frequency of a batter's appearances against a given hurler did not significantly increase his chances of making a hit. That there should be so notable a contrast between that era and now in batter/pitcher relations is a puzzle worthy of the SABRmetrics' attention. Of these five, Frisch and Collins each hit hard fouls that just missed being safe in fair territory. In one extra inning, center fielder Jo Moore rushed in to grab a hard-hit low liner off Collins, but that was it in the luck element.

Not luck, but the winner's brilliant hurling, has made the game memorable. In reflecting on it, Hubbell recalled that his screwball broke extremely well and that his alternative pitches were equally effective. Freedom from excessive reliance on his "out" pitch may have helped.

The box score reveals some of the lean southwesterner's deeds. Through eighteen opportunities, the visitors could hit safely only six times — two doubles and four scratchy singles. The Giants' defense helped with an error-free game. In the infield, a routine double play succeeded once, leaving the Cardinals with only five left on base in so long a game. It is amazing that in twelve of the innings, their hitters went out 1–2–3. The hits were evenly divided between the two halves, so as the game went on and on, Hubbell gave no sign that his continued labors were wearing him down.

By the later extra innings, how did the Giants' fans respond? "The throng grew ... hoarse ... weak from the tension."[3] "As the tension increased, the thrills crowded one another." "The fans were fascinated by the long duel."[4] Again and again the Giants, ineffective batters, let opportunities slip away. In the twelfth and fifteenth especially, they failed to hit when a run was at the door. In the latter inning, Terry tripled, yet no tally resulted. Altogether, the home team left nineteen on base.

On the thirtieth anniversary of this memorable game, Hubbell declared this to be his greatest pitching performance. He considered it to be even greater than the All-Star exhibition a year later. Another time, Carl asserted, somewhat improbably, that neither in this, his longest effort, not any other prolonged games he pitched, did he feel especially weary afterwards. He did add, however, that pitching so long in a scoreless tie left him "emotionally exhausted."[5]

In the eleventh inning, Cardinals manager Gabby Street sent up his aging but still hard-hitting Rogers Hornsby to pinch-hit for shortstop Leo Durocher. Earlier that season he had slammed seven straight pinch hits. This time against Hubbell he tapped back to the pitcher for an easy out. Street tried again in the seventeenth and sent up Bob O'Farrell, so recently a Giant, to pinch-hit for the weary Carleton. Hubbell got him on a "sweeping curve"[6]—a called third strike.

In such a long game, any reader would be bound to wonder how many pitches he threw. Since this was long before the day of pitch counts, there is no way of knowing for certain. The usual games Hubbell pitched lasted about an hour and forty-five minutes, give or take a few either way. This game went four hours and three minutes! This equaled two, two-hour games, much longer than his average. Carl had a dozen strikeouts. To make these 12 strikeouts, he had to pitch at least thirty-six pitches. More than likely, it was about forty to forty-two pitches. He gave no walks, which saved pitches. Hubbell probably averaged about eleven pitches per inning to the fifty-nine batters. Therefore, in the whole eighteen innings, many tensely pitched, he threw a staggering total of around 200 pitches.

How did this struggle ever find an ending? It came via an opening that the veteran Jesse Haines, Carleton's relief, provided to start the Giants' half of the eighteenth. Jo-Jo Moore, the first hitter, worked him for a walk. Catcher Gus Mancuso advanced Moore with a sacrifice. Travis Jackson, batting for

Blondy Ryan, received an intentional pass. Up came Hubbell to bat. (That Terry let Carl bat suggests that if there had been a nineteenth inning, he still would have been pitching.) Hubbell forced Jackson, advancing Moore to third. A moment later, Hughie Critz, up for his ninth time at bat, drove a single to center for the winning run.[7]

At the moment the Giants won the game, in tribute to Hubbell, "a deafening roar went up and straw hats, torn programs, and other debris rained upon the turf."[8] In another's description, as Hubbell "wearily trudged toward the clubhouse ... he was tendered an ovation that must have been heard in the distant reaches of the Bronx."[9]

In the general game analysis by reporters there was widespread agreement that they had witnessed the game of a lifetime. The *New York Times* scribe concluded that the "tall, somber ... Hubbell gave one of the most outstanding examples of endurance and mound skill seen in many years."[10] His *New York Herald Tribune* equivalent wrote that he had pitched "the game of the century"—which was supposed to be the coming All-Star game—"four days earlier."[11] In John Wray's *St. Louis Post Dispatch* column, he averred the season Hubbell was having, along with the game he had just pitched, elevated the Giants' southpaw onto a plane equal to Lefty Grove, making Carl one of the major league's two great pitchers. Six years before the Hall of Fame was created, Wray foresaw these two as "certain entries into this Valhalla."[12]

Peter Williams, in his 1994 book *When the Giants Were Giants*, mused, "Hubbell's performance was truly incredible. It still stands as among half a dozen or so candidates for the greatest game ever pitched."[13] Williams's judgment was made decades (and many more games pitched) after Hubbell's July 2, 1933, remarkable performance.

In addition, this particular game was, to some extent, an expression of the time in which the game was pitched. The "lively ball" stage of the game was a time of hitters' preponderance. The early '30s constituted a brief interlude in this "lively ball" era of superiority by the pitchers. Hubbell's gem illustrated the ultimate in pitching during this interruption.

Many, if not most, famous baseball records are closely related to the conditions that produced them. In 1968, Bob Gibson, the Cardinals' pitching star of a later generation, lowered Hubbell's 1933 National League ERA of 1.66 to 1.12 and deserved the plaudits that came his way. It should be noted, however, that it happened in another interlude of pitching predominance. Similarly, Barry Bonds did not hit his 73 home runs in dead ball days, but in the era of home run dominance from the late 1980s and early 1990s on. In like fashion, at most defensive positions, the fielding records are no leftover from the "small glove" dead ball days. They blossomed after hand protection and favorable field conditions reached their highest level of development. To say of a particular record that it is illustrative of its setting is not to dim its luster, but only to observe that few sports accomplishments can be divorced from their settings.

To estimate Hubbell's achievement in an historical context, one must look at it in relation to similar feats in both the dead ball age and the principal's own lively ball era. The criteria would have to comprise a very long game, almost eighteen innings hurled, and especially "whitewash" flinging all the way.

In terms of the first comparison requirement, there have been numerous examples of tossers who not only equaled but exceeded eighteen innings-pitched. The totals range from nineteen to the absolute high of twenty-six. However, in every instance, the pitcher gave up at least one, sometimes several, runs. Thus, with regard to the shutout stipulation, all are disqualified.

Comparing to other scoreless pitched games, there are only two early specimens. However, there were three other later cases in which the innings pitched requirement fell more or less short, but otherwise featured a scale of shutout hurling worthy of at least some comparison to the Giant portsider. These are described below.

If pitching a double-header shutout can be regarded as equal to a single game of eighteen innings, which seems fair enough, then the first of the two comparison games is quite well known. On September 26, 1908, Ed Reublach, one of the Chicago Cubs' dead ball era's pitching stars, threw a double-header shutout over the Brooklyn Dodgers, 5–0 , and 3–0. In the two games together, he gave up eight hits to Hubbell's six, a walk to his successor's none, and made an error.

A close look at the box scores and other statistics makes it obvious that the 1933 pitching jewel sparkled much more brightly. In 1908, the Dodgers were 53–101 W-L. The 1933 Cardinals were 82–70. The Brooklynites' hitting was so feeble as to reach only .213. The Redbirds hit .276. In 1908, the National League batting average stood at only .239. Twenty-five years later, when Hubbell pitched his remarkable game, it was .266.

A much closer comparison, but still not quite matching Hubbell's achievement, took place on May 15, 1918. On this day, the great Walter Johnson of the Washington Senators shut out the White Sox and Claude Williams, 1–0 in 18 rounds, the same as Carl. However, Johnson gave up ten hits to Hubbell's six, three walks to his emulator's none, and ten strikeouts to his successor's lively-ball twelve. In wartime 1918, the White Sox hit .256. In 1933, the Cardinals were twenty points higher. The 1918 American League batting average was .254 to the aforementioned National League one of .266 in 1933.

Three other prolonged struggles, all after Hubbell's own time, bear some resemblance to his feat. One came along just after World War II. On September 11, 1946, the Cincinnati Reds and the Brooklyn Dodgers held each other scoreless through nineteen innings until darkness ended the engagement. What keeps this game from being lost in obscurity is that Johnny Van Der Meer — he of the double no-hitters in 1938 — pitched the first fifteen for the Reds. While he fell three short of Hubbell's innings total, he struck out an impressive fourteen hitters and walked but two. Eleven hits marked his tenure.

Thirteen more years elapsed. Then on May 27, 1959, left-hander Harvey Haddix of the Pirates produced a new form of pitching uniqueness. Before losing to the Milwaukee Braves 2–0 in the thirteenth inning, he pitched a record twelve perfect innings. His deed equaled Hubbell's twelve but actually outdid one aspect of the Oklahoman's accomplishment: Haddix's dozen were consecutive. No pitcher ever matched Haddix's work. Pitching conditions have changed and no current pitcher would be called upon to go more than ten innings. Haddix finally lost because in the thirteenth, an error, a walk, and a double scored a pair of runs. As compared to Hubbell's game, he pitched five fewer innings, did not finally pitch a shutout, and lost rather than won.

The game that most resembled Hubbell's happened appropriately on July 2, 1963, the thirtieth anniversary of Hubbell's eighteen-rounder. This battle took place between the San Francisco Giants and the Milwaukee Braves. The opposing hurlers were the Braves' great left-hander, Warren Spahn, and the home team's Juan Marichal, also very good but not quite Spahn's equal. After fifteen scoreless innings, Willie Mays hit a home run to win it for the Giants. Marichal had won a 1–0 sixteen-inning thriller.

As impressive as are the statistics for the Giants' pitcher's performance, they are not quite the equal of Hubbell's in his eighteen-inning one. He matched his predecessor in winning a lengthy 1–0 shutout, but two innings short of the 1933 St. Louis–New York Giants game. He, too, gave up only six hits but again, the two-inning difference suggests his performance, while very, very good, was still not the equal of Hubbell's dazzling one. What is most suggestive of a difference between a high quality of service and an almost unbelievable one is that he allowed four batters to reach base on walks, to no Cardinal runner reaching base against Hubbell in that manner. In sum, the San Francisco hurler pitched a game worthy of high compliments, but Hubbell's thirty years earlier was a great one, challenging fans' belief that it had actually occurred.

After the Marichal-Spahn struggle, the number of lengthy extra-innings games between two moundsmen diminished. Greater attention to the possibility that a hurler could hurt his arm permanently in such long service explains why. By twenty or so years after the San Francisco instance, pitching struggles of this sort had dwindled to eleven or twelve innings as the length of service in which a pitcher was allowed to engage.

By the later decades of the twentieth century, continuing into the early years of the twenty-first, baseball passed through an interlude of extensive changes. By the early 2000s, a hurler throwing more than a regular-length nine innings was limited to a ten-inning maximum, happening only once in several years. Possibly it may never occur again.

As for Hubbell's greatest game, what he managed to accomplish on July 2, 1933, ought to be given attention as the greatest single one-game pitching performance in the last ninety or more years, but it is not. That it is not is partly due to the peculiarities of record keeping. In any typical record group, the reader will find a section listing hurlers' record achievements, plus and minus. But nowhere will he or she find a reference to Hubbell's greatest game. It is because, strictly speaking, what he did was not unique. There are several instances from "dead ball" days when a pitcher accomplished a like feat. The vast difference in pitcher/batter relations before 1920 and after is not taken into account. Thus nowhere does Hubbell's masterpiece appear. Such is the official status of Hubbell's actual realization of what for almost any hurler of his time would have been the ideal game to pitch.

Chapter 5

Meeker's Celebrity

·To almost anyone conversant with baseball, the July 2, 1933, achievement by "Oklahoma Carl" amounted to a great season in itself. Nevertheless, another remarkable accomplishment lay immediately ahead to be followed by yet other outstanding ones.

Thursday, July 6, arrived with its much anticipated All-Star Game. Almost 50,000 fans crowded Comiskey Park. The game is remembered chiefly because the first-ever All-Star home run had the one and only Babe Ruth as the clouter. Rarely noticed in reports of the game is that the later innings featured two of the greatest pitchers of the era: Lefty Grove and Carl Hubbell. During this game, they were locked in combat for the only time.

Overwhelming fan sentiment required septuagenarian Connie Mack and John McGraw to be the first All-Star Game managers. In the latter's case, this bore a relationship to Hubbell's role in those later innings. His old mentor intended to make him the National League starter. However, Terry intervened and talked him out of it, presumably on the ground of his pitcher's prolonged service on Sunday. Hubbell probably would not have pitched at all, despite the crowd's desire to see him at work, had he not volunteered to do so. Probably there was an understanding that if one team or the other established a substantial lead, he would make a token appearance. As the events unfolded, however, he pitched the National League's last innings under circumstances requiring fairly concentrated efforts.

Fixing upon a left-hander to deal with the American League's predominantly portside hitting, McGraw switched to Bill Hallahan. He had a fine fast ball and had won big ball games. However, he had had only a brief rest since his last game. Likely due to this, he gave up Ruth's home run as well as two runs early in the game. The Cubs' best, Lon Warneke, who pitched the next four innings, did much better, giving up only one tally.

On his side, Mack used his three hurlers so as to have Grove be his finisher. With the National Leaguers having scored two to their opponents' four going into the seventh, the stage was set for Grove. Remembered primarily as a formidable starter, he was simultaneously a ferocious closer. He could overwhelm the last couple of batters in a closely played game. Or, if needed, he could go three innings. Once in a while he would do long relief.

As the seventh round started, the Nationals began well. This was due to Pie Traynor's double to right center. To some it looked as if a faster right fielder than Ruth might have collared it. Despite the good start, Grove squelched the National Leaguers without a run.

Still behind, but by only two runs, the National Leaguers needed to hold their opponents scoreless. In the last half of the inning, the American Leaguers got their first runner to base when Hubbell walked Gehrig on four pitches. He succeeded in getting Al Simmons to hit into a force-out. The Athletics' Jimmy Dykes added a single. Hubbell then got Joe Cronin to foul out, followed by Rick Ferrell's rolling into a force-out.

In the eighth, both pitchers handled the opposing hitters. In Hubbell's case, he retired his rival, Grove, on a grounder, struck out Ben Chapman, and disposed of Charlie Gehringer on a fly to center. For Grove, it was not quite so routine, but again the National Leaguers could not score. The same was true in the ninth, with Grove retiring second baseman Tony Cuccinello, the last batter, on a strikeout. Perhaps it was fitting that the two great pitchers, in their only confrontation, surrendered nothing.

All in all, the American League win fit the times. For at least the first thirty years of the lively ball era, the American League clearly showed itself the better league. Off and on, the National League would win, but several times as upset winners. The first All-Star Game National League manager visited the American League clubhouse afterwards to congratulate his old managing rival and his players.

With the All-Star Game behind them, teams returned to their regular schedules. For the Polo Grounders, this meant a trip through the west, starting at Chicago. Then came St. Louis unless, as in some years, these two were reversed, followed by Cincinnati and Pittsburgh — or vice versa. In that year, the schedule called for them on their return eastward to play their irksome neighbors, the Brooklyn Dodgers.

The post–All-Star Game Sunday in Chicago added up to an important occasion. With the Cubs and Pirates trailing the Giants by 3½, the Sabbath double-header loomed large. By that day the Giants had lost four straight and needed at least a split. To their dismay, the Polo Grounders lost both. Hubbell faced Warneke in his effort. The Cubs' best blanked the visitors. A combination of errors, poor judgment, semi-intentional walks, and solid hits caused Terry to remove his ace in the fifth. It was his sixth loss compared to eleven wins.

Fortunately the travelers regained their equilibrium in St. Louis. Hubbell pitched the Thursday, July 13, game against a familiar foe, Tex Carleton.

Again, Hubbell won by a run, 3–2, when Johnny Vergez hit a ninth-inning homer. The situation put the Pirates in third place, 3½ back, and the Cubs continued in second.

That day, the Cardinals scored their last run in the sixth. At the time, the tally drew no remarks. Later, however, it attracted attention. The reason was that the league's batters were not able to produce one single run off Hubbell for the remainder of July.

In that stretch, the hitters had five opportunities to put this menace to their respectability in his place for a change. Two were Pittsburgh games. The Pirates were by far the best-hitting team in the league. Also, Hubbell's appearances against them were only two days apart. Yet in 17⅓ innings, the Pittsburghers, although able to make 14 hits, could not score one run. Nor did the other three teams do any better.

The reporters, struck by the batters' diminution into midgets, began to look back to whenever anybody had scored off Hubbell. This led them to the St. Louis Cardinals' July 13 game, and the last feeble run scored in the recent past.

Altogether, Hubbell's scoreless string reached 45⅓ innings. At the time, he thereby broke the National League record. By the 2000s, however, it had slipped to sixth, and fourth among National League hurlers. First is Orel Hershiser with 59 innings, set in 1988. Second is Don Drysdale, with 58, achieved in 1968. However, among left-handers, Hubbell's total remains tops. This fact demands attention to be paid several features of the streak.

The frequency of his appearances is one remarkable aspect. The Giants moved on from St. Louis to Cincinnati. Two days after he defeated Carleton, Hubbell faced off against the Reds' best, Paul Derringer, on Sunday, July 16, in the second of a double-header. The first the travelers had lost 1–0 in extra innings. Hubbell defeated Derringer by the same score in an hour and forty-one minutes.

Back when managers assumed starters would hurl complete games most of the time, there was a criterion often used to identify an outstanding start, as distinguished from an average one. This criterion held that if the team scored only one and that run in the first, the moundsman in use should be able to hold the one-run lead throughout. In this game, Derringer allowed a first-inning run, but held the Giants runless thereafter. Meanwhile, Hubbell held the Reds scoreless from the first through the ninth, meeting the criterion for an outstanding start.

Keeping in mind that Carl had only two days' rest since his last game, and the ninth-inning crisis he managed to scrape through, he did very well. Granted, the Reds were the league's weakest team, and it was easier to shut them out than any other team; still, this was an exemplary performance.

The Reds began their ninth promisingly with hits by their best batters, Chick Hafey and Ernie Lombardi. The next batter bunted. The Giants let it roll, hoping that it would roll foul, but it did not. Thus Cincinnati had three on with none out. Surely even the Reds could score in this situation. Not at all. Their next batter tapped into a force-out at home. The following one did the same. The last one flew to the left. Presto! In a twinkling, the Giants had won a 1–0 shutout.

The Polo Grounders moved on to Pittsburgh, their final western stop. The Pirates had caught up to the Cubs as a threat. Therefore, the Giants badly needed to avoid anything like a repeat of the Chicago series.

On Wednesday, July 19, the teams went at it in a double bill. Pittsburgh won the opener. The Giants needed a split. Watty Clark, Hubbell's one-time nemesis and Giants addition, opened the nightcap. The Giants scored, but in the Pirates' half, Clark coughed up three runs and four hits. With an out left, Bill Terry rushed Hubbell in as relief despite once again having had only two days off. The manager had Hubbell pegged correctly, just as Mack knew his Grove. The Oklahoman went on to pitch 8⅓ innings with no runs. The Giants won 7–3. Today it would be unheard of for a pitcher to be used so often. With the diminished rosters of the depression, not just Terry, but other managers as well, used their pitchers frequently. The reporters of those days did not criticize managers for so doing. Most significantly, Hubbell himself did not.

Saturday, July 22, the wanderers faced another double-header with Pittsburgh. A crowd of 27,000 attended, the largest there in three years. After his usual two days off, Hubbell pitched and won one of the two set-tos. The Pirates put their best, Larry French, to confront the visitors' best. Along with Bill Hallahan, French was looked upon as second only to Hubbell among the league's southpaws. Quoting John Drebinger, the *New York Times* correspondent, the Giants' star — in another "matchless performance" — stopped French in front of his home crowd.[1] Once again the Giants scored in the first and that was that. Because both hurlers worked promptly, Hubbell polished off his skillful opponent 1–0 in an hour and thirty-two minutes.

At the end of their trek, the Giants found themselves still holding their 3½-game margin over whoever happened to be second that day. At 8–9 in 17 games, they might easily have lost ground. Good fortune smiled on them. All season long their rivals, the Cubs and the Pirates, along with the party-crashing Boston Braves, who showed up unexpectedly as a contender, were quite evenly matched. Each would slow one another one or two just when it was helpful to the Giants. When the season ended, only 9½ games separated the second from the fifth placers.

For Hubbell, with the Giants back home, he did not appear until five days later, July 27, to take on Van Lingle Mungo, the Brooklyn fastballer, at the Polo Grounds. The game remained scoreless until the seventh. The Dodgers landed two on with only an out in their eighth, but the next batter hit into a double play. The Giants won 2–0. The Dodgers made four hits, one scratchy. The pitching duel lasted an hour and forty-eight minutes. By this time, Hubbell's runless streak had reached 38⅔ innings and had begun to attract attention. Meantime, the Giants had extended their lead to 5½ games.

On July 30, after another two days off, Terry inserted Carl, his ace, as a reliever in a game the Giants were losing to the Braves, 5–3. With two times at bat still left, the manager felt the Giants had a chance to win or tie; therefore, he wanted his best on the mound to prevent the Braves from scoring again. They did not. Neither did the Giants. Hubbell, however, did add two more innings to his scoreless streak. For the month of July, his ERA was 0.82.

With the Braves still in town, Hubbell appeared again, this time as a starter. As of that moment, the league record for consecutive scoreless innings was held by Ed Reulbach. In 1908, he had stopped opponents from scoring for 44 straight innings. When Hubbell went to the mound that day, his streak stood at 40. He needed to make it through five more rounds to outdo Reulbach. This was a weekday game and only 7,000 fans were on hand to see him try. Had it not been for the possibility Hubbell would break Reulbach's record, there probably would have been only about half that many. The Oklahoman pitched his "customary shrewd game,"[2] and Carl succeeded in holding the Braves scoreless through the fifth, thereby breaking Reulbach's record by a single inning. However, the Braves scored a pair in the sixth, ending Carl's streak, and eventually winning 3–1.

In the Giants' half of the sixth, Terry pulled Hubbell for a pinch hitter. As the Oklahoman walked to the clubhouse, the crowd "cheered him to the echo."[3] Thirty-five years were to pass before another National League pitcher would break Carl's record. Even though such great left-handers as Warren Spahn, Sandy Koufax, Steve Carlton, and Randy Johnson came after him, none of them equaled Hubbell's scoreless streak.

The Braves left and the Polo Grounders moved over to Philadelphia. In a game there on August 4, the manager used his prize left-hander again in the late innings. Watty Clark had been pitching quite well while the Giants built up a 7–1 lead. However, in the Phillies' seventh, they succeeded in putting two on base with two outs. This was hardly a hair-raising danger for the visitors. Nevertheless, Terry decided to relieve Clark. Either Luque or Bell could have been a sufficiently safe replacement with a six-run lead. Nonetheless, Terry brought in Hubbell, who got the third out, then went on to hold the home team scoreless thereafter. Meanwhile, the Giants broke the game wide open, winning 18–1. Hubbell had been used for 2⅓ pointless innings.

After only one day off, Hubbell was matched opposite Mungo again, this time at Ebbets Field. The manager and his team got hurt. Mungo beat the best and won 6–3. Errors hurt the Giants, but mostly Carl had very little to give. He gave up ten hits and four walks to account for the six runs.

It looked as if Terry realized, at least temporarily, that he was overworking his best, because Hubbell received a full week off. With the Phillies as the opponent again on August 13, the rested-up ace pitched a solid game against the easy-to-beat Quakers. Nonetheless, they lost 2–1 to "Fidgety Phil" Collins, usually not a formidable foe.

After another five days off, Terry started his ringleader against the Cubs on August 19. Hubbell pitched so-so ball at best, giving up four runs on five hits and three walks in seven rounds. Terry then removed Carl. However, with the Giants scoring eight against three Cub hurlers, Hubbell garnered a rather cheap win.

After this, the way Terry used Hubbell depended upon how well the Giants' lead stood up, or whether the particular opponent represented a serious threat. At this point in the season, the Giants were playing at home and clicked for an eight-game winning streak. It provided the opportunity for Hubbell to rest up.

In what followed, the Oklahoma portsider gave another demonstration of how brilliant he could be when in fine fettle. In the space of only a week, from Saturday, August 26, through Friday, September 1, Hubbell pitched three fine games — one going ten innings — against the other three leading contenders. Carl won all despite low run support. He allowed only a single tally in 28 innings.

The Pirates arrived in town. Hubbell had received a full week's rest by August 26. This enabled Carl to make the .285 hitting Pittsburghers his first of three victims. The game was a typical Hubbell exhibition. The "master screwball manipulator" held "the straining Corsairs to a skimpy five hits," winning 2–1.[4] Accomplishing this win required just one hour and forty-five minutes. Played as the first game of a Saturday double-header, the "two-for-one" drew 42,000 ardent fans. At the end of this day, the surprising Braves occupied second, the Cubs third, the Pirates fourth, and the Cardinals fifth.

On August 29, Hubbell came out to tackle the Giants' next foe, the St. Louis Cardinals. Frank Frisch, the new manager of the Redbirds, replied with Bill Hallahan. Despite only two days off, Hubbell performed amazingly well, giving up no runs in a 3–0 shutout. He fanned no fewer than a dozen and permitted the Crimson Birds only a quintet of hits.

The Giants immediately hit the road for five important stops. First, they went to Boston, then on through the usual Western stops, three of which figured to be no easy going. With their varying four- to six-game lead, what the Giants most needed was to prevent the westerners from plunging them into a losing streak. If they could avoid one, then their middling lead would be enough to carry them through.

First were the surprising, pesky Braves. For this reason, this series, especially the first game, provided the most exciting play of the five series. The Beantowners were like an inferior version of the New Yorkers. They had almost as good a starting pitcher lineup, the best defense in the league, and offense even weaker than the Giants. They had only one proven power hitter, Wally Berger, their center fielder. He had hit half of the team's mere fifty-four home runs. Boston's team batting average was .252 — ranked next to last.

Several extraordinary happenings occurred on Friday, the first day of the Labor Day weekend. The Braves scheduled a double-header. Despite the depths of the Depression, the pennant-starved Boston fans turned out in droves. The 59,000 present included 7,300 school children let in free. This constituted the largest crowd at the time ever to gather at a Boston sports event. So jammed was the Braves' field that standees several deep occupied all three outfields. This made cheap hits easy, seemingly, but not actually, handicapping each pitcher.

Winning the opener was very important to both teams. Regardless of the risk to his ace's arm, Terry sent Hubbell out to do his team's pitching. McKechnie countered with his best, Freddy Frankhouse, for a repeat of the April duel.

The game exposed the Giants' hitting weakness. Because of the close outfield, Frankhouse pitched around the Giants hitters whenever possible. Through the Giants' ninth, he held them scoreless despite giving up nine walks. Of course, he gave up several hits and his Braves committed two errors. The result was the New Yorkers left an unbelievable sixteen on base.

In a very different way, Frankhouse's opponent also pitched an exceptional game. In this game Hubbell demonstrated the art of expending the least amount of exertion to achieve the maximum positive effect. Connoisseurs of pitching excellence have cited it as the perfect example of Hubbell's hurling at its peak. It is stated that he gave no walks in the ten-inning game and did not once fall behind in the count. Every batter swung at no more than the fourth pitch.

This is true in essence but not in fact. In the Braves' half of the tenth, they put a runner on second with one out. Terry did the obvious thing, since the next batter was Wally Berger, and had his pitcher give him a base on balls. Thus did Hubbell, due to instructions, provide four balls to one batter. Every other batter made a hit or an out on four pitches or fewer.

In the Giants' tenth, three Braves errors, along with hits off Frankhouse, enabled the Giants to score two runs and win the game. They also won the second game. The double defeat for the Bostonians ended the overachievers' days as a serious threat.

On Hubbell's side, the three complete games in a single week is an extreme example of what in his age might be asked of a hurler. By contrast, twenty-first century baseball illustrates especially well how a later day and age in baseball can present a very different conception of handling pitcher duties. By the 2000s, the average starter might equal Hubbell's three in seven days with his third by the close of the season.

With the Braves series out of the way, the Giants staggered through the west on a Pittsburgh-Cincinnati-Chicago–St. Louis pathway. In Pittsburgh, a five-game set gave cause for worry. If the Pirates should behave like their name, and hack up the visitors by winning four — or even worse, all five — of the games, they would have as good a chance of winning as the guests. Accordingly, on September 5, Terry assigned Hubbell, after a reasonable three idle days, to pitch the first one. The Buccaneers racked him up in only three-plus innings of a 6–1 win in which Larry French did their pitching. Pittsburgh also captured two of the next three. This raised the stakes for the last one. Who but Hubbell appeared to pitch for the Giants on two days' rest yet again? He came back strong, repulsing the Corsairs, 2–1. To get their lone tally in the eighth, the chastened threateners needed three hits, a walk, and a force-out. The Giants departed with their several-game lead still intact.

The travelers moved on to their Cincinnati haven. Since any of his starters other than the kingpin probably could beat the Reds almost as easily as he could, the manager did not have his ace make a start. This did not mean, however, that he received an off-days respite. On both September 10 and 11, Terry had Carl pitch three relief innings to protect 6–1 and 3–1 wins.

Next it was on to the Windy City. There they faced a double-header on a cold, windy and rainy day: September 13. That 18,000 Cub fans turned up in these conditions convinced the *Times*'s John Drebinger that they had to be the most "rabid" fans in baseball.[5] In the first game, Hubbell went against Guy Bush. The Cubs scored two immediately. Then after the second inning, a two-hour rain delay occurred. Terry removed Hubbell. Bush went on to win, 2–0. Hubbell's early removal enabled him to pitch again in the finale three days later on September 16. He hung on to win 2–1 despite twelve hits. In the first inning, the Cubs obtained no runs out of two singles and a double. Carl also took a line drive in the left wrist, but pitched to the end regardless.

On September 18, depending on the Pirates' showing in their game and a Giants win, the wanderers stood on the verge of clinching the pennant. They were in St. Louis. With the visitors scoring three early against Carleton, they held a slim lead over the home team in the latter's fifth inning. At the moment, Terry again displayed the recklessness with which he risked overstrain to his ace's arm. This time Hubbell had only one day off. Terry brought him on with one out to protect the lead. It cost him the game. Hubbell had nothing. Carl gave up two runs on seven hits in the remaining 3⅔ innings. In the eighth, a Leo Durocher triple and a Steve Carlton single brought in the winning run for the locals for their 4–3 win. If no one else did, Carleton must have enjoyed the win, though his stalker lost via a relief.

Just how unnecessary Terry's use of Hubbell as a reliever had been became evident the next day. The Giants lost, but so did the Pirates. This enabled the Giants to win the pennant as a loser on clincher day.

Meantime, in New York, an elaborate reception awaited the winners. When the team rolled into Grand Central Station in Manhattan from Pittsburgh, 10,000 eager fans greeted them. Two brass bands offered a deafening serenade. Terry, Ott, Hubbell and "they can't beat us" Ryan received the loudest applause.

On September 21, the following day, the players gathered in the rain on the steps of the mayor's mansion. Despite the weather, 5,000 waited a couple of hours to see their heroes. On hand to give speeches were Mayor O'Brien and former manager John McGraw. McGraw received applause as usual. Also present was league president John Heydler, whom McGraw had dressed down so publicly only two years before. In the photo of the occasion, McGraw and Heydler stood far apart. Each player was introduced. Hubbell was cheered the loudest.

On the competitive front, the Giants' four pursuers pulled one another down so effectively that they provided the winners with a lucky break. They were able to wrap up the pennant fairly early. With almost two weeks of the season remaining, it enabled the players to obtain ample rest before beginning the World Series. In the remaining games, the manager gave his regulars respite midway in games or occasionally did not use one or another at all. Over in the American League, the Washington Senators captured the pennant only one day after the Giants. Whichever team should win the World Series, the loser could not claim exhaustion as the excuse.

Terry, perhaps showing belated realization that he had pushed his ace to the absolute limit, provided Hubbell extra time off. From his disastrous September 18 relief job to the season's end, Hubbell made only one appearance, on September 27. As a tuneup for what was to come, Carl defeated the Phillies without trouble 3–1, his 100th major league triumph. With the World Series scheduled to start Tuesday, October 3, Hubbell had an ideal five days of rest before facing the Senators.

When the season statistics appeared, they made evident the extent to which the Oklahoman had blossomed into the outstanding hurler in his circuit. He led in the most important column: ERA. Hubbell's was 1.66, considerably below the runner-up at 2.00. This was the lowest ERA in the majors since the later dead-ball days, during which Johnson and Alexander had finished still lower. Hubbell's low held up in the National League for thirty-five years.

Further, the southpaw deceiver finished first in wins with twenty-three, first in innings pitched (309), and first in shutouts with ten. Five of these shutouts were by 1–0 and another was 2–0 in ten innings. No one had blanked the opposition so often since Alexander's record sixteen in 1916. In other categories Carl rated second in winning percentage at .657, second in strikeouts at 158, and was tied for second in saves —five. In games pitched, Hubbell tied for third. He tied for fourth in complete games with twenty. This figure probably would have been higher, but a dozen relief appearances diminished opportunities to some degree.

Chapter 6

The World Series Wizard

Regardless of the economic conditions, with the World Series imminent, fan interest shot up. For the nation's favorite spectator sport, this event drew more attention than any other in the year. Even only lukewarm fans, and people who weren't fans at all, kept track. Since the vast majority had no chance of attending a game, broadcasting the series by radio became a public service.

The contrast between the teams drew immediate comment. The Nationals — or Nats, as the Senators were often called — had outhit the Giants during the season by a whopping .287 to .263 margin. They had four .300+ hitters to the Polo Grounders' one — Bill Terry. Usually Mel Ott surely would have been one, but 1933 was an off year for him. The Giants doubled their opponents in home run production, but the Senators did the same in triples. The difference lay mostly in park dimensions. The Polo Grounds was quite home-run accessible, while Griffith Stadium's deep fences lent themselves to triple hitting. More important, the Senators averaged about five runs per game to the Giants' much inferior four.

On defense, the contestants were close to equal. The Nats led their league in fielding percentage. However, the Giants' outfielders were faster and had better throwing arms. Their infield was better on the right side. On both, there was shortstop error-proneness. At catcher the backstops evened out. In a time when base stealing accounted for little, there was only a single steal in the Series, and it had no bearing on the outcome.

In pitching, the Giants featured a wide ERA superiority: 2.71 to 3.82. Nevertheless, the Senators displayed four capable starters. Two of their starters, Al Crowder and Earl Whitehill, were twenty-game winners. Both teams possessed solid relievers. The Senators' starting pitching nearly equaled the Giants'. However, none matched Hubbell in brilliance.

The opponents were not as far apart in skill as they appear on paper. The National League's higher-seams ball boosted good pitching, while the American League's lower-seams sphere did the opposite. Had each team been in the other's league, the difference would have been lessened. Probably by a small, or at most medium, margin, the Senators were a better club. Jack Doyle, the betting majordomo, rated the Senators as "strong favorites."

The games were scheduled for every-day play. When the distances between clubs did not require prolonged travel, the custom in these pre-television days was to play without a travel break after the second and, in an extended series, the fifth games. For a team whose fourth starter was a little dubious, it could put a manager in a tough spot in deciding who would start the fourth game.

The Senators' manager was Joe Cronin. His fourth starter was Monte Weaver. Terry's fourth starter, Roy Parmelee, did not equal him. Parmelee had an excellent fast ball, but he had spells of wildness. Weaver, though arm trouble doomed him to a short career, was very reliable. Before play began, Terry let it be known that he intended to use his ace as much as possible. This implied that he would solve the fourth starter problem by using Hubbell for that as well as the first. It also hinted that if the series should go to the limit, Hubbell likewise would start the last one.

Cronin also had a problem, but it was different from Terry's. Cronin's problem was deciding whom to start in the opener against Hubbell. Should he go with one of his two aces or try Wally Stewart, his third best? Stewart also had a good won-lost record, but not a twenty-win one.

The pre-series press gave considerable attention to how baffling Hub-

bell could be. Trying to anticipate, the Senators hired St. Louis Browns' Garland Braxton, the American League's only left-handed screwballer, to throw for a couple of hours of practice to their hitters. They hit Braxton quite well, thus boosting their hitters' confidence that they could hit Hubbell, too. However, Braxton did not throw his screwball as hard as did Hubbell. Probably Braxton's did not break as sharply as Carl's.

Hubbell is holding the ball in his partially outstretched hand a moment before he intends to twist it downward and inward to fling his screwball at a presumably frustrated batter.

Though Cronin sometimes gambled on a starter, it looks more likely that so much ballyhoo concerning the Oklahoma whiz kid may have put him a little on the defensive in his choice of whom he would have challenge Hubbell. Instead of going with Al Crowder, who had average stuff but a big-game reputation, or Earl Whitehill, a left-hander who perhaps could stop the Giants' two good hitters and neutralize their right-hand hitting mediocrities, he chose Wally Stewart, his third best. Was he worried that Whitehill or Crowder might lose a close one to Hubbell, thus wasting one of his two likely starts? If he started Stewart and lost, he had his aces to follow immediately, so his position would still be very good. If Stewart upset Hubbell, the Senators might win in a walk. It was a mistake not to counter the enemy's ace with his own.

The home field advantage fell to the National League in 1933. Reporters and prominent hangers-on began to gather in New York City as soon as the regular season ended. Most were from either New York or D.C. A few from other metropolitan areas also would be on hand. Significantly, in this particular year, one from Tulsa, Oklahoma, appeared.

As always, "experts" were on hand. They offered their predictions and opinions, whether they were closely read or listened to or not. Among those whose views showed more than average perspicacity were "Doc" White, a newcomer, and Babe Ruth. The Babe had simply become part of the World Series environment.

Doc White was the long-ago White Sox southpaw remembered for having twice defeated the Chicago Cubs in the 1906 World Series upset. White likened Hubbell's screwball to Christy Mathewson's "fade away." White opined that in the first game Hubbell, like Matty before him, would have an edge over the Senators because of the novelty of his pitch. Further, it was White's opinion that as the Senators became familiar with Hubbell's best pitch, they would be able to break through in a second appearance. Nevertheless, increasing familiarity by opponents with Matty's pitch had not increased their ability to defeat him.

Ruth, though usually not credited by onlookers with special acuity, occasionally would express views of surprising shrewdness. Like many others, especially American Leaguers, the Babe anticipated a Washington triumph. It would come through superior hitting and — a point not usually emphasized — their excellent defense. However, Ruth's forecast was not as unqualified as that of most American Leaguers. Stating that Hubbell was "a great pitcher," the Babe said he would be a problem for the Senators.[1] If they managed to beat Carl in the first game, Washington could win the World Series going away. If Hubbell should win the first, the Senators might have something to worry about. Hubbell was about to show baseball how accurate Ruth's estimate was.

That Ruth ranked Hubbell so highly a year before their 1934 All-Star Game encounter is mildly surprising. Could it be that he recalled the Toronto exhibition game of long before? It seems unlikely. To Ruth, that one could have been hardly more than just another "show-up-and-play" exhibition. Neither had he nor Hubbell ever directly referred to the fact that the Babe had battled against him at that time. Could it have been that so much talk about the new star among the moundsmen impressed him that much? More likely, either in a spring training game or on a Yankee off day, he had witnessed him pitch and decided that he was no ordinary pitcher.

On Tuesday, October 3, a crowd of 50,000 enthusiastic rooters nearly filled the Polo Grounds to cheer on their favorites. The sky was sunny, but the air was chilly. In order to enhance luster, the National Anthem was played just before the game started. At the time, it was heard at ballparks only at the summertime national holidays and just before the World Series opener. It increased people's feeling that something special was about to unfold.

This assuredly was how Hubbell responded. In an interview in old age, he harked back to how he felt just before the beginning of the first game. Standing while he listened to "The Star Spangled Banner," aware that after the last note had died out, he was destined to walk in a dignified way out to the pitcher's mound to cast the first pitch of the 1933 World Series, sent thrills and chills up and down his spine. Though at different times and speaking to different people, he varied in his estimate of what he felt was his greatest moment in baseball, his description of this occasion reads as if he really felt it deeply.

Just prior to this sendoff, the photographers had Wally Stewart and Carl Hubbell shake hands. Struck by the fact that the two had been teammates seven years before in Toronto and had not seen each other since, they wanted a photo of them as a sentimental gesture. The imminent foes gladly obliged. Back in their Toronto days, Stewart had been the promising pitching star, Hubbell only the hanger-on. As the years passed, Stewart had a major league career of occasional noteworthy success, but intermixed also with several years of mediocrity. Meantime, Hubbell had developed into a great star. When they shook hands, Stewart had become the underdog, his opponent the one from whom the crowd expected great things.

The preliminaries ended, Hubbell took his warm-up tosses and set to work. Acute embarrassment immediately befell the Senators. Leadoff batter Buddy Myer struck out. Second batter, Goose Goslin, a power hitter, struck out. The third hitter, high-batting-average Henry Manush, struck out as well. All three had had a few times at bat against Hubbell in the 1926 exhibition games, but none showed any signs that it had benefited them at this moment.

Up to this day, never in the history of the World Series had the very first three batters struck out. The New York crowd cheered mightily while Hubbell — as he usually did — walked to the Giants' dugout without a change of expression.

Afterwards, the visitors' inept start drew ridicule from the press. The *New York Herald-Tribune* writer decided that, not only in the first inning, but for the first two-thirds of the game, the Nats' hitting was "pathetic."[2] Worse yet, the *Washington Post's* reporter, H.L. Phillips, described his own team's hitters as swinging their bats "like a blindfolded golfer at a submerged ball with a rubber hose."[3] Possibly such severe ridicule shook the Senators' confidence a little.

If so, the Giants' home half of the first also contributed to the shaking. After a Buddy Myer fumble, Mel Ott drove a Stewart pitch into the right field lower deck for a pair of Giants' runs. Better yet for them, in the fourth, they tallied another two. Out went Stewart; in came Jack Russell, Nats reliever. He, and briefly Al Thomas, stopped the Polo Grounders the rest of the way.

In the first half of the fourth, the visitors eked out a cheap run on a Critz error and two singles. There matters stood until the eighth. The Nats registered their first out behind the infield in the seventh on a pop-up behind short.

In their eighth, the Nats came close. However, they were in a two-out situation and this was followed by a tough third out. Hubbell gave up a pair of walks between outs, putting runners on first and third, with Goslin coming up. After a long foul, he drove a hard liner that Terry stabbed on a fine catch. Had it gone through, it surely would have scored both runners. Two runs on top of two outs would have been encouraging to Washington. Instead, it was three outs with two runners left on base.

The game reached a peak of tension in the ninth. The Senators were handed an opening when Ryan fumbled Heinie Manush's grounder. Cronin singled to right. Fred Schulte hit a hard grounder that Travis Jackson could not handle cleanly, producing an infield hit.

At last the Senators had backed Hubbell into the ropes. The score was 4–1. The bases were loaded. They had not used up any of their valuable outs. A couple of hits, one preferably for extra bases, would tie up the game. More than one extra baser and the battle would be theirs.

On his side, Hubbell had to show whether he could stifle a club with harder hitters than any the National League team had in his previous — and frequent — late inning turning off of their spigots. Terry, still clinging to a three-run lead, decided to play his infield back.

The Senators did not hit another ball out of the infield. Joe Kuhel grounded to Ryan, who threw him out, a run scoring. With still two outs to go and runners on second and third, the Senators were in excellent position to tie if either Bluege or Sewell got a hit. Bluege struck out. Sewell grounded to Jackson, whose throw easily retired him.

The Giants had won, 4–2. The Giants' fans saluted them with a storm of applause and the Senators got a lesson in how tough a clutch pitcher Hubbell could be. In their postgame views, however, they conceded nothing. Stewart lamented how he had ever given up four runs to a team of such feeble hitters. Senators batters complained that National League umpire Charley Moran had given Hubbell all the borderline calls. Several felt the battle had simply been an instance of the breaks going the Giants' way. Actually, Hubbell's good luck on Goslin's liner was the only notable instance in his favor. The Nats batters, having familiarized themselves to some extent with Hubbell's slants, felt confident that they could catch up to him on a second try in Griffith Stadium.

The visitors suffered their second jolt the next day. Schumacher, a nineteen-game winner, hurled for the home team. Cronin started Al Crowder, reputedly his most reliable pitcher. The Senators led 1–0 on a Goslin home run in the sixth. But in the last half of the sixth, the Giants broke the game wide open. They loaded the bases with Davis coming up. Terry sent O'Doul, a career .300+ pinch hitter, to bat for Davis. He cracked a clean single; two runners scored. This opened the door for the locals. They racked up a six-run inning. With the Giants ahead, Schumacher's task for the rest of the way was eased. For the second time, the Giants won: 6–1.

The next day the scene shifted to Griffith Stadium. Clark Griffith, the owner, anticipated a large crowd and had temporary bleachers installed in front of the regular ones. They shortened the playing area, but not extensively. However, in two of the ensuing games, this did have an effect on the scoring. Both times it was in the Giants' favor.

Griffith was worried about the Depression's impact on attendance. He convinced the new president, Franklin D. Roosevelt, to be on hand for the game. This was expected to increase attendance. To Griffith's disappointment, the crowd numbered only slightly under 30,000. While this may have been a result of the hard times, New York City's attendance of 50,000 makes one wonder.

With the Senators facing an all but insurmountable 3–0 deficit should they lose, they had much at stake when they took the field. As expected, manager Cronin turned to his second ace, left-hander Earl Whitehill. Terry relied on the ever-reliable knuckleballer, Fred Fitzsimmons.

With the home crowd behind them, the Senators lived up to expectations, winning handily, 4–0. Whitehill pitched a fine six-hit shutout. As a left-hander pitching to left-handed batters, he collared Terry, Moore, and Ott in eleven tries among them. The six hits were scattered harmlessly among the Giants' right-hand hitters. As for Fitzsimmons, like Charlie Root with the Cubs, he was never to win a World Series game. In this one he pitched a sub-par game, giving up four runs in three different innings over seven rounds. Senator batters steadily peppered him on three doubles and six singles.

Along came the important fourth game. Though Terry had in mind from the beginning to start Hubbell again, with a two-one lead he easily could have taken a chance on Parmelee after all. If they won, the Giants would be up three-one. If they lost, they would still be no worse than two-two. Some managers would have chosen the fourth starter.

Terry probably saw using Roy Parmelee as a possibility. However, if he used Parmelee and the series went to seven games, Terry would not have had Hubbell available to start the last one. He would pitch the fifth and not be rested enough to pitch the seventh. Terry decided to go with his ace in this one. He would then be available for use in a hypothetical seventh game.

On the other side, Joe Cronin had Monte Weaver, a first-class fourth starter. The manager had no difficulty selecting him. Furthermore, since Al Crowder and Earl Whitehill had been so recently used, neither could start again so soon. Stewart, in view of his poor showing in game one, would have been too risky. From any standpoint, therefore, Weaver was Cronin's man. Also, their position had improved some with the Nats' winning the day before, looking good in the process. They were playing at home with the crowd behind them. It seemed a promising possibility that they could even the series at two-two.

Despite the home team's encouraging win the day before, the crowd again fell short of 30,000. As the starting pitchers warmed up, they were a contrast in degree of rest for the occasion. Weaver had not pitched since the last day of the regular season. "Hubbell," as the *Times* reporter remarked before the Giants spring training in 1934, "was ... tired and under tremendous strain."[4] That this was so seemed entirely credible.

Yet, as the reporter added, he then went on to pitch "greater ball in Washington than he did here [i.e., New York City]."[5] The box score shows that this was no overstatement. In spite of the Senator hitters' confidence that they would get to him on a second try, they did not get a runner on base until the fourth inning. Nor did they make a single extra base hit. In eleven opportunities they managed a single unearned run. How did the magician bring it off?

It looks as if Hubbell foresaw that if he pitched pretty much in the same pattern as in the first game, the Nats' hitters might get to him as they claimed they would. Therefore, he altered his pitching motion on his second go. At the plate calling balls and strikes was the American League umpire, Red Ormsby. Later he said:

> The Senators ... figured they had begun to get a line on it [i.e., the screw-ball], and that the next time they saw it, they would knock the cover off it. In the second game, they were all set for it — and Carl showed them one that came up straight as a string and then dropped sharply as though he had rolled it off the end of a table. I have looked at many a delivery, but I never saw one like that before.[6]

Hubbell pretty much confirmed this. He seemed to regard what others would call a sinker (a pitch that sinks abruptly as it nears the plate) as a variant form of his screwball. In the second game, he switched to what others would call a sinker, but to him was a screwball that simply dropped downward, without the break so characteristic of his "pure" screwball.

In the first three innings, the Senators were toppled one, two, three on five outfield flies, two infield pop-ups, and two ground outs. Gone were the strikeouts, replaced by outfield flies, thus confirming that Hubbell had indeed changed his delivery.

From the fourth inning on, the Senators pecked away, but futilely. Three times they advanced a runner to third, but with two outs. In each instance the next batter registered the third out. Respectively, they were a force-out, a strikeout — Cronin — and a pop-up. In the tenth, again with two outs, they had runners on first and second, but then the next batter — Cronin again — hit into a force-out. Otherwise the Senators continued their early inning pattern of frequent fly outs and pop-ups.

In scoring, the Giants equaled the Nats in ineffectiveness. In the fourth they did tally one. Terry lashed a drive to center that just cleared the low fence fronting the temporary bleachers. In the regular season without the extra bleachers, it would have been a long triple or a very deep fly out.

In the seventh, the Senators tied it up. In a lapse into his early fielding ineptitude, Hubbell bobbled Joe Kuhel's bunt. After a sacrifice, Nats catcher Luke Sewell singled in the tying run. Without the error, Hubbell would have shut out the Senators, 1–0. The batter following Sewell was the pitcher, Weaver. Cronin did not put in a pinch hitter for him and Carl got him easily on a pop-up.

The game continued into increasingly tense eighth, ninth, tenth, and eleventh innings. In the series-deciding inning, the Giants scored but the Senators could not. In the first half, Travis Jackson beat out a surprise bunt. Gus Mancuso's sacrifice succeeded. Then the weak-hitting, but sometimes timely Blondy Ryan singled to the left to bring Jackson in for the winning score.

Among exciting World Series games, the last half of the Senators' eleventh has often been recalled. Schulte singled to left. Joe Kuhel laid down a foul-line-hugging bunt. Terry let it roll, hoping it would trickle foul. It did not.

Thus the Senators gained a break — a hit, not a sacrifice. Ossie Bluege sacrificed. Just as in the first game, the Senators had Hubbell backed up against the ropes. Better yet, with only one out, runners on second and third and just one run behind, their chances were better than in game one. On his side, Terry had his pitcher walk Sewell, hoping for a killer double play.

The series had reached its climactic moment. Mancuso commented later that the Giants were relieved when Cronin chose Cliff Bolton, rather than the veteran Sam Rice, as pinch hitter for the pitcher. Bolton, a back-up catcher, had done very well in the season as a pinch hitter.

Had Bolton stroked a solid hit, the Nats would have won the game on the spot. For Terry, the question was how to play the infield: drawn in, as he usually did in this situation, or keep the infielders back for a double play? If the infield was in close, the chance of a double play depended largely on a force at the plate. Most times this brought only one out. It was risky for the catcher to throw the batter out at first because it could easily happen that the ball would hit the base runner as he hurried to that base. If this happened, the opponents would be sure to score one run and perhaps two.

On the mound, the infielders and the catcher conferred with Hubbell as to which alternative they should use. At first, Terry favored playing the infield in, and settling for a force-out at home if a grounder were hit. Shortstop Ryan and second baseman Critz, however, urged him to play them back in order to try for a double play brought off by the infielders on a grounder. From the bench, Charley Dressen sent them a message telling them that he had seen Bolton run, and that he was very slow-footed. Playing the infield back, therefore, would be the better choice. Terry agreed, Hubbell acquiesced, and the players returned to their positions. The pitcher and catcher decided that Hubbell would throw only his "dipsy-doo" stuff.[7]

With the crowd holding its breath, Hubbell pitched to the pinch hitter. The umpire called his third delivery a ball, giving the batter a two ball–one strike advantage. It put Hubbell in danger because another two balls and he would be walking in the tying run. Because of this, Bolton should have let the fourth pitch go by. If it were a strike, he would be no worse off than he was after the previous pitch. On the other hand, if it were called a ball, the count would be three-one in his favor. Hubbell was in imminent danger of surrendering a run-scoring walk and would all but have to throw a pitch the batter would have a good chance of hitting solidly.

Hubbell threw his fourth pitch, another screwball low and outside. It was close enough so that the umpire could call it either way. Bolton, instead of letting it go by, swung at it, probably out of a newcomer's nervousness. He hit a perfect double-play grounder to Ryan. The shortstop threw it quickly to Critz for the force-out at second. The second baseman fired a throw to

Terry at first. Bolton was out by several steps, and in a flash, the Giants had won the fourth game of the World Series, 2–1.

With the Giants players racing to the visitors' dressing room, Hubbell called over to Terry to give him the ball as a souvenir. The manager did so. Thus did the Oklahoman acquire a lifelong souvenir for the most dramatic one-run win of his career.

Still the Series had not quite ended. Down three-one, the Senators still had an outside chance. For the fifth game on Saturday, October 7, Cronin went back to Crowder as his starter, while Terry countered with Hal Schumacher, Crowder's second-game rival.

Until the home team's sixth, the game looked headed for a comfortable Giants wrap-up. In the second, they registered a pair on a hit, a walk, a sacrifice, and a single by Schumacher himself. In their sixth they added another on doubles by Davis and Mancuso.

Schumacher got the first two Senator batters in order in their sixth. Then a couple of singles were followed by a score-tying three-run homer off Schulte's bat. When the shaken Schumacher allowed two more hits, Terry replaced him with Dolph Luque, who got the final out.

Luque was a small but hard-working right-hander whom McGraw had for years coveted from Cincinnati. When he finally signed him in 1932, the forty-plus Luque was only a free agent looking for a job. McGraw took him on and the Cuban went on to give the Giants three years of excellent relief pitching, including this World Series appearance.

In the Senators' case, reliever Jack Russell had replaced Al Crowder in the middle of the first half of this inning. He, too, stayed in until the game ended. No more runs were scored until the tenth. With two outs in the Giants' half, Mel Ott banged a long fly to left center. With Ott a left-hander who usually hit hard to right, center fielder Fred Schulte had shaded him toward right center. Schulte had a long run, only to have it tip off his glove over the low fence of the temporary bleachers for a home run. For a second time, the extra seats had done the New Yorkers a favor. The Nats, in their half, threatened Luque by getting two on. However, they also had two outs. Luque struck out the last batter.

That a hard-hitting aggregation such as the Senators could score only three runs in two games off Hubbell is astonishing. It amounted to a tribute to Hubbell's amazing skill in this, his greatest season. Moreover, had it not been for his teammates' errors in the first battle and his own in the second, the Nats would have been shut out twice. As it actually turned out, they amassed three consolation runs and he had a 1933 World Series ERA of 0.00.

The Giants' combination of fine pitching — featured by a superlative ace-team spark, and lucky breaks — had enabled them not only to win a pennant but a World Series as well. All the Senators' players could do was to straggle home bemoaning their upset. For the star of the series, honors and awards were about to be showered upon him.

Hardly had the World Series ended when the first prize arrived. The players from rival clubs chose seventeen Associated Press writers to decide who had been the Most Valuable Player for the series. Hubbell, who received 82 votes, won out over Mel Ott, the runner-up with 66. In the *New York Times*, John Kiernan, with his own column, thought up inflated titles for the players who distinguished themselves. Hubbell, the "mild mannered man from Meeker, Oklahoma," he designated as the winner of the "Grand Order of the Stingy Arms."[8]

The very next day, the Baseball Writers Association of America voted the "Meeker man" winner of the coveted Most Valuable Player Award for the National League. In the days before the Cy Young Award was available as a unique honor for pitchers, it was more difficult for hurlers to win the MVP award than it is to win their own specialty award today. In any year, there were potentially player candidates from eight positions for each team against three or four pitchers who might have a chance. Hubbell's two leading competitors were outfielders Chuck Klein of the Phillies and Walter Berger of the Braves. The former obtained 48 votes, the latter 44. Hubbell garnered 77 of 80 possible votes. In addition, every single writer had his name listed, although not everyone listed Carl as first. The last time a pitcher had won the MVP in the National League, it was won by Carl's old adversary Dazzy Vance in 1924.

Two months later Hubbell landed a third honor. On December 18, 1933, "a nationwide jury of sports editors and writers"[9] bestowed upon him the title of Outstanding Athlete of 1933. Both amateur and professional athletes were included in the canvass. Thus, his new prize exceeded in distinction his single-sport baseball titles. Out of 207 votes cast, Hubbell received 56. The runner-up, Jack Lovelock, track star, obtained 26. Johnny Goodman, golfer, made third.

All contestants were white. Had blacks not been unofficially excluded, the result may have been otherwise. It was not until three years later when Jesse Owens in the 1936 Olympics set records that a black athlete could not be ignored.

Given the constraints within which the voters chose to operate, the choice of Hubbell as the winner was fair. All the athletes were excellent in their own way. However, that year, Hubbell had dominated his sport on a scale unequaled by the other contestants in theirs, so the submitters of ballots selected wisely.

Chapter 7

The Hero at Home

The impressive awards that the "Meekerite" had earned were one thing. The unofficial honors that the local folk were about to shower on him were another, even better. Probably he felt a sense of pride appropriate to the triple honors. Through a decade of work, he had reached the pinnacle of pitching endeavor. He may also have felt a sense of fulfillment. After all, the dark days after Detroit released him were only five and a half years behind him.

Given Hubbell's background, disposition and local attachments, the local honors, though unofficial, may have offered him an equal or greater pleasure than the formal prizes that officialdom granted him. Carl and his wife Sue were homebodies through and through. However, insofar as Carl was concerned, over the next few years, increasing familiarity with big-city life brought about a diminishing attachment to rural living.

After the World Series, Hubbell, along with several other players, lingered in the vicinity. As late as the 1930s, vaudeville remained a popular entertainment. After a World Series, the players on the winning team could easily make some extra cash by signing up to perform on the vaudeville circuit. They would learn a few comic skits, recall a few anecdotes for the season or the World Series, and go about, from city to city, reciting them until such time as the attendance dwindled and the promoters closed shop. Hubbell, more or less reluctantly, agreed to participate in this form of post-season easy money. However, negotiation with the promoter dragged on. Carl was reluctant to appear onstage before an audience under artificial circumstances, and both Hubbells may have longed to return to Meeker. Carl decided to cast aside the vaudeville opportunity.

On October 16, he telegraphed his father-in-law from Columbus, Ohio: they would be back in Meeker by Thursday, October 19. The couple probably left the Northeast in a state of considerable exhilaration. While still in their New York City apartment after the World Series, they had received hundreds of letters and telegrams of congratulations. One was from President Roosevelt himself. From Columbus, they succeeded in driving 850 to 900 miles in two and a half days. They tried to arrive inconspicuously. However, news of the telegram had alerted the villagers to the local hero's return.

In the eyes of Meekerites, Carl represented the epitome of the traditional American success story. Even better, he was one of their own who had gone out and made it big in the big leagues. Before him, who had heard of Meeker and its 562 citizens? The locals themselves, of course; the neighboring farmers — one of whom was his father on the Hubbell farm southeast of town — and many of the folk in Lincoln County. Possibly, too, an occasional traveler who whizzed through on Highway 62 might have remembered the village. But who else?

Once Hubbell and the Giants reached the World Series, that changed. Readers of the sports pages and radio listeners at last became aware that Meeker existed. For that, Meekerites had their own favorite son to thank.

Best of all, Hubbell — unlike many of those who had departed from small towns rarely, if ever, to return — continued to be theirs. True, through life in the big city, he had acquired a "slim and polished" appearance in contrast to the "rangy farm boy who stumbled over the mound in his professional debut." Nevertheless, he was still *their* Carl. The "lanky Oklahoman forsook crowds, turned down a vaudeville contract, and returned to the farm for the winter" with the "same unassuming, appealing personality."[1]

The gratitude of the townspeople took the form of prolonged celebration. It began on October 3, the first day of the World Series. Usually Cardinal backers, everybody in Meeker, on the neighboring farms — and probably in all of Lincoln County — had become ardent supporters of the Giants to win the World Series. The Meeker school let out for the day so the children could listen to the game on the radio. To celebrate the occasion, the town was bedecked with flags and banners. There was even talk of making the date into a town holiday to be named "Carl Hubbell Day."[2]

For listeners on the radio, it was a tense afternoon. Nevertheless, "their own Carl was bound to win"; "Carl couldn't lose." In the nerve-wracking ninth, there was cause for worry, but "Carl was not the weakening kind." And sure enough, he hung on to win it for the Giants. "We knew he'd do it."[3]

When, a couple of weeks later, the Hubbells arrived, villagers and farmers were ready to resume their celebrating. One of the town leaders was the honored guest's father-in-law. They knew the Hubbell couple would be back sometime later in October. This enabled them to push forward their plans for the "greatest day in Meeker history"[4] well in advance. Once they learned the travelers would arrive on October 19, they were able to finalize their plans quickly. They decided to allow the returnees a day to rest up, and arranged for Saturday, October 21, 1933, to be the great day.

The neighboring towns were quickly notified. Expectations were that crowds from all of Meeker's neighboring villages would appear in large numbers. Speculation ran high. Stories had it that people might turn up from all over the state. There were guesses that 10,000 people might line up along Meeker's one paved street — Highway 62 — and crowd the dusty side streets. At 1:00 P.M., there was to be a parade, and at 2:00 P.M., a ball game at the local diamond. In the Community Building, at 7:30 P.M., there would be a banquet for the modest celebrity. During the Depression, the charge of a dollar a head meant quite an outlay to listen to speeches and eat a banquet-caliber meal. Nonetheless, since it would be Lincoln County's most famous citizen who was being honored, the crowd was expected to reach 400.

On the whole, expectations were realized. That 10,000 showed up is extremely unlikely. It is even less probable that the rumored statewide representation included fans from as far distant as the Oklahoma Panhandle. Nevertheless, people from all over Lincoln County were on hand and quite a few from Oklahoma City, fifty-odd miles away on a two-lane highway.

The parade began at 1:00 P.M. Two marching bands provided the noise. At 2:00 P.M. came the ball game. Of course the crowd was enormous. As his way of expressing his gratitude for the locals' support of him, Hubbell had promised to pitch a few innings. After all, this was the primary reason most were there. Some probably had never seen a game with a major-league pitcher in it before.

Actually, apart from the leading figure, the exhibition offered other better-than-average players. From Oklahoma City came a makeshift team comprising good semi-pros and several lower minor leaguers. The locals, in addition to the star, included his two in-game pitching successors, Merritt Hubbell and Jim Winford. Merritt was Carl's younger brother and was also a left-handed pitcher. The younger Hubbell had helped Baton Rouge win the Dixie League championship that fall, while Winford had been an important pitcher on the winner of the Columbus Little World Series. (Winford went on to a brief career with the Cardinals.) In addition, one of Hubbell's older brothers, Jay, handled second base.

Hubbell pitched the first five innings. One wonders whether he chanced throwing a few screwballs to the hitters. Since the pitch was what had made him famous, and he was performing for the home folk, he probably offered a handful to satisfy their curiosity. Who won, who lost, what Carl pitched, all went unreported. At the time nobody cared. The crowd was there to see Hubbell pitch, not to pull for one spur-of-the-moment team over the other.

The banquet came off as expected, with the exception of one aspect. On hand to serve as master of ceremonies was Carl's former manager and booster, Ned Pettigrew. All of Carl's life, when Pettigrew's name came up, he gave his one-time Cushing and Oklahoma City manager a great deal of credit for guiding him on the road to success.

The M.C. introduced the honored guest. Then something unexpected happened. This person, who had not long before stood up under the pressure of pitching eighteen innings before a large crowd and had resisted shaky nerves through two tight World Series games, found himself tongue-tied. He was in front of 400 of his own hometown people! But he was expected to give a speech, not pitch. After cajoling and coaxing, he managed to stumble through a few sentences of appreciation for all of the honors bestowed upon him. Presumably the banquet then went on as planned.

About a week later, in Oklahoma City, a repeat celebration concluded the festivities. On Friday, October 27, another parade took place. This time it wound its way through the downtown streets of the state capital. The parade was followed by a luncheon at the Chamber of Commerce. The *Daily Oklahoman* scribe warned possible visitors not to expect an eloquent address from the guest. Hubbell was simply not the "talkative type."[5]

Nevertheless, this was the city where eight years before, Hubbell had first impressed baseball fans in any sizeable numbers with his promise as a pitcher. No doubt there were some who remembered him from those days. They wanted to see the pitcher whom they had observed as a minor league aspirant return to the town as a dazzling major league success. They were not particularly concerned that the star from their own state was not a skilled speaker. There was no report that the Chamber of Commerce luncheon had suffered for a shortage of guests.

Incidental to the celebrating, but quite helpful from the standpoint of gaining insight into Hubbell's pitching outlook, were two interviews that he gave to sports writers from the vicinity. One took place on October 19, apparently soon after the couple's arrival. The other came on Sunday, October 21, after all the hometown celebration was over.

Meeting the scribes from home seemed to make Carl a little more talkative than when he was interviewed by metropolitan reporters. Even so, the *Daily Oklahoman* representative noted that he had to be "pumped for information" and "weighs his answers carefully."[6]

Of course the recent World Series invited questions. "I was kinda nervous before the first game."[7] Then came some remarkable comments about how he felt in his two starts. He conceded that in the late innings of the first game, he had tired. As a result, he had to hang on for dear life to hold his lead. He attributed this to too much rest, rather than too little. Noting that late in the season he had pitched very little, he gave it as his opinion that often pitchers in this scenario who had exceptional stuff early — thus his fanning of the side in the Senators' first — ran short of stamina later.

Carl's comments on his second performance were even more surprising. "I didn't tire at all, and had as much stuff in the eleventh as the first."[8] The idea that Hubbell had "more stuff" pitching on less rest rather than more is astonishing.

It looks as if Hubbell believed (as did many old-time pitchers) that the arm, like other muscles, did not deteriorate through frequency of use, but benefited from it. While obviously this is true of the proper exercise of the muscles in their natural motion, the twirlers of that day did not take into account their arm movement was anything but natural. In Hubbell's case with his screwball, it was doubly unnatural.

The subject of Hubbell's in-season pitching arose. He offered the opinion that he had pitched as well in 1931 and 1932 as he had in 1933. This certainly was not the case for his pitching in the '31 season. Perhaps he mixed up the year with one or two other better ones. At any rate, he was correct about '32's comparability to '33 in the quality of his pitching. His great success in 1933 he credited to the much better performance of the team and to how many of the players behind him helped. Strangely, he failed to mention the diminished potency of the ball as a major factor.

Inevitably, the topic of his screwball came up. From what Hubbell said, he used the word loosely to embrace two or three variants of how he threw his "out" pitch. Others would have described one of the forms as a sinker rather than a screwball. Hubbell as much as said so himself. "There isn't a whole lot of difference between the sinker and the screwball."[9] From his description, it was this pitch that Umpire Red Ormsby had found so impressive. Hubbell's "pure scroogie" that broke away as well as down required a much greater snap and twist to the wrist than a regular sinker or screwball.

Hubbell's relations with the Giants also became a topic of the interviews. In this sphere, Carl became more reticent. He felt the club had treated him fairly. However, he admitted that after the season he had just had, he was going to ask for a raise. When asked what his salary was, he refused to divulge it. As for Bill Terry, he was an excellent manager. Later in life, he was not so generous in his assessment of Terry's managerial skills.

How did his arm feel? He said he did not once let it worry him. He hoped to last another ten years. As events were to show, his hope was exactly realized. However, he made the tenth year just barely and not in the manner he had in mind in this interview.

Finally, what did he plan to do with himself in the off-season? At first, he would watch a few football games, mostly in Oklahoma City. Nearby Shawnee had a golf course and he expected to play there a few times. Later he and some teammates intended to go on a two-week hunting trip to Mexico.

Presumably, it took some persuading for the wives to approve a nifty little junket like this.

Over several more years, Hubbell gradually overcame his shyness. For a professional athlete, the competitiveness of whose calling invites the development of a rough-hewn exterior, he appeared to have a surprisingly sensitive disposition. McGraw's harangues seemed to bother him more than they did most of his teammates. Self-consciousness made him uneasy in the presence of unfamiliar, urbane northerners. The "polish" the *Daily Oklahoman* reported that he had acquired served as a helpful surface protection against such "city slickers" as took him for an "Okie hick from the sticks."[10]

For a long time Carl felt most comfortable in the presence of southwesterners, especially Oklahomans. During warm-up at one of the World Series games, a youth leaped from the box seats and raced across to the Giant dugout. There he introduced himself to Hubbell. He was Edwin Carnett, a high school left-handed pitcher from Oklahoma, just as Carl once had been. Hubbell replied, "I am tickled to death to meet anyone from Oklahoma," and made a point of introducing the young fellow to Bill Terry.[11]

Carl's wife, Sue, may have helped him to gain more confidence when in the company of worldly people. Either as the daughter of a prominent businessman she was more sophisticated than he, or she adjusted quickly to the expectations of social life in the cultural capital. In 1936, at the time of the first game of the World Series, her name appeared in the syndicated column of Dorothy Roe, a prominent women's page reporter of the day. In her box seat for the game, Sue "appeared to be the 'belle of the ball.' She wore a gray tweed suit and small black hat, with a bright green scarf knotted about her throat."[12] Among the nearby celebrities was Mrs. Babe Ruth, wearing a mink cape.

Those who silently pegged Hubbell as socially awkward were only a handful compared to those who solicited Carl for autographs or a few words of conversation and found him very affable and likeable. Despite his fame as a pitcher, he was not in the least pretentious or egotistical.

Carl's relations with teammates and opponents illustrate why fans liked him so well. After games that were hard won, he regularly gave credit to his teammates. For instance, he went out of his way to praise Gus Mancuso as an adept and knowing catcher. He was not slow either in complimenting other teams for how hard they had played, whether the Giants won or lost. For example, after the first game of the 1933 Series, he was much more generous to the Senators than they were to him. "They're good, all right," he drawled. "They are dangerous every minute. But once we got the lead today, they had to try to slug ... and that gave me an advantage."[13] The absence of self-inflation in such remarks was one of the reasons why folk were so pleased to have him back for the winter in Meeker. They could greet him as an equal.

Chapter 8

Ups and Downs of Fame

The seasons of 1934 and 1935 brought disappointment to the Giants. They ended up as "also-rans" both times. In '34 they finished an eyelash-close second. In '35 a late slippage brought them down to a third-place finish.

In the thirties, until 1939, the top three regular contenders were so evenly matched that whichever prevailed in a particular year easily could be overtaken by one of the others the next. Overconfidence may have overtaken the Giants in both '34 and '35. The breaks that helped them in '33 largely evaporated in the following two years. Further, the other teams, through quick personnel improvements and effective trades, as well as through luck, overtook the '33 winners.

As victors, for the most part, the Giants approached the '34 season as "standpatters." The only major change took place in the outfield. In the off-season, Terry traded center fielder Kiddo Davis for the Cardinals' George Watkins. The latter had been a better hitter. With the Giants, he did not live up to expectations. When Watkins fell below expectations, Terry sometimes substituted with Hank Leiber, a farm product whose hitting fell short in this, his first year in the majors.

Otherwise, the lineup stayed nearly the same. Jackson moved back to short while Ryan became a utility infielder. With this exception, the infield remained the 1933 one. Starting pitchers also remained the same. However, not far into the season, a bad break struck the team. For quite a while, they lost Roy Parmelee because of an emergency appendectomy and a slow recovery. This necessitated the use of three semi-starters — Joe Bowman, Al Smith, and Jack Salveson — during Parmelee's absence. Sometimes they were also used after Parmelee returned. None was particularly helpful.

As spring training arrived, the players learned that a chronic problem had been solved over the course of the winter. A near-complete agreement between the leagues ended the debates over the velocity of the baseball, at least for a long time. In the National League, there had been complaints, not only from the fans, but also the batters. The hitters felt that the raised-seam ball tipped the batter-pitcher balance too much in favor of the slingers. The National League owners agreed to adopt a ball with the same degree of velocity as the American League sphere. For a couple of years thereafter, the National League continued to use its own baseball manufacturer. However, for all practical purposes, the sphere from 1934 on traveled the same distance in both leagues.

For the World Series champions, spring training came and went uneventfully. An innovation of the later weeks featured the launching of a Giants–Cleveland Indians long-term relationship. As the two teams headed north from their Deep South training bases, they played each other from one selected city to another. It was long before the advent of television. The opportunity for fans in the south and

In a slightly puzzling photograph, Hubbell poses with what appears to be an oversized fielder's glove on his right hand.

west to observe stars compete in competition near the regular season usually brought favorable attendance figures. The Indians and Giants quickly developed a congenial rivalry. For years their series provided welcome dividends to both clubs.

Hubbell had long since become a spring training veteran. The stretches, the extended running, and the semi-serious practice games passed routinely. At one moment, a reporter asked Carl whether he expected the new ball to diminish his effectiveness. Hubbell shrugged and replied that if it did, it would bother every other National League hurler just as much.

From the winners' and expectant reporters' standpoint, the season moved along in an agreeable fashion until late in the summer when the first clouds and then thunderclaps arrived. The Giants reached first place in June, and maintained it steadily week-by-week. Their lead averaged about three to four games, usually over the Cardinals. They could not shake off the Cubs, but that had been true through much of the 1933 season, and they had prevailed. As expected, the new ball brought a hitting improvement. Manager Terry hit a rousing .354, second in the league. Mel Ott led in home runs. Travis Jackson reached double figures in homers, as unexpectedly did Jo-Jo Moore. The pitching starters continued their 1933 pace. Schumacher even won more than Hubbell. Fitzsimmons had a good season, and Parmelee, after his return, did quite well.

As for Hubbell, he stood at 12–5 at mid-season, and 17–8 W/L by mid–August. Among his wins were three 2–0 and one 1–0 shutouts. However, up to the later date, he showed only 1–3 against the Cardinals, losing the three-some to the Dean brothers. Up to mid–July against the Cubs, Carl stood 2–2. He won against their second-tier starters, but against the Chicago ace Lon Warneke, he lost 4–0. He also lost 2–1 against Chicago's fast-advancing Bill Lee.

At mid-season, in the second All-Star Game, Hubbell reached his 1934 peak. He fanned five consecutive Hall of Fame sluggers. This event caught the public's imagination to a greater degree than did any of the other remark-able achievements of the Oklahoman screwballer. For instance, he received more publicity from the consecutive strikeouts than he did from the eight-een-inning shutout in the prior season. However, the latter was probably the greater feat.

When events commemorative of the summer classic come to mind, the most familiar is Hubbell's masterpiece. At the time, the game was still a doubt-ful proposition. Hubbell's wonder helped transform the second-year novelty into a summertime staple. Afterwards, baseball's All-Star special set the prece-dent for the other professional sports to adopt the same format.

The first All-Star game had been played in Chicago. New York City became the setting for the second. The Polo Grounds drew the nod as the site. The custom by which each league's previous pennant-winning manager took the reins as All-Star boss started up. In this instance, it meant Bill Terry and Joe Cronin. Given the location of the game and Hubbell's 1933 season, there was no way that Terry could fail to make his "Meal Ticket" the National League's starter. Joe Cronin chose the Yankees' left-handed ace, Lefty Gomez, as his. Hubbell was probably helped by the knowledge that the home crowd was cheering him on.

On this famous day in baseball's annals, July 10, 1934, more propitious weather could not have been found. The sun shone brightly, but it was not too cool. Neither was it too hot or humid. A crowd of 50,000 awaited a great game. Most were, of course, Giants fans. However, there were some Yankee rooters, too. Just before the start of the action, Hubbell received his 1933 MVP award. Also, in deepest center field, a plaque was hung in honor of John McGraw, who had died in February.

The batting statistics printed in The *New York Times* a couple of days before the game revealed that Hubbell would face a formidable array of American League batters. Exclusive of the last hitter, weak-hitting pitcher Lefty Gomez, the others threatened with a .330 collective batting average. In home runs, they averaged out at 13 each. With the season only halfway over, the two highest — Gehrig and Foxx — had 24 home runs each. Every single player in the American League lineup eventually made it to the Hall of Fame, unique in All-Star Game history.

Nonetheless, in the first and second innings, Hubbell felled one great hitter in the middle of the lineup after another. This was an almost unbelievable feat. How did he do it?

Prior to game time, Hubbell and the Cubs' Gabby Hartnett, his catcher for the occasion, conferred on what pitches to try in order to subdue the American League powerhouses. The two were so much in accord they had very little to iron out. Hubbell felt that since the hitters he was about to face had seen better fast balls, curves, and change-ups than he could serve up, he had better use these pitches only as out-of-the-strike-zone tantalizers. He would use his "out pitch," the screwball, in greater numbers than in a regular game since he would only need to pitch three innings. Hartnett agreed, and on the basis of this understanding, the two went out to start their work.

Over the years, Hubbell answered many questions concerning how he had pitched the famous hitters. The answers to these questions, along with what the pair had decided, make it possible to reconstruct Carl's pitching pattern in this game. He mentioned that every one of the five succumbed to a screwball on the last pitch. However, not every pitch was a "scroogie." Early in the count, two or three of them swung at a "baiting pitch." But the third strike that each hitter, except Ruth, swung at and missed was a screwball. Ruth took a called third strike.

Why were the batters so vulnerable to this pitch? It was for the same reason that National League players who encountered his "out pitch" for the first time found it so difficult to hit the ball out of the infield. Even after facing him for years, teams would occasionally hit grounders off him over and over again.

To the American Leaguers, Hubbell's screwball, as it approached the plate, looked like a so-so fast ball — nice to jump on. Gehrig, in his later description of what happened to him, conveyed very well the frustration hitters would feel. Just as the apparent fast ball came close to the plate, it would slow up and abruptly break. This was why hitters swung and missed it entirely or pounded it into the ground. Hubbell observed that of the four hitters who swung at the third strike, each was in front of the pitch — swung too soon, mistaking it for a fast ball.

At 1:37 P.M., plate umpire Cy Pfirman signaled Hubbell to begin pitching. Almost immediately, leadoff batter Charley Gehringer rapped a clean single to right center. When center fielder Wally Berger fumbled the pickup, Gehringer hurried to second. The next batter, Henry Manush, had been easy for Hubbell in the 1933 World Series. However, this day Carl walked him.

As pitchers' predicaments go, it is difficult to imagine a worse crisis than the one that the Giants' pitching star had created for himself. The very next batter was to be the "Sultan of Swat" himself, Babe Ruth. From one end of the country to the other, the children's idol, the Babe, created more future adult fans — and their descendants — than any other player in history. However, by 1934, thanks to the increasing age of the player, as well as his "eat, drink, and be merry" living habits, he had declined somewhat from the great hitter he had once been. Nevertheless, pitchers continued to pitch to him with the utmost care, conscious that one small slip on their part might produce one of his mammoth home runs.

If Hubbell should get by Ruth, there were his immediate successors to confront: Lou Gehrig and Jimmie Foxx. By this time, each had surpassed the Babe, and ruled as the new greatest sluggers. The crisis brought a brief conference at the mound, with the infielders joining Hubbell and Hartnett. The consensus reached was an obvious one. Hubbell should relax and not let the hitters make him throw their pitches by falling behind on the count.

After all was over, John Kiernan, the *New York Times'* sports columnist, recalled Hubbell's predicament and wrote, "It was a good spot for a pitcher to turn in his uniform and go back to farming. But Carl stood there and started a fanning run that was pitching in a pinch."[1]

As the Oklahoman began to pitch to Ruth, many in the crowd held their breath in anticipation. If Hubbell should slip and throw a pitch near the middle of the plate, Ruth still could hit a baseball farther than anyone else playing the game at that time. But on the first three pitches, Hubbell gained a one-two pitch count advantage. On his fourth pitch, low and on the edge of the plate, outside, Ruth chose to let it go by, guessing "ball." However, Umpire Pfirman called him out on strikes. The Babe's vast array of fans groaned. Ruth, walking away, made no complaint. *Strikeout number one.*

Gehrig came up next. A mixture of balls and strikes brought the count to three and two. On the next pitch, Gehrig swung hard and missed, producing a huge outburst of cheering. *Strikeout number two.*

On the three-two screwball to Gehrig, Manush and Gehringer stole second and third. If anything, this made Hubbell's position even more precarious. If Foxx, his first right-hand hitter, should hit a homer, it meant three runs. If Foxx hit only a single, the Americans still would be up two.

Having fanned the first two poster hitters, he pitched to Foxx, and a "deafening roar" accompanied every Hubbell pitch. On two-two, Foxx swung mightily and missed, and the "crowd went wild."[2] *Strikeout number three.*

After the National Leaguers tallied one in their first, Hubbell returned to the slab. After three whiffs in the American Leaguers' first, the crowd awaited expectantly for the appearance of Al Simmons, then Joe Cronin, both right-hand swatters, with Bill Dickey, a "southpaw" swinger, to follow.

Simmons and Cronin were meat for the voracious screwballer, who subjected them to the same outcome as their three predecessors, but in this case, it took only four pitches per batter. Each, given an unbroken string of borderline high and outsiders, looked ungainly in flailing at the beyond-reach pitches. *Successive strikeouts in a row — numbers four and five.*

Catcher Bill Dickey finally broke the spell with a single to left on the one-two pitch. It meant nothing. Lefty Gomez immediately struck out. *Strikeout six, after one hit, but no runs.*

Because of all the strikeouts, an oddity of the first two innings was that infielders and outfielders had no putouts. Hartnett had all of them. From a different perspective, the two rounds had cost Hubbell plenty in pitching effort. It had taken him twenty-three pitches to navigate through inning one, fifteen more to do the second. Thirty-eight tosses in many of the regular in-season games would have taken him to the fourth inning.

The Nationals did not score in their share of the second. Hubbell, back up for his last inning, did not let his phenomenal success in the first two innings make him overconfident. With the top of the lineup back at the plate, he pitched cautiously to each batter.

In turn, the American League sluggers showed that they had learned something from their first-round experience. Though again they could not score, they completely eliminated the strikeouts. Further, two of their outs were solidly hit balls.

Gehringer flied deep to Kiki Cuyler, eventually a National League Hall of Famer, who made a nice catch. Manush, as at the World Series, grounded out easily. With Ruth up again, Hubbell, despite his whiff of him in the first, pitched cautiously, finally walking him. Gehrig lined to Cuyler in right to close the inning.

The National Leaguers enjoyed a three-run third. In the middle of it, Hubbell departed for a pinch hitter. At the time, it looked as if he would emerge an easy winner. However, the American Leaguers rallied, finally winning 9–7, due to their hitting and Mel Harder's five innings of scoreless pitching. In so doing, Harder violated the unofficial understanding that pitchers would go only three innings. However, the year before, Warneke had gone four.

It made no difference insofar as the fame of this particular All-Star Game is concerned. It is always remembered as the one in which Carl Hubbell struck out five Hall of Fame sluggers in a row.

An added dimension to understanding Hubbell's accomplishment emerges from the comments of the victims afterwards. Because of the closeness to the time of the actual event, that of the American League manager conveys the greatest authenticity. Another reflection dates from long afterward, but carries the air of unembellished recall. Two others are also helpful. However, the words expressed suggest that the authors had decided to fit their remarks to the increasing legendary status of Hubbell's feat. A fifth had interest because it was voiced not by one of the strikeout quintet, but by another of the participants whose occupation was the same as Hubbell's.

In the American League dressing room after the end of the game, Manager Joe Cronin held court. Naturally he was delighted by his players' rallying for the victory. Likewise, he probably felt this helped even up scores for the Senators' humiliating World Series loss the year before. He praised his own players exuberantly for their league's obvious superiority. Then he added: "I say this for the National League, Carl Hubbell is the greatest pitcher I've ever seen."[3] This judgment came from a hitter who, for six and a half years, had been batting against Lefty Grove. At that moment in the clubhouse with Cronin was the great retired pitcher Walter Johnson. Cronin looked over at Johnson as he offered his assessment, and Walter "nodded approvingly."[4]

Long after the Senators had lost the '33 World Series to the Giants, Cronin mentioned to Hubbell that in 1934, the other American League players — and particularly the Yankees — had razzed him about the Giants' win. How had his club ever lost to such a ragged hitting outfit as the Polo Grounders? Cronin's answer became, "You'll know why when you see Hubbell pitch."[5] After the All-Star Game, Cronin noticed that his rivals' cheap swipes petered out.

Lefty Gomez, a Hall of Fame pitcher himself, knew another when he encountered him. He said of his former portsider rival, "Hubbell had a screwball and a good one, the best I ever saw. He had excellent control and he was pretty quick." Then, recalling the hitters as they came back to the bench, he added that at the moment, they gave Carl only "grudging praise.... They keep saying, 'We'll get him next time....' Hitters always said that. They'd strike out ... and somebody would ask, 'What's he got?' They'd say, 'Nothing.'"[6]

As for himself, by the time the story was lapsing into legendary status, Lefty chose the roll of buffoon. By the time he stepped to the plate to end the American Leaguers' second inning, the five great hitters had already become victims. According to Gomez, he turned to Hartnett and said, "You are now looking at a man whose batting average is .104. What the hell am I doing here?"[7]

Gehrig's remarks come not from immediately afterwards, but while he was still playing the game. They convey quite well why hitters, mistaking

Hubbell's screwball for a fast ball, had so much trouble with Carl's "out pitch." "I swung at all three pitches, and every time I took a swing, I thought to myself, 'This is a home run for sure!' It looked so easy."[8]

Jimmie Foxx, while still playing, sounded in his remarks as if he was caught up in the legendary tempo. Pretending that nobody could solve Hubbell, he said, "Oh, sure, I struck out — but I hit a long foul off Hub. That's more than those other guys could do." (The *New York Times* account makes no reference to a long foul hit by Foxx.) "Any time you hit a foul off Hub, you are practically in a hitting mood."[9]

Charlie Gehringer was the former player who was not a strikeout victim, but who commented on the flurry of them. As a long time Detroit player, he had good reason to remember Hubbell. Years after, Gehringer recalled Carl from the Tigers' 1926 spring training — but apparently not from the Toronto exhibition game.

Recalling the 1934 All-Star Game, Gehringer described his frame of mind at the time: when he and Manush got on base to start the first inning, "I figured we were good for at least a couple of runs, that there was no way he could get by our three best hitters. But he struck out Ruth. Gehrig and Foxx were still coming to bat.... But he struck out Gehrig. And then he struck out Foxx. To start out the next inning, he struck out Simmons. And then he struck out Cronin. Bill Dickey finally broke the string. I'm glad he did. It was starting to be embarrassing."[10]

To his interlocutor, Gehringer added, "I guess what he did in that game still ranks as one of the greatest pitching performances of all times.... When you strike out those five guys ... in a row, you have to figure that's really something."[11]

In the thirties, Detroit had a top-notch team, barely inferior to the Yankees. They had Hank Greenberg, in addition to Gehringer, as well as high-class hurlers Schoolboy Rowe and Tommy Bridges. They won three pennants, counting 1940, and one World Series. Gehringer lamented Hubbell's departure from the Tigers, saying that if he had been on hand as their ace in the thirties, they might have won another pennant or two and perhaps even another World Series.

And what did the principal himself have to say about his most publicized achievement? To questioners, Carl agreed that it provided him with his greatest baseball thrill. Why? He never regarded himself a strikeout pitcher, nor had others viewed him in that light. Striking out these five elevated him momentarily to the status of "strikeout whiz," to be recalled ever so briefly with the great fastballers.

What Hubbell did on that July 10 left very little that he could possibly do in the second half of the season that could equal what he had already done.

Consequently, the post–All-Star Game stretch was almost unavoidably anti-climactic. Neither their ace nor the Giants sensed how great a letdown was in store for them. There were no acute immediate worries. They maintained their lead, albeit a small one, through the rest of July, August, and almost all of September. Given the favorable signs, it was easy to dismiss the worries as minor ailments.

An important worry, but an unmentionable one, was Manager Terry's use of his "Meal Ticket." For instance, including the three strenuous All-Star innings, Hubbell pitched on July 4, 7, 10, 12, and 15. In twelve days he appeared five times, pitching two complete games, relieving twice, and appearing in the All-Star Game. Further, in six days, July 29 through August 3, "King Carl" pitched two complete games on either side of a four-inning relief job, for a total of 22 innings. Judging by certain signs that appeared in July and August, sharply augmented in September, this was simply too much.

At the Polo Grounds on July 17, the first instance of a problem that beset Hubbell for the remainder of the season appeared. Whereas he would continue to win the low score, one-run games against the array of lowly clubs, he would lose the close ones against the team's major pursuers. This was only to a minor degree due to a lapse in his clutch pitching skills. It was mainly because his good luck ran out. The Giants, though improved in hitting and leaders in home runs, were only fifth in overall hitting. Against the top-notch pitches that he took on, his teammates failed miserably at the plate.

In the July 17 midweek Chicago double-header at the Polo Grounds, 44,000 were present, the largest in several years for non-weekend games. The Giants won the opener, 5–3, and with Hubbell ready to go in the second, they were hoping for a sweep against the Cubs. However, in the words of the *Chicago Tribune*'s reporter, "The Chicogoans, with Bill Lee pitching a fine game, defeated the 'Great Carl Hubbell,' 2–1."[12] Billy Herman pestered the home team's best hurler with three hits, both resulting in runs.

Nine days later, with the Cardinals in town, Hubbell absorbed another loss, his third straight. Paul Dean defeated him 7–2. The Giants' southpaw lasted only four innings. During these four, he was pelted for seven hits and three earned tallies. An infield error and an outfield misplay, not identified, did damage, but mostly it was because "the frequently hypnotic" Hubbell had very little to offer.[13]

The Giants scrambled along in August but continued to retain their lead. In mid–August in Pittsburgh, their ace went through the wringer of another tough loss. This game is a mild historical curiosity in that the three pitchers who appeared became Hall of Fame designees. For Hubbell, the game also harbored a curiosity in that for eight innings, his foe was his very first antagonist from back in 1928, Burleigh Grimes. "Old Stubble Beard" was in his third and last stint with the Pirates. Constantly shuttled about because only Brooklyn manager Wilbert Robinson could stand him for any length of time, the ancient spitballer battled his much younger opponent even until the eighth, when new manager Pie Traynor lifted him for a pinch hitter. In the ninth, Waite Hoyt replaced Grimes at the mound with the score tied at two. It took Hoyt only seven pitches to retire three Giant batters. In the Pittsburgh ninth, Hubbell retired one. Then former teammate Fred Lindstrom doubled and first baseman Gus Suhr singled for a 3–2 Pittsburgh win.

After only a couple of days off, Hubbell went against the Pirates again on August 17. Provided with plenty of runs by his teammates, he easily defeated the Pirates 8–3. Nonetheless, he did give up ten hits.

With last-place Cincinnati next, to be followed by St. Louis and Chicago, Terry used his ace as he had in '33. Rather than have Hubbell use up a start against the last-place Reds, he employed him to close out wins on August 19 and 20.

Hubbell had been used on August 14, 17, 19 and 20. Then he received two full days off. On August 23, he was back as a starter, with Paul Dean, the younger member of the Dean family, as his opponent for the Cardinals for the third time. In a game the Giants won, 5–3, the Oklahoman showed signs of wear and tear. He lasted only five innings and gave up eight hits and three runs. He did not receive credit for the win. Because of going only five, after just a day off, Terry had him back for two innings on August 25 against St. Louis in relief of Parmelee. Carl allowed another run on two hits in two innings. The Giants did win, 7–6, but again, Hubbell received "no decision."

At the end of this grueling road trip, the Giants reached Chicago for another important series. This time Terry gave his ace the standard starter's three days off in order to have him ready to pitch the final game on August 29. With Lon Warneke his opponent again, Carl had 20,000 expectant Cubs fans on hand for the pitching duel.

They got their wish. In a "tense game,"[14] the two went at it neck-and-neck through eight fast-played innings with neither team scoring. In their ninth, the Giants did nothing. Then Hubbell's downfall arrived. A Critz error to start the Cubs' ninth turned out to be too much to overcome. A force-out placed Augie Galan, a fast runner, on first. Kiki Cuyler came up to bat. He lashed a double down the left field line. Galan raced home all the way from first. The game took only one hour and thirty-nine minutes from start to finish. Of course, Cubs fans went home delighted with the exciting finish.

The *Chicago Tribune* reporter on the Cubs' beat had had a high opinion of Hubbell ever since the time in 1929 when Carl had pitched the game in which the outfield had no putouts. The reference to him in the account of this game was that the Cubs had defeated the "matchless Hubbell."[15]

In spite of the defeat, the Giants returned home feeling relieved. Their success against the Cardinals just prior to the Cub series enabled them to hold their four-and-a-half-game lead. The Cubs were a close third. With quite a few home games immediately ahead and only a month of the season remaining, their chances of maintaining their lead seemed fairly probable.

In Hubbell's mind, however, there probably was some cause for worry. Sometime in August or September, he developed a tender arm. Later Carl attributed the soreness to too much relief pitching. This seems plausible. Decades later, Carl remarked that by this season he noticed that his left arm had begun to "crook up."[16] Whether this also contributed to the tightness is not certain. Unlike four years later, the soreness may have been intermittent at this stage; in some games he pitched very well, in others, poorly.

Did he inform the manager? One cannot know for certain. However, the way Terry used him toward the end of the season suggests that either through observation the manager figured out something was wrong with his ace, or Hubbell did tell him. Carl probably should have asked for time off. In a tight pennant race, that was difficult. Probably to his own disadvantage, Carl went out and pitched when asked as long as he could pick up a baseball.

In August, Terry turned to Hubbell as reliever five times in addition to six starts. Surely this was too much. In September, the manager eased up and used him in relief only once until the very end of the season. At that point, the Giants' desperation was increasing by the day. Nonetheless, in the last week, with the race tightening daily, Terry might have started Hubbell twice but did not start him at all.

In September, Carl had pitched unevenly — as if his arm hurt at times, but not all of the time. For instance, he won three one-run games against second-division teams — the Phillies, 3–2 on September 4; the Pirates, same score, on September 12; the Reds, 4–3 on the 20th. However, against first-division teams, Hubbell lost two — to the Cubs, 4–2 on September 7, and to the Cardinals, 3–2 on the 16th. On the 23rd, Carl had a "no decision" against the Braves in a game the Giants lost, 4–3. The losses to the closest pursuers hurt. Both games were lost at home.

Part of the reason for the losses was that during the final month, the Giants' hitters fell into a horrendous batting slump. They offered Hubbell only minimal help when he needed more than a stingy two runs to go on at a time when his arm was probably hurting. Against the Cubs, Carl lasted only five of the innings in the 4–2 loss. In the fifth, his All-Star Game battery mate, Gabby Hartnett, delivered a home run *coup de grâce*. Terry relieved him at the end of the inning although Carl had allowed just two runs on three hits — a little odd, unless Carl's arm was sore. For Lon Warneke, his vanquisher, it was his twentieth win.

What was later recognized as the decisive day of the season came on Sunday, September 16. The Redbirds were in town for a double bill. Frankie Frisch had the Deans ready to handle the Cardinals' hurling. An immense crowd of 62,000 jammed the Polo Grounds. Terry decided on Parmelee and Hubbell to go against Dizzy and Paul Dean, respectively. In the 1933 season, the manager had consistently had Hubbell pitch the first of a double-header and then another one of the starters took the second. In 1934, for some unknown reason, he reversed the pattern. Parmelee lost to Dizzy Dean in the first game, 5–3. This left Hubbell to take on Paul Dean, who had bothered him all season, in the nightcap.

The Giants needed only a split, but they needed it very badly. In this situation, a split meant the status quo; a double loss would shrink the Cardinal deficit by two. Therefore, the second game was fought with very high stakes. If the Redbirds won the nightcap, they would be just 3½ back. This put tremendous pressure on Hubbell to capture the closer. If the Giants' batters had been up to providing two measly runs, their tender-armed ace could have won in nine. Hubbell held the Cardinals scoreless until Rip Collins tagged him for a homer in the seventh. Earlier the home team had tallied but once.

Paul Dean and Hubbell battled each other through three tense and scoreless innings: the eighth, ninth and tenth. Finally, in the eleventh, the Giants' ace cracked. Pepper Martin got to him for a home run. This was followed by another tally later in the same round. When Paul Dean stopped the Giants in their half, the Cardinals had won, 3–1. The double-header was theirs. They were in the thick of the race and there were still two weeks to go.

Of course, the next day the New York newspapers bewailed the Giants' double loss. In St. Louis, the press reaction was opposite. Martin Haley in the *Globe Democrat* hailed the Redbirds' twin triumphs. He also observed that the Giants had an additional worry: their ace's recent predilection to give up four-base swats. This was a reference not only to the two homers the Cardinals had hit off Hubbell the day before, but also to Hartnett's homer in the Cub game, as well as a scattering of them across the season, not the least of which had been the one by a washed-up Hack Wilson. At a later time, of much greater average home run production, the total would not have been enough to draw notice. The relative frequency of home runs off Carl may have been another indication of his arm's tenderness.

In the final weeks, the Cardinals also wilted some, thus giving the Giants the chance to widen their lead again. However, they muffed it. Utter exhaustion overtook them during the last two weeks of the season. On Thursday,

September 20, the southpaw succeeded in defeating the basement-dwelling Reds. On the last day of the week in the second game of a double-header against the Braves, Hubbell made his final start. He hung on to the eighth in a game the Giants lost in extra innings.

On September 26, Wednesday of the final week, a day on which the Cardinals lost, the Giants badly needed a win over the 59–93 W-L, .376-winning-percentage Phillies. Instead, they got slapped for a 5–4 loss. In the eighth, Hal Schumacher's weariness brought his removal, with Hubbell as his replacement. As the reliever, Carl coughed up two runs on five hits in two innings. In the ninth, Dolph Luque lost it on a wild pitch.

On the final weekend, disaster overwhelmed the 1933 pennant winners. The fates seemed to destine them for defeat. The Cardinals had only to beat the basement-dwelling Reds at home, with the Dean brothers at the ready. The Giants, on the other hand, had games against their cross-town enemies: the accursed Dodgers.

Worse, thanks to the blunt Manager Bill Terry's indiscretion the previous winter, the Flatbushers were sure to be eating their hearts out to beat the Giants in the last two games. A reporter had asked Terry about Brooklyn's prospects in 1934 and he had replied mildly, but disparagingly, "Are they still in the league?"[17] In Dodgers-Giants games all season long that year, the Flatbush supporters had been "on" the Giants for Terry's remark. With the Cardinals on the Giants' heels, Dodger fans were ready to crowd the Polo Grounds and fill the air with their jeering of the home team.

By Friday, the Cardinals had narrowed their deficit to only half a game. The Giants had an off day, but St. Louis played Cincinnati before an enthusiastic home crowd. Dizzy Dean easily beat the Reds, drawing the Cardinals into a dead heat with the "Terrymen."

On a dreary Saturday afternoon, in the season's penultimate Giants-Dodgers meeting, the former's players and fans alike carried on as if thoroughly disheartened. Judging the jeers versus cheers from the crowd, the Flatbushers greatly outnumbered the home fans. Against the Dodgers' best, Van Lingle Mungo, the Giants offered little resistance, losing 5–1. Out in St. Louis, with Paul Dean emulating his brother Dizzy, the Cardinals won easily again. With one game to go, they had gone one up on the Giants.

It was the season's last day and the home team had only a slim hope of obtaining a tie through a win and a Cardinal loss. Nonetheless, the players put up a battle to close on a victorious note. With the weather much better, a crowd of 40,000 was on hand. However, once again the majority seemed to be Dodger rooters. Worse, in mid-game, the scoreboard showed the Cardinals with a lead in their game. Dizzy Dean was hurling for his thirtieth win on one day's rest.

Back at the Giants-Dodgers struggle, they were tied at five after nine innings. In the Brooklyn tenth, the Dodgers put two on with none out. At this point, Terry relieved Schumacher with Hubbell. Why he bothered is puzzling. By that time, it was obvious that the Cardinals had the pennant all but sewed up. At any rate, in his final appearance of the season, Hubbell could not help. After he retired the Dodgers' pitcher, there came a walk, then an error by Ryan, letting in a run. A long fly scored another run and a single provided the third. The Dodgers won 8–5. Dodger fans, with final raucous jeers and boos, returned to Flatbush enjoying the typical losers' pleasure for dragging down those above them. Giants players and fans alike dispersed disconsolately, having to swallow their bitter ending.

Over the winter, Hubbell could take some consolation in his final statistics. In ERA, he led all National League pitchers again at 2.30. It would have been better had it not been for the late season overload. It was the fifth straight year he finished first or second in that revealing category. It would be interesting to locate other great pitchers who have done as much. It would be futile. There are none.

Otherwise, the Oklahoman finished fourth in total wins, at twenty-one, and second in innings pitched, at 313. He had five shutouts that tied him for second in that category. Carl had twenty-three complete games, a tie for second. Total appearances were 49, again a tie, for fourth-fifth. For any other pitcher, this set of statistics would have meant an outstanding year. For both the team and for Hubbell, the season's dismal ending largely destroyed the glitter associated with his All-Star Game feat, and made 1934 into a disappointing year.

In light of the late season fold-up by the Giants, when Hubbell arrived home, there was no grandiose celebration awaiting him, either in Meeker or in Oklahoma City, as had been the case the previous year. No doubt, Carl neither expected nor wanted one. Moreover, in the four winter months before the next spring, he surely must have worried now and then as to whether rest would relieve his arm of the discomfort that had set in during the latter part of the season. One wonders whether he recalled and rued the day the year before when, queried by state reporters as to whether he ever considered the possibility of developing a sore arm, he had replied that he never let it worry him.

Chapter 9

Marking Time

At the 1934–35 winter meetings, Manager Bill Terry consummated an important trade. He obtained Dick Bartell, the Philadelphia Phillies' regular shortstop, in exchange for four Giants. In 1934, the shortstop position had developed into a serious problem. Travis Jackson, with his frequent injuries, covered insufficient territory and had committed 43 errors. Nor did Blondy Ryan prove up to the mark as oft-used utility infielder. His upbeat spirit failed to offset his hitting and fielding shortcomings.

By comparison to Jackson — who in 1935 shifted to third — Bartell served as a solid, well-established left side mid-fielder. He was very alert and aggressive as well as a hitting asset. Pitchers disliked him. Dick was a push batter, insisting on standing close to the plate. Hurlers regarded him as a crybaby. When they pitched him inside, as most did, Bartell would complain to the umpires that the pitchers were throwing at him. Not that he was intimidated. It was simply his way of obtaining a batting advantage.

In their pre-teammate days, Hubbell — usually so accommodating — had viewed him as other twirlers had. However, once Bartell became a Giant, he and the others found him to be an asset. He unfailingly played hard, slid aggressively into bases, argued with umpires when close calls went the opposition's way, and yet cooperated nicely with teammates.

For Bartell, Terry provided the hard-up Phillies with Vergez, Ryan, Watkins, and a minor league pitcher. Constantly forced to trade their few good players for cash or prospects, the Phillies deserved to have at least one, preferably two, of the four turn into a solid regular player. None amounted to anything in his Phillies uniform.

At the winter meetings, the rumor mill spun one particularly startling tale. Whispers had it that Terry actually considered trading Hubbell for Larry French. As good a hurler as French was, it was fairly common knowledge that the Pirates were in a mood to trade him. In fact, at the meetings, they did part with him and Fred Lindstrom, in exchange for Guy Bush and others from the Chicago Cubs.

Whether there was substance to the rumor remains unclear. For Terry, even to consider trading his "Meal Ticket" surely would have struck Giants fans as gross ingratitude, and the idea raised eyebrows in both leagues. Yet he really did not deny the story quickly and vehemently. Also, Hubbell had had a semi-painful arm late in the season, while French had not been troubled by any adverse arm symptoms. If Terry did momentarily consider it, he may have recalled Connie Mack's move of the winter before. In the latter part of the 1933 season, his pitching star-of-stars, Lefty Grove, after throwing his great fireball for eight and a half seasons, had pitched at times with a sore arm. Over the 1933–34 winter break, Mack had traded him to the Boston Red Sox for a huge cash outlay and some players from their new owner, Tom Yawkey. Possibly Terry gave brief thought along the same lines with regards to Hubbell. But, in any case, he did not trade him, to the Giants' subsequent benefit. As for Hubbell, when asked later for his reactions, he — ever the team player — replied that he did not resent it because every manager had to do whatever he thought was best for the club.

When the 1935 spring training arrived, it produced one development very reassuring to the Oklahoma newsmaker. After working the kinks and unevenness out of his arm by carefully nurtured winter disuse, he found there was no lingering soreness. He was ready to go for a new season. It proved another successful one. In one or two aspects, 1935 was better than his 1934 season. In other ways, however, it was less. At any rate, it was no match for the 1933 season.

As a team, however, Hubbell and his Giant mates underwent another disappointing season. They were again non-winners, this time dropping out of first place much earlier than the year before. Eventually, sheer weariness drew them down to a third-place finish.

In the larger view of baseball and its 1935 dimensions, the chief surprise came through the inauguration of night baseball games for the first time in the major leagues at the Cincinnati park in May of that year. The lighting system struck most players and fans as up to playing standards. Cincinnati was long low in the standings, and therefore accustomed to smaller crowds, so the attendance increase for their night games clearly indicated the value of the innovation. Although by late in the decade a few other clubs had adopted night ball, most, despite the economy, were slower to seize upon the all-lighted ballpark and night games than a retrospective observer would expect.

A climatic element in the 1935 season was the extreme heat that enveloped the East and Midwest in midsummer. Heat waves were numerous through the thirties, made worse by the absence of air conditioning — except in movie theaters — until at least the end of the decade. There were no cooling facilities on the baseball field, so playing hard-fought games in temperatures often in the high 90s was extremely hard on the players. It was especially hard on the pitchers. In the Giants' case, it did direct damage, causing Schumacher to collapse on the mound in the heat during an important later-season game in St. Louis.

When the season got underway, Hubbell began with a spectacular debut. This time, however, he was not the victor, but the victim. For the Boston Braves' home opener on April 16, there were 25,000 in the stands. The day was sunny, but extremely chilly, or else the crowd probably would have been much larger. Still, 25,000 was a large turnout to see the colorless Braves play. Judge Fuchs had hoped for a much larger audience. Why could he possibly expect more? In the Depression, a 25,000 turnout on a cold opening day was a good showing for a team like the Braves. The reason was that Babe Ruth had become a Beantown addition — as surprising a development on the sports scene as could be imagined.

The Yankees, aware that the Babe was about finished as a player, had released him the previous fall. Considering what Ruth, despite his epicurean lifestyle, had accomplished for the Yankees, and for baseball, his unceremonious dismissal reeked of astigmatic ingratitude. Ambitious to become a manager in the winter of 1934–35, Ruth waited in disappointment for a major league owner to offer him a job as a field boss. Finally, the Braves' owner, Emil Fuchs, offered him a position as assistant manager to Bill McKechnie, and Ruth jumped at the chance. He was also to appear as a player once again.

Thus, when the game began, out in left field was Babe Ruth. It was more than half a year since Hubbell had struck out the Bambino in the All-Star Game. There was great anticipation of how the two would do against each other this time.

The laurels went entirely to the Babe. In the first, he drove in a runner on a hard single and later scored. In mid-game, with Ruth up and a runner on, Hubbell evidently threw a pitch a little too much toward the strike zone. Ruth waded into it, and drove a 430-foot home run into the right center field seats. Predictably, the crowd went wild. The Giants lost 4–2, with Ruth accounting for the four Braves runs. After six innings, Terry removed Hubbell, who had, in addition to the runs, surrendered nine hits.

In the *Times*, James Dawson had nothing but superlatives for Ruth: "The greatest figure baseball ever knew, Babe Ruth never was greater than he was today."[1] Actually, it was the first of only two outstanding days Ruth had in his dismal two months' stay with the Braves.

In surrendering that one home run, Hubbell became the eleventh and final Hall of Fame pitcher against whom the Babe struck four-base smashes. Among the preceding ten were such super-greats as Walter Johnson and Lefty Grove, against whom Ruth had belted nine each.

As the first half of the season moved along, the Giants played well, advancing to first, and by Independence Day, had developed an encouraging seven-game lead. Prospects looked good for regaining the pennant from the St. Louis interlopers of the year before.

Within this framework, Hubbell continued to hold the dominant position among the team's pitchers in spite of the fact that Schumacher was actually pitching slightly better ball than he. For a change, the Giants' batters hit reasonably well for Hubbell. For instance, in a stretch of later May and the first half of June, Carl ran off a succession of five straight wins of complete games. In three, the hitters provided seven runs twice, and ten runs once. It enabled him to ease up a little, allowing double-digit hit totals and nineteen runs in the quintet, four of them unearned.

A little bit prior to the start of the run, Hubbell had won a game against Pittsburgh, 3–1, which had more than average interest to him. His opponent was Cy Blanton, a newcomer. Until Blanton's arrival, the two contemporary Oklahoma major leaguers who attracted attention were Hubbell and Pepper Martin. The latter's home run in the eleventh in a critical game the year before had damaged the Giants and Hubbell severely. For a while, Blanton made it a trio of Oklahoma sports attention getters. Born in Waurika, he lived his early adult years near Shawnee, only twenty or so miles down the road from Meeker. Martin, the "Wild Horse of the Osage," had been born in Temple, also not far from Meeker. All had small-town or farm origins and a common lust for baseball.

Blanton, however, after winning eighteen for Pittsburgh as a rookie, slowly faded. He ended up with a fairly short career, a slightly sub-.500 twirler. Nevertheless, in this season, late in August at the Polo Grounds when the Giants badly needed wins, he defeated Hubbell 6–1 in a rematch.

In the earlier going, Hubbell split two against the Giants' perennial leading competitors. On May 13, the Giants' ace encountered one-time roomie Bill Walker, in his third year as a Redbird. In a nifty left-handers' weapons finessing, Walker got the better of Carl, 3–2, in ten hard-fought rounds. This was in spite of the fact that Hubbell allowed only four hits.

On May 25, the Meeker mainstay did better against a competitor he dearly wanted to overcome. This was Lon Warneke. Lon had prevailed in two important games the year before. This time it was Hubbell who won out in Chicago, 3–2. He pitched with a "machine-like screwball delivery"[2] before about 12,000 disappointed Wrigley fans.

On July 8 in Cleveland came the third All-Star Game. Again the American League triumphed, 4–1. However, this time Hubbell was a non-combatant. This had the advantage of providing him more than an average length of time between starts.

In the All-Star aftermath, the Giants watched their lead steadily shrivel. This was in part due to close ones slipping away and partly due to Fitzsimmons' loss caused by arm soreness. By the close of their second western trip in later July, their lead had dwindled to three and a half games, varying with the day. The major damage was caused by a four-game wipeout in the Windy City.

That year July, August and September were especially hot and humid. For days the temperatures would climb into the nineties. It was on just such a day, Sunday, July 21, that the Polo Grounders suffered a double loss to the Cubs to wind up the series. The day was ferociously hot. Seemingly half of Chicago was at the north and southside beaches seeking relief. The other half was at Wrigley Field.

Jammed into the park were 46,168 paying customers. Management handled the overflow by allowing a field crowd of standees five or six rows deep in front of the left field wall. Several thousand others were excluded. In the *Times*, the flabbergasted James Dawson described what he observed. "Those unable to obtain admission watched from roof tops, porches, fire escapes, and telegraph poles"[3] — and this was in the Depression. So huge a number crowded into a confined area added to the discomfort of the heat and humidity.

Such were the conditions in which the players had to go out and perform. So exhausting was it for the pitchers that three of the four starters had to be removed in mid-game, either through ineffectiveness caused by the heat or for a pinch hitter for the same reason.

With his astonishing stamina, Hubbell was the one of the four who lasted out an entire game, and an extra-inning one at that. Since the first game of the double bill lasted almost two and a half hours, and he gave up six walks — two of them intentional — his pitch count for the total of an eleven-inning game had to be much higher than usual. Both teams surrendered a run more than ordinarily would have been the case due to field-crowd doubles. Hubbell's starting opponent, favorite foe Tex Carleton (by 1935 a Cub), wilted in the heat after only three innings. Charley Root was his replacement. At the end of nine, the score stood four apiece.

Nothing happened in the tenth, but in the eleventh the Cubs finally cornered Hubbell. Even then he came within an eyelash of escaping. Augie Galan opened the inning with a left field foul line double. Herman bunted and Hubbell's throw, attempting to catch Galan advancing to third, failed. With the Giants' infield drawn in, Giants fill-in shortstop Mark Koenig fumbled Phil Cavaretta's roller, filling the bases. Up came Hartnett. Hubbell got him to hit a high bouncer to the mound. A quick throw to the plate forced Galan, and the peg to first doubled Hartnett. The next batter, Frank Demaree, singled cleanly and the Giants had lost a big one, 5–4.

In the second game, Terry — desperate for starters — had to start Allyn Stout, a shaky reliever. The Cubs pounded him and his successor, 11–5. From ten and a half in arrears on the Fourth of July, the Bruins had climbed to a strong third in less than three weeks. This put them only four back and legitimate contenders from this time on.

The Giants were saved from immediate disaster when they went on to St. Louis, where they won four of six in the continued boiling heat. Terry, after giving Hubbell only two days off to recover from Chicago's searing temperature, sent him out against Dizzy Dean on July 24. Allowing only six hits and two runs, one unearned, he beat the Dizzy 4–2.

What struck down the Giants was that during August, when they were at home except for brief interruptions, they did no better than a split against the eastern teams. They mostly lost against the western teams. During this stretch, Hubbell went 4–2 W-L, so he shared at most mild responsibility for the slippage. Meantime, the two rivals, Chicago and Cardinals, were drawing closer and closer.

Hubbell's pitching during the month constituted mediocrity at best. It looked better than it was because the Giants' batters usually kept up their hitting for him. In the two losses, he pitched unimpressively. One he dropped to Curt Davis of the doormat Phillies, 6–3. The other was the aforementioned loss to Meeker neighbor Cy Blanton of the Pittsburgh Pirates.

Of the four wins, one on August 14 over Paul Dean stands out for the crowd at the Polo Grounds. Fans, 50,568 strong, came to watch a weekday double-header, with Paul Dean and Hubbell in the first encounter. This was the largest weekday gathering in National League history up to that point. The year before, Hubbell had lost to the younger Dean. That he finally beat him 6–4 brought Carl satisfaction even though he pitched only a so-so game. The next start the "Meal Ticket" made was against the Reds. He beat them by the same score.

The other two were relief successes. One was a brief service, also in the Cincinnati series, that gave him a quickie 6–5 verdict. The other was a 9–4 win over the Cubs in a 6⅔ relief stint for the walk-prone Roy Parmelee. The game had some interest, less because of Hubbell's pitching, than because of a recent acquaintance whom Carl had good reason to remember.

In a box seat sat Babe Ruth, baseball's most distinguished retiree, accompanied by Mrs. Ruth. When asked for a comment, Ruth replied that he attended several Giants games recently and they had won them all, so he had begun to consider himself the team's mascot. Since at the time Babe was decidedly down on the Yankees, it is possible, as his words implied, that temporarily he had become a mild Giants fan.

Once having lost the lead, the Giants did not regain it at any time in

September. They stayed close to the Cardinals until their final western trip. However, at one of the four stops, disaster overtook them, resulting in a fade-out into third place. This made for an unimpressive finish.

By mid-month, both the Giants and the Cardinals were trailing the Cubs. Through early season "wet grounds" cancellations, the Bruins obtained what, even for that time, was an exceptionally long final home stand. Through a combination of brilliant play before enthusiastic home crowds, overachieving, good luck, and the best pitching staff the team had had since the days of "Three Finger" Brown and his hurling mates, they ran off a twenty-one-game winning streak. Nearly all the wins were at home. In all the decades since, the streak has not been matched or surpassed. It won them the pennant.

Until the Giants reached Chicago, the last western stop, Terry felt — as also did his team, no doubt — that the club still had a fairly good chance to win. Therefore, he worked his understaffed starting pitchers — and his ace — to the limit. Against Cincinnati, the first stop, Hubbell won a 6–4 game, two of the opposing runs unearned. However, he did allow a conspicuous dozen hits. At Pittsburgh, the second station, he pitched and won an excellent 3–1 six-hitter. That brought the New Yorkers to St. Louis. By then they had slipped to third, 3½ back of the Redbirds, 2½ behind the Cubs.

For the opener on Thursday, September 12, with 15,000 present, each manager had his ace ready. Hubbell was no match for Dizzy Dean that day, losing to him 5–2. In five innings, the Giants' best allowed four runs and seven hits. Terry withdrew him, as he sometimes did when Carl fell behind early to a pitcher who was likely to beat the Polo Grounders anyway.

In the next two of the four-game set, the Giants won close ones. The second Cardinal loss moved the Cubs into first place by half a game.

A September 15 double-header brought the series to a close. With five games in five days, the quintet brought the rare instance of ace versus ace twice in the same series. Both Frisch and Terry used their best over again after just two days off. In John Drebinger's words, it was a battle of "voluble Dizzy Dean versus the silent Carl Hubbell."[4] Their fame helped pack Sportsman's Park with a crowd of 43,000. Again this led management to allow an on-field group in left.

The "terrific strain and heat" showed Hubbell to be more of a temperature-endurer than Dean.[5] The Giants beat St. Louis, 7–3. Toward the game's end, even "King Carl" showed wear and tear, surrendering a couple of runs. Nonetheless, he endured through the last out. In Chicago, fans and players were delighted. It increased the Cubs' lead over the Cardinals.

Exhausted from the series with the Cardinals, the Giants moved on to Chicago and the red-hot Cubs for another four-game series. Before improbable mid-week daily crowds of 30,000, the Cubs swept the weary visitors. In the third game on September 19, Hubbell — starting his third game in a week — was hit hard by the Cubs. Carl gave up five runs on ten hits. Terry pulled him after seven rounds. The Giants were through for 1935.

The weary left-hander pitched twice more before winding up the season, but against the Boston Braves. In 1933 and 1934, McKechnie had done a fine job of bringing the team to fourth spot. In 1935, the failure of the Babe Ruth experiment, and the rudderless chaos that accompanied and followed it, led to the Braves' completely losing their bearings. So awful were they that it enabled the Reds to jump up two notches to sixth place in this season. At 38–115 W-L, the Braves ended up with a .248 winning percentage. This was the second lowest in major league history since the advent of the twentieth century.

Against the morale-ruined Bostonians, Hubbell should have made them easy victims of two wins for himself. However, he could only win the home game of the two, 3–2, a nice six-hit effort. In his final start on September 27 in Boston, Carl lasted only two innings. He gave up eight hits and six runs, three unearned. Terry pulled him.

On this sour note, Hubbell's 1935 season ended. Two days later, September 29, his team's season also ended.

The Sooner sensation's season statistics looked worthy of him in spite of the disappointing third-place team finish. At a .657 winning percentage, he was fifth among starters. With twenty-three wins, he was second among starters. Dizzy Dean's twenty-eight was the only one ahead of him. In strike-outs, Carl reached second to Dean at 150 whiffs. Hubbell was also second to the Cardinal ace in innings pitched, 302, and complete games, twenty-four. To almost any other pitcher, this added up to a high-quality season, and to some extent it did for Carl. Aside from the raw statistics, a favorable development for Hubbell and the team was that he finally managed a two-one showing against the Dodgers. The wins were an easy 9–2 victory on June 7 and an impressive 6–0 shutout, July 28. The one loss was a 3–2 defeat at Mungo's hands on June 29, in a failed three-inning effort.

Beneath the surface of the 1935 season, there were two or three negative signs that had no aftermath in the two succeeding seasons, but possibly were faint harbingers of what was to come three years later. For one, for the first time since 1928, Hubbell dropped out of the first five in ERA. In all, eight regular starters did better than he. Second, while the 302 innings pitched were cause for praise, the total was also worrisomely high in relation to possible overuse of his arm. Moreover, Carl's hits allowed exceeded innings pitched. Sometimes this was a tell-tale sign of trouble to come. Finally, Hubbell gave up a startling twenty-eight home runs. In the decade of the thirties, this was a very high total. Over the winter, these facts surely gave pause to Terry, to his teammates, and especially to Hubbell himself.

Chapter 10

Composition of a Mound Artist

In the last half of the 1936 season, and the first quarter of the 1937 one, the Meeker maestro established another pitching record. Like the preceding two, it represented a uniqueness of its own.

If baseball has had few hurling master craftsmen, Carl Owen Hubbell surely ranks as one. Prior to exploring the dimensions of his twenty-four-game winning streak, the elements composing Hubbell the person and Hubbell the pitcher bear examination. The personality sheds some light on the mound wizardry.

In most athletes, exposure to compliments and praise from their early years, followed by success in early adulthood, easily produces a confident, assertive, expectant personality. For the extremely successful, glamour and glory become their companions. Most of the inconveniences and annoyances associated with daily living for everyman escape them. Others people handle the tasks that ordinarily would devolve upon them.

In the sports world that is their wont; the obvious forms of living to excess exist all around them. Quite a few cannot resist the temptation to overindulge in one or more varieties of loose living. At least for a while, their admirers feel disappointed in them when sometimes flagrant behavior reaches the press. Their juvenile followers are bewildered, disillusioned.

A common source of scandal in Hubbell's day, and in practically every decade after, was marital crises. At that time, there might have been a greater number of these indiscretions than reached the press, since many sports reporters "cooperated" with players in a tacit understanding that the athletes' private lives should be kept so. No marital embarrassment beset Hubbell. By 1936, Carl and Sue Hubbell were parents of a son born the year before. He was named after his father, Carl Owen Hubbell Junior.

None of the excess-loving, assertive, glory-seeking nature was true of the man from Meeker. On the contrary; through his early years with the Giants, sportswriters often mistook him for a rare introverted athlete. For instance, the scribes' descriptions of his physical appearance bear some resemblance to each other. They called attention to his serious, almost somber manner. To one reporter, he seemed "awkwardly angular, gaunt, lean-visaged."[1] Another was struck by the "slight look of worry"[2] that often characterized his face. To sportswriters, Hubbell's "colorlessness" made it difficult to extract much from him beyond the obvious. With the fans, Hubbell felt more at home. They found him "always affable and obliging."[3]

It seems reasonable to assume that Hubbell's conservatively tailored clothes, his caution in interviews, his serious, often unsmiling expression, stemmed from his days growing up on an Oklahoma rented farm. Living with five brothers, a sister, and his parents surely encouraged self-restraint and denial. Recalling those days in old age, Carl described the setting:

> We worked from sun up to sun down, and there weren't any five-day weeks. It can get pretty hot in Oklahoma. When you're out there in that 100 degree weather chopping cotton, you don't forget about it. I knew I was going to do everything I could to keep from going back to the farm.[4]

Hubbell's teammates, unlike the reporters, did not find him especially cautious in relations among themselves. Something that probably helped gradually to make the young man feel increasingly at ease was that in the 1930s, the Giants players developed a high degree of camaraderie. This was probably not unlike the closeness that existed among Carl and his brothers. Jo-Jo Moore, one of Hubbell's dearest friends, described the bonds the players shared after leaving the Polo Grounds:

> Our ball club was a family in those days. We lived in the same neighborhood, up on Manhattan Island, with several of the families living in the same building. We ... lived up there, and had good family relationships; the kids played together, etc.[5]

Bill Werber, the Cincinnati Reds' alert hot corner occupant of their first-rate late thirties team, had, by 1942, moved to the Giants. His description of Hubbell suggests a person easy to get to know in circumstances in which he felt at home:

> He was quiet, introspective, and a model of decorum. He did not have an aggressive bone in his body, and he had a sly sense of humor that made him enjoyable to be around.[6]

So seriously did Hubbell pursue his craft that it engendered an anecdote from the early spring training in Havana. Terry felt that Hubbell and Fitzsimmons were taking the early practices too seriously, too soon. Encountering the two one evening in the hotel lobby, about 6:30 or 7:30, he invited them to go out on the town in pre–Castro Havana. If they liked, they could come back in the small hours of the morning.

A bit surprised, Terry ran into them again about 9:30 or 10:00 P.M. He remarked that Carl and Fitz evidently had decided to embark upon their big evening pretty late. They informed him that they had already had their big blowout, enjoying a sumptuous meal, appreciating the unrestrained fun, and had returned in order to have a good sleep for the morrow.

If possible, Hubbell's relations with the front office were even better. Not once in his major league career did he hold out. He felt that the Giants' brass treated him fairly. His peak salary reached between twenty and twenty-five thousand. This made him one of the half dozen highest paid pitchers. Compared to super hurlers of a later period, his top salary added up to small change. In a modern setting, his teammates probably would see him as too accommodating, too close to serving as a front office shill, to the disadvantage of his own income and that of his fellow players. However, this was the Depression, and steady employment was a prize in and of itself.

An anecdote of how Hubbell could underestimate his value came from Charles Stoneham, the Giants' president. A friend of his inveighed against the players for being selfish and salary hounds. Stoneham bet him that in the case of Hubbell, at least, this was not true. Then he mailed a blank contract for Hubbell to fill in with the pitcher's own estimate of his worth. He returned it with such a moderate raise that Stoneham felt bound to tear it up and send Carl a new contract with a couple of thousand added.

Like other prominent athletes, Hubbell's fame enabled him to acquire supplementary income. For instance, an Oklahoma oil firm took him on as vice-president. Whether this entailed serious duties in the season seems very improbable. More than likely, Carl did not have to work very hard in the off season, either. How much of a stipend this title provided was, of course, not divulged. Hubbell endorsed Dodge among automobiles. Also receiving Hubbell's endorsements were Wheaties cereal for children and Camel cigarettes for adults. How much income these endorsements provided was, once again, not divulged. Carl's income from outside sources probably was considerable, but without his pitching success, he would not have obtained it.

In the sphere of amusements and pastimes, Hubbell was — as might be easily surmised — primarily an outdoorsman. In the fall and winter months, he loved to hunt small game and to fish. He also liked to ride balky broncos. This was a pleasure that he probably did not call to the attention of Giants' management. In the spring and fall, golf was a favorite amusement. By middle life he had become an excellent golfer.

Hubbell's tastes in indoor pastimes were entirely conventional. He enjoyed popular movies, with teammates on the road, or with his wife at home. He and Sue also enjoyed stage shows. Spencer Tracy was his favorite actor. Band music also amused Carl, with Ted Lewis his preferred band leader.

Poker at twenty-five cents sufficed for gambling. Free time also included reading.

In season, Carl, the product of farm life, put strict limits on his evenings. Reporters did not find him among the lobby loungers kidding among themselves or flirting with the hat check girl. He and Ott would return to their room early. They would share a bottle of beer or ale. Hubbell would make it a point to go to bed by 11:00 P.M. His aim was to sleep nine hours a night. Refreshed, he would eat a hearty breakfast, study the box scores, and then head to the ballpark by the early afternoon.

The discipline with which he lived his daily life in season carried over with rare exceptions to his relations with umpires. By not constantly arguing with the plate ump on balls and strikes, he probably did himself a favor. On borderline calls, umpires, perhaps unconsciously influenced by his willingness to accept their decisions, as well as his reputation as a control artist, may have given him the benefit of the doubt more often than not. They called pitches strikes that just as easily could have been labeled balls. In the first game of the '33 World Series, the Senators' batters thought so.

Not once in his major league career, nor probably in the minors, did an umpire order him off the field or impose a fine. One writer went so far as to assert that Hubbell never challenged an umpire's call. Of course, every once in a great while, he would offer an objection. One particular example has survived. Babe Pinelli, who umpired many of the years that Hubbell pitched, remembered an occasion in which Carl did object to his call. On April 30, 1937, at the Polo Grounds, the Giants and Hubbell trounced the Dodgers 11–2. In the first inning, when the game had just started, Pinelli called a pitch by Hubbell to Jack Winsett, Dodger outfielder, "ball three." Hubbell felt otherwise. It bothered him, because he then passed Winsett, never a successful major league hitter, but a good minor league one. Immediately after, Heinie Manush, a Hubbell cousin, cuffed a home run off him. After the half-inning ended, the pitcher went up to the umpire to complain about his two-one call to Winsett. However, Carl did it so unobtrusively, in Pinelli's opinion, as to attract no attention to his objection.

Despite unusually restrained behavior in the setting of rude, competitive sports, Hubbell, like 99 percent of the people anywhere, did not aspire to be a model of moral rectitude. Like many (if not most) people, on rare occasions, Carl engaged in slightly questionable conduct. He did so only when it was not likely to draw much attention. His endorsement of Camel cigarettes provides an example. According to the endorser, "Camels are so mild ... they never get my wind or ruffle my nerves. And Camels have real flavor mildness — rare combination."[7] Not a hint appears that cigarette tobacco might be a health hazard. For a reimbursement of $500 to $1,000 perhaps, he succeeded in overcoming such qualms as he might have had at the omission. In the same advertisement, several other athletes also found it easy to sidetrack their consciences.

A more intriguing example survives from his pitching career. As every fan is aware, a pitcher, in order to record outs, must throw inside to batters. In the course of a season, a twirler is bound to hit a number of swingers. In this era, prior to batting helmets and other protective gear, a batter could be severely injured if hit in the cranium. If hit elsewhere on the body, serious injury could also result. A few pitchers would try to hit batters intentionally. Occasionally, "bean ball" pitchers would produce near riotous conditions. Nothing was done about the "bean ballers." Umpires, not then required to dismiss obvious suspects, preferred to avoid being "mind readers" by saying what the intent of the hurler was.

Hubbell definitely was not one of the suspects. In the six years from 1932 through 1937 in which he averaged high innings-pitched totals, he plunked only an average of four to five a season. It suggests a little more than normal effort not to hit batters. If so, it fitted his character.

Nevertheless, strong circumstantial evidence indicates that at least once — and if once, why not a few other times? — Carl deliberately hit a batter. The circumstances resembled those of the cigarette advertisement: When a superior required a little looseness, he complied.

Bill Herman recalled the episode. As usual with recollections, Herman's overall depiction was sound, but the details were somewhat awry. Actually, even the immediate postgame accounts in the *Tribune* and *Times* did not agree. In a New York–Chicago series in the Windy City in May of 1934, the Cubs won a tight game on May 14, 3–2. The game went ten innings. In the last of the tenth, Chuck Klein, who was starting his two-year tenure with the Cubs, slammed a two-out double down the right field line. This enabled a runner on first to score from there and win the game.

The next day, early in the game, Hubbell threw consciously at Klein in retaliation for the way he had ended the previous day's engagement. Carl hit Klein in the arm. In the Giants' half of the very next inning, Charlie Root, Hubbell's opponent as the Cubs' starter, threw a duster at Bill Terry and hit him in the neck. According to Herman, "Terry yelled at Root, 'What the hell did you do that for?' Root replied, 'Why did you make Hubbell throw at Klein?'"[8] After the umpires prevented an on-field brawl, the game went on. Neither pitcher was expelled. This was how umpires handled a run-of-the-mill "duster duel" then. Hubbell and the Giants proceeded to win the May 15 game easily, 10–3.

As for Hubbell's role, could he have decided to aim at Klein on his own? This is extremely unlikely. In their comments on Hubbell, no batters remembered him as a "hit batter" specialist. His low HBP annual total indicates the same. In 1934 he hit only two batters all season. As Root yelled to Terry, the Cubs knew that at first base, Terry had signed Hubbell to fire a few at Klein. As ordered, his hurler did, and hit him with one, but only in the arm. As with most people, when circumstances were demanding enough, Carl could stretch his usual rules to accommodate the situation.

Presumably such episodes were a rarity. As for Hubbell's overall reputation as a National League pitcher, it is enlightening to read what several of his hitting opponents who had to face him all season long — unlike the American League ones who met him only in All-Star and World Series games — thought of Carl's hurling. Billy Herman, who gave Hubbell fits as a hitter, said, "When he was pitching, you hardly ever saw the opposing team sitting back in the dugout. They were all on the top step watching him operate.... He was an absolute master of what he did ... and he got every last ounce out of his abilities.... I never saw another pitcher who could so fascinate the opposition."[9]

Frank McCormick, long the Reds' first baseman and a better than average hitter, confirmed Herman's assessment: "I was sitting in the dugout when Carl Hubbell went out to warm up. You should have heard the moaning on the bench. 'Oh, it's that guy again' ... 'Here's where I get the collar.' Talk like that."[10]

A pair of Cub teammates, one a left-handed swinger and the other right-handed, described how a batter from each side responded to the break on Hubbell's screwball. Phil Cavaretta:

> Hubbell's screwball was the funniest pitch you ever want to see. [He'd] throw it, and as the ball was in flight, it would look like a fast ball, but not very fast.... To a left-handed hitter like myself ... it would start on the outside part of the plate, and as it got to you, the ball would spin way inside on you. You would swing and miss it or get jammed.... Right-handed hitters, I don't know how they made contact."[11]

Woody English said, "Carl Hubbell was the best pitcher I ever faced. The other guys who threw the screwball you could pretty well see it coming all the way; but Hubbell's ball was right on top of you, almost on the edge of the plate, boom, down it went and that was his strikeout pitch."[12]

Except for his "freak" one, the elements composing the Oklahoman's craftsmanship were not otherwise distinctive. Every major league hurler featured a fast ball, a curve and a change-up. When possible, they would also have a "specialty" toss. Herman shrewdly observed that what advanced Carl to the head of the pitching class was the persistence with which he practiced his different deliveries until he reached the highest level of skill in their use that "he had within him."

For instance, Hubbell largely overcame his wildness tendency by 1928. This he did by constant practice with each of his pitches. Also he worked on overcoming a psychological barrier. Carl noticed that when he dwelt to himself on how he must not surrender a walk, he was more likely to do so. He banished from his mind any thought of inadvertently handing out a base on balls. This mental practice enabled Carl to overcome the obstacle. His thinking was reinforced when in his first conference with McGraw, the latter stressed that to succeed in the majors, Hubbell would need to get ahead of the hitters — advice that he always remembered.

Similarly, for years, Hubbell's curve was only average at best. Carl kept working on it and finally, in early 1936, he improved it through altering the elevation of his arm in throwing the curve. This brought about considerable advance in its effectiveness in throwing to left-handed "swat smiths."

Hubbell received countless questions concerning his mastery of the "reverse curve." Conceding that the pitch was hard on the arm, he did not flatly advise other moundsmen not to try it, but opined that only ones with a slender build like his own, along with very flexible hands, wrists, and elbows, should use it.

Illustrating how dangerous the screwball could be, Carl took some blame for Cliff Melton's ruining his arm with it. Melton joined the Giants in 1937 and had a brilliant opening season. Nevertheless, he kept asking Hubbell to show him how to throw the screwball. The older pitcher advised him not to, because he did not have Hubbell's wrist dexterity. Melton pestered often enough that finally his teammate taught it to him. As a result, in a 1939 game, Melton hurt his arm throwing the screwball and never again approached his earlier pitching results.

Once Hubbell joked about his "scroogie," saying that his arm had become so twisted that for him the pitch had become a "natural," not an unnatural one.[13] However, this statement could also be a warning to others. About a year after this remark, the subject was no longer one Carl could treat lightly.

Later in his life when the topic would come up, Carl strongly emphasized that for the pitch to be truly effective, it must be thrown directly overhand. Then the batter could not distinguish it from a fast ball or a curve before the pitch was on him. Thrown otherwise, the pitch would not be effective for long. Hitters could more easily adjust to it when it was thrown sidearm since pitchers did not usually throw many pitches that way. Overhand, batters time and again would mistake it for a second-rate fast ball, only to be deceived in their swing by the combination of sudden speed diminution and rapid drop-off.

Hubbell recalled that while he pitched, Larry French used the pitch quite effectively, and after them, Warren Spahn had done so as well. However, neither of the others threw it directly overhand. For them it was a secondary feature of their repertory. When finally Fernando Valenzuela came along a half century after him, Hubbell pronounced him the only practitioner of the screwball who threw it exactly the same way he had.

Gus Mancuso estimated that, on occasions when Hubbell had his best stuff, the pitch broke about a foot directly down. Harry Danning, Hubbell's third regular backstop, went further. Danning claimed it sank as much as two feet. Though this was probably an overstatement, it does help to account for the batters' expressions of amazement that they could swing at a Hubbellian "scroogie" and miss it as much as they did.

By their calling, pitchers tend to view batters as their eternal enemy. Thus, Hubbell, like his brethren, did not hold most hitters in high esteem. He felt that too many fixed upon a single batting stance and never varied it. He liked to pitch to the fixed-position hitters. It enabled Carl to develop a pitching sequence that he could follow consistently, sometimes for years at a time. He could usually extract easy outs from them.

For instance, Carl noted that certain batsmen were susceptible to 2–0 counts. In pitching them, contradicting his usual rule of trying to get ahead of the hitter, he would deliberately go 2–0. This type of hitter, Hubbell observed, would go for the 2–0 offering, confident it would be a fast one. Instead he would make the next pitch anything but what they were expecting. They would usually oblige with an easy grounder or fly-out. Sometimes Carl would do this for years against particular batters who never seemed to learn. Moreover, he did not have to throw more than three pitches per batter in most games to these hitters. Of course, this form of pitching requires excellent control. In the words of Billy Herman, "Hubbell ... could throw strikes at midnight."[14]

Hubbell offered another criticism of hitters. This was the tendency of so many to swing for the long ball. Since he feasted on the lesser variety of this type, Carl was only too glad to encounter them. Their prevalence did not elevate his opinion of the "batsmiths."

Nevertheless, certain batters did give him trouble. Hitters such as Kiki Cuyler, Pie Traynor and Ernie Lombardi were conspicuous examples. However, through experiment, Carl would catch up to them sooner or later. In the opinion of C.M. Black, Hubbell had "the canniest pitching mind in baseball."[15] Carl's canny ability to think about the different hitters and strategize different approaches to match them probably explains why he usually caught up with most, eventually.

Nonetheless, in spite of every variant, a few hitters bothered Hubbell indefinitely. Joe "Ducky" Medwick was one. Carl could explain Joe's case easily. As a "bad ball" hitter, he was apt to swing at anything. Hubbell found no way of developing a pattern to deal with him.

The two who were the cleverest examples of his "headache" hitters were Billy Herman and Paul Waner. Interestingly, neither was a power hitter, though Waner came close with his high double and triple totals. For each, Hubbell had high praise. Speaking of Herman, a right-hand hitter: "He ... gets up differently every time he comes to the plate. One time he crowds it, another time he stands back and steps into the ball, a third time he'll wait for me. He's so smart, that Herman."[16] Years later, Carl elaborated further on Herman's methods: "He moved up in the batter's box, used a heavy bat, and hit the screwball to the right field before it could break. After he did, others tried it, but he did it better than anybody."[17]

Paul Waner, Hubbell commented, "was the greatest I've ever seen at hitting any kind of pitch to an infield or outfield hole. Say you threw him an inside pitch, and figured he would have to pull; Waner could smash it to left if a hole was there. You had to play Paul straight and take your chances. [He] gave absolutely no tip-off of his intentions.... It was all in his wrists."[18]

Turning to the soon-to-be 1936–37 winning streak of 24, Hubbell lived for over fifty years after it. Yet in that length of time — and since — no pitcher has equaled or surpassed it. His own comments relative to that season were remarkably free of braggadocio. Once in early May 1937, while the streak was still intact, Carl's answer when asked was, "All I do is go out and throw the 'screwball.' The boys pick up the hot bounders, throw out their men, catch long flies, and hit the runs that have won the games."[19]

Soon after, speaking in the same vein, Hubbell referred to the Giants' "foolproof infield."[20] That he was very generous in his compliments is evident from the fact that in 1936, the infield quartet committed 97 errors. Fielding figures, even more than other baseball statistics, are closely related to time and circumstances.

Hubbell also mentioned that insofar as his own role was concerned, his improved curve made his pitching better that season. Did his greater use of it mean lesser resort to the screwball? He did not say so directly, but seemed to imply it. More curves and fewer "scroogies" meant less strain on his arm.

Most often, however, Carl cited "luck" as a key ingredient in the long winning streak. Every pitcher understands just how important luck can be as a factor in winning or losing, but few are as willing to call attention to it as was Hubbell. Even a very good pitcher understands when running a streak that sooner or later another hurler in a particular game is going to be even better than he is, beating him to end the streak. Just how vital a factor luck could be is shown in the case of Lefty Grove. Five summers before Hubbell's run, he clicked off sixteen straight in the 1931 season. His team was a better-hitting one than the Giants. Yet on August 23, 1931, pitching against the lowly St. Louis Browns, Lefty ran up against a chronic underachiever, Dick Coffman. That day Coffman beat Lefty 1–0 for the game of his career. Since Grove then won another six straight, had he not been shut out by Coffman, he would have had twenty-three straight in a single season. Such is luck.

After the Oklahoman's own great run, it took a little more than a score of years for another to come close. This originated from a surprising source: Elroy Face, the Pirates' long relief hurler of the late fifties and early sixties. In 1958–59, he strung together a twenty-two-game winning streak. Since they were relief wins, sometimes several-inning ones, the circumstances were not as stiff as for Hubbell or Grove. But a streak is a streak.

Roger Clemens' 1998–99 twenty in a row was in roughly comparable conditions to Hubbell's of 1936–37. More than sixty years after Carl, *New York Times* reporter Dave Anderson noted that Hubbell in his hurling had been steadier than Clemens. The latter's streak reached as high as it did because once he gave up seven runs in three early innings, and in another instance five in the first three, but the Yankee lineup had rescued him both times.

On the whole, Anderson's assessment is correct, but as Hubbell readily recognized, he had his good luck, too — but not on Clemens' scale. Hubbell pitched numerous brilliant games; his belated successor, few. In 1936, Hubbell won ten one-run games, eight of them during the streak.

Clemens, informed that Hubbell had completed nineteen starts, was very much impressed, saying "That's awesome."[21] Actually, in the year to which they were referring, he stayed to the end of twenty-five games. Mel Stottlemeyer, a twenty-game winner three times with the Yankees, added, "Complete games ... are ... what takes it out of you."[22]

Had the subject of Hubbell's eighteen-inning game been raised, their reactions would have been even more interesting. The interviewer probably was unaware of the three-in-a-week, or it, too, would have elicited startled comments.

Chapter 11

Superlatives Recaptured

Spring training of 1936 offered no surprises for Hubbell. Working assiduously on improving his curve, Carl succeeded so well that in the season just ahead, the home run susceptibility that had so plagued him the previous seasons dropped precipitously.

Over the off season, Manager Bill Terry, in view of the disappointments of the previous two years, brought about a few personnel changes. In '35, the infield on its right side had developed leaks. Hughie Critz had played only part-time, and at season's end, retired. At first, Terry himself, having severely bruised legs, had diminished mobility.

To remedy the second-base weakness, Terry secured Burgess Whitehead, the Cardinals' reserve infielder. Terry had to pay a rather high price. Parmelee, his fourth pitching starter, went to the Cardinals along with three so-so prospects. Neither team benefited much, if any, from the trade. Parmelee lasted only a year in St. Louis. Whitehead played several seasons for the Giants. However, he was quite erratic. In 1936, he made numerous brilliant plays. Yet he also led the league second-sackers in errors at thirty-two. Further, he showed a penchant for inexplicable misplays.

The manager sought a first-class regular first baseman as his own replacement. Failing in this, he regained Sam Leslie from Brooklyn, for whom he had toiled for some two and a half years. Though not a Terry as a batter, Leslie could hit respectably. As a fielder, again Sam was adequate, but no more than that. Reluctantly at times during the season, Terry would drag himself out to play as Leslie's replacement.

By 1936, Luque and Bell were no longer satisfactory as relief pitchers. From the St. Louis Browns, the manager obtained Dick Coffman, who until then had never lived up to expectations. As the Giants' chief reliever, he did better than he ever had previously.

Soon into the season, a disappointment appeared in the starting pitching. During 1935, Clyde Castleman had quickly advanced into a successful new starter. Terry figured him for Parmelee's replacement. But in the new pennant

Carl Hubbell, in the dugout long before the start of a game, is about to reach into the team's ball bag to pick up one to his liking.

run, he quickly deteriorated. Al Smith, mostly a reliever in '34 and '35, succeeded to Castleman's starting slot. He did his best, hurling about 50–50 ball. However, more was needed.

To make matters worse, Hank Leiber, who in 1935 had had an excellent season, slipped into mediocrity in '36. To replace Leiber at times, the Giants acquired Jimmy Ripple, a minor-league late bloomer who hit surprisingly well for the Polo Grounders.

Overall, the personnel changes only produced a half-game improvement over '35. In that year, it would not have been sufficient to lift the Giants out of third place. The primary reason why in 1936 virtually the same record won them the pennant came from the stellar work of their star moundsman. At season's end, the Polo Grounders' familiar pair of rivals ended up deadlocked for second/third in the stretch run. Three of the most costly defeats each suffered were administered by the Giants' hurling kingpin.

In general, from an overall perspective of the National League, the 1935-

36 winter passed quietly. This was in contrast to the immediately preceding years when the problem of the carrying force of baseballs stood out. The only important news focused upon the Boston franchise. The team's 1935 disaster led to new ownership. With fan help, the newcomer owners decided upon a fresh name — the Boston Bees — for the club. The team went nowhere. It soon became evident that "Bees" was not a wise choice for the name. Cheap jokes were made about the "stingless" and "buzzless" ones. In only a few years, the ownership reverted to the name of Boston Braves.

For the Giants, the annual race, once launched, soon resembled the immediately preceding ones. Surprisingly, at times the Cincinnati Reds showed signs of coming to life, only to wilt later. The Pirates, as was their wont, stumbled along between third and fourth. In consequence, occasionally — for brief times — the Giants found themselves in fifth.

Until mid-season, Hubbell's hurling was defined by a certain amount of unevenness. A couple of times he pitched brilliant games, the outcome of which brought only losses for him and the team. On the other hand, several times he was only mediocre, but won anyway or came out with a no-decision. Once he was plainly inadequate. By the All-Star break, he stood at 10–5 W-L, and 3.20 ERA. Both of these statistics were good, but not remarkably so.

Looking at his losses until this point in the season, they seem to indicate that a stretch of bad luck tagged him. Once he was shut out 3–0; twice 1–0. Another was a painful 2–1 setback in a memorable seventeen-inning marathon. A fourth defeat he incurred, losing 3–2. The fifth loss, 5–3, was the one in which he pitched unmistakably poorly, giving up the runs in less than four innings. His last setback occurred shortly after the All-Star Game, 1–0. After that point in the season, there was no stopping him.

In hurling prior to the mid-season specialty, four times an in-game feature sufficiently distinctive as to need elaboration occurred. The first came on April 29, the date of the seventeen-inning struggle, the second longest pitching stint of his major league years. It bore a remarkable resemblance to the 1933 endurance contest. The two struggles are sometimes bracketed together.

The opponents were identical: Giants versus the Cardinals. Two of the pitchers in the July 2, 1933, double-header went at it: Hubbell and Roy Parmelee. There the resemblance ended. On the earlier occasion, Parmelee had pitched the second game behind Hubbell, and — helped some by the approaching semi-darkness — had also defeated the Redbirds, 1–0. This time he was Hubbell's opponent. Angry at Terry for trading him to St. Louis, Parmelee was itching to get at the Giants in this, his first opportunity. This time the Cardinals were the home team and they emerged the winner. However, it was because Hubbell's "foolproof" infield forsook him.

A measly 4,500 spectators attended this remarkable game. Had it not been that the visiting hurler was so well known, such a mid-week game in the midst of the Depression probably would have drawn half that number.

Though Hubbell did not match what he had accomplished in the eighteen-inning game in 1933, he pitched very well, nevertheless. Parmelee likewise was at his best, so the first eleven innings were quickly reeled off with both teams scoreless. In the twelfth, each hurler finally gave up a run.

The battle resumed. Parmelee and Hubbell each blanked his opponent's team four or, in the case of Parmelee, five more innings. The seventeenth brought Hubbell's defeat. His situation began very inauspiciously when Redbirds catcher Spud Davis doubled down the right field line. Nevertheless, Hubbell probably would have squirmed out of his predicament had it not been that the left side of the infield cracked. With runners on first and second and one out, Parmelee, batting for himself, hit a double-play roller to Dick Bartell at short. Bartell fumbled it, loading the bases. Terry Moore grounded to Jackson at third. Throwing home for a force-out, his peg drew Mancuso off the plate, enabling a pinch runner to score the winning run for a 2–1 Cardinal victory. Hubbell gave up eleven hits and four walks, with two of the latter intentional. To walk off the field the loser after pitching into the seventeenth inning must have been a dismal experience, but Hubbell managed it.

For once, the manager gave his "Meal Ticket" time off commensurate with his seventeen innings of work on April 29. The Giants were on their first western tour. While in Cincinnati on May 4, Terry sent Hubbell back to the slab. Again the Giants underwent a frustrating loss. As Hubbell's opponent, there appeared a pitching unknown, likewise a fellow Sooner, Lee Stine. In his major league career, Stine won only three games, 250 fewer than Hubbell.

Though the Giant batters whacked Stine for eight solid hits, in the nine innings they could not score. Hubbell held the Reds to four puny hits in eight. Then came the ninth inning. Just as in St. Louis, it started very unfavorably. The first batter was Kiki Cuyler, often a problem for Hubbell. At mid-season the year before, the Cubs, thinking that Cuyler was worn out, released him unconditionally. This had enabled the Reds to pick him up. In 1936, he hit .326. Cuyler lashed out at Hubbell's first pitch to the right center for three bases. After that, Hubbell got the Red shortstop out on an infield play and walked Ernie Lombardi and Babe Herman to load the bases.

Up came Sammy Byrd. Two or three years before, Byrd had been Babe Ruth's "caddy" in late innings of Yankee games, when a slowed-up Babe would retire. Later Byrd enjoyed a successful golf career, winning one major tournament. In this game, at bat, he hit a fly to Ott in fairly short right field. Still fast, Cuyler streaked for the plate, beating Ott's slightly off-line throw by a hair. "Nobody" Stine had shut out pitching "ace" Hubbell, 1–0.

After a third straight loss, against the Phillies on May 9, in which he pitched poorly against Curt Davis, the Oklahoman's luck changed. He proceeded to hurl four straight wins. The last of the foursome had a special event as its feature. In an extra-inning struggle against the Dodgers on May 27, Hubbell defeated them 5–4. The game went to twelve innings. In relief, Fred Frankhouse, a recent Brooklyn acquisition, came out the loser. Momentarily, the win placed the Giants in first. This was the first of three wins Hubbell obtained over the Dodgers that year, losing none to them. This broke the Flatbushers' jinx over him, but for only this 1936 annum.

In June, the Giants' "Old Reliable," though pitching a little unevenly, won three of four. One, on June 20, garnered Carl a lucky win against the Cardinals. In 7⅓ innings, his opponents scored four runs on ten hits. He almost lost a substantial lead. Fortunately, Dick Coffman saved it for him with a 7–6 win.

Shortly before the All-Star Game on July 2, the fourth instance of an unusual event occurred. It was in a game at Boston against the Bees. The Giants won it, 7–6, but again Hubbell lasted only half of the game, giving up five runs and eight hits. This time, however, his difficulties were due to an inadvertent injury he inflicted on a Boston player. In the Bees' fifth inning, their first batsman was Bill Urbanski, shortstop. On Hubbell's first pitch to Bill, he hit him in the cranium. Urbanski crumpled to the ground. It unnerved Hubbell to such a degree that it led to his withdrawal.

The time in Chicago two years previously when his pitch had hit Chuck Klein, Hubbell had shown no concern. This time, hitting the batter, especially in the head, disturbed Carl a great deal. His flustered hurling quickly jeopardized the Giants' three-run advantage. Two of the next three Boston batters made hits. In addition, an errant Hubbell toss produced a passed ball. Terry decided that his pitcher was too disturbed by what happened and lifted him from the game. The Giants were lucky to win this one.

A break in the schedule came with the fourth All-Star Game on July 7. For the first time, the National Leaguers were the winners, 4–3. Players from the circuit's three best teams brought it about. Dizzy Dean pitched three scoreless innings. Hubbell followed with three more. The four runs were provided by the hitting of the Cubs' Gabby Hartnett and Augie Galan.

Hubbell's role consisted of allowing a single to Gehrig in the fourth, to Rip Radcliff, Chicago White Sox outfielder, in the fifth, and a walk to Gehringer in the sixth. No run was allowed, however. In three games, the American League had yet to score off him. Perhaps their players felt their diminished strikeouts represented improvement.

Regular play returned immediately. On July 10, Terry's "Meal Ticket" pitched 7⅓ inconclusive innings in a 5–4 loss to the Cardinals. After two days off, Carl was back in a starting role against the Cubs at Wrigley Field.

With several teams closely bunched, the game had a certain measure of mid-season importance. With Bill Lee as his opponent, Hubbell lost 1–0. In the fourth, the Cubs scored their run on a pair of "Texas Leaguers": bloopers between infielders and outfielders. Also, Whitehead had a foolish miscue. This put the Cubs in first by a half game over the Cardinals, while dropping the Giants briefly into fifth.

At mid-month, in Pittsburgh, the Giants' 1936 pennant hope appeared to be in the scrapheap. Fifth place, they trailed the Cubs, who were in first, by eleven games. However, in the Corsair series, they suddenly rewired, capturing three straight. The last was a 6–0 win, with Hubbell turning in a "walkless" five-hit effort, on July 17. It was the first of his long streak. For another month or more, it went unnoticed.

Returning home, the Giants played great ball through the remainder of the month of July, as well as August. In the latter month, they ran up a fifteen-game winning streak, emulating the Cubs in 1932 and 1935. With this momentum, they continued to do well into early September. As usual in a multi-contested race, the close pursuers did the ultimate winner a continuing favor by damaging each other at just the wrong time for themselves, but the right time for the Giants. When the New York visitors won out over the Cardinals in a vital early September series in St. Louis, their lead reached four games. They held onto it fairly consistently to the end.

In the Giants' exciting late season upsurge, Hubbell's pitching probably did the most to put them over. His winning streak, after it reached ten, began to be noticed. The six more to the end required winning extremely important games uninterruptedly, which he did. Altogether, from the start of the streak to season's close, he pitched nineteen times, four of which were relief tasks.

Afterward, when Hubbell stressed good luck as important, in that he avoided being shut out, he was only partly right. Even more helpful, his teammates won three games in which he pitched. These were games where the great majority of the time he would have been the loser, had his teammates not scored for him.

In one, particularly, the Giants emerged victorious only because three episodes occurred in which the chances were about one in a thousand that they would happen in the same game. With regard to the other two, in one he pitched poorly, but luck was with him because the New York batters in the early innings were wearing their "hitting clothes." In the other, last-moment relief help saved him. Had he stayed in, his own weariness probably would have lost it for him.

Putting the 1936 season in a broader context, Hubbell, with the exception of these three instances, hurled magnificent ball from mid–July to the season's end. Altogether, he appeared in nineteen games. In fifteen of them, he served as starting pitcher. In fourteen, he also was the finisher. In a close race, this helped the manager a great deal. Terry was able to save his relief hurlers for duty in aid of the other starters most of the time.

In August alone, Hubbell started six games, completed six and won all six. In baseball's domain of the trivial, it would be interesting to know how often, if at all, other hurlers before or after Carl ever did as much.

Hubbell even succeeded in winning two of the sixteen as a reliever. In one, on July 19, he hurled 2⅓ innings to pick up the win, 4–3 over the Reds. The other, a very important success against the Cardinals on September 14, he won 7–5 with a five-inning relief stint. Overall, in 145 innings of hurling during the streak, his ERA came to 2.07.

In retrospect, the game that to the Giants' players started their great leap forward came on July 21. Though the contest at the Polo Grounds offered a Dizzy Dean/Hubbell collision, the Monday date brought only a small crowd. It was characterized afterward as a "titanic pitching struggle" between the "silent King Carl and his loquacious duelist."[1] The Giants won 2–1 in the tenth on a Dick Bartell home run. The Cardinals all but had it won in the ninth when Frank Frisch was the batter. The bases were loaded and there was one out. However, Hubbell induced Frisch to top one back to him which he threw to Mancuso for the force at home. The catcher then doubled the batter at first. In the *Globe Democrat*, Haley paid tribute to the Giants' pitcher for his skill in obtaining double plays at vital moments.

The game that, by every reckoning except the final score, Hubbell should have lost, happened at the Polo Grounds on Sunday, July 26. By the Giants' seventh inning, the home team trailed the Cincinnati Reds' best hurler, Paul Derringer, 4–2. Terry removed his starter for a pinch hitter.

Earlier, Cincinnati should have obtained two or three more runs but for the bizarre base running miscalculations. For example, in the fourth inning, with their first baseman Les Scarsella on first and Kiki Cuyler at second, catcher Ernie Lombardi crashed a terrific drive to deep left center. It looked uncatchable, so the base runners raced forward. But Hank Leiber in center field made a great catch. The result was that Cuyler, racing past third, could not get back to second in time. Therefore, Leiber's throw to second resulted in Cuyler's making the second out at that base. Meantime, this forced Scarsella, near second, to return to first. Ernie Lombardi was in his way and he got tagged for the third out on the same play. The Giants had completed a triple play on two base-running mishaps and a great catch. For their efforts, the Reds obtained exactly nothing.

After Hubbell left, trailing 4–2 in the home team's ninth, they succeeded in winning after all on two more lucky breaks. First, through three hits, the Giants scored one run, leaving them behind only 4–3, with the tying run on third. Then the second break occurred. Balks are very infrequent and are rare with a runner on third. But Derringer, shaken by all that had happened, balked in the tying run, while the possible winning run stood at second. Leiber singled to left. Babe Herman snatched up the ball on the first bounce. He had a reasonably good chance of throwing out the prospective winning run at the plate. However, "enthralled" by the "amazing drama" of the Giants' rally, Herman, like a "true artist," stood holding the ball while the winning run scampered in.[2] When the 1937 season came, the Cincinnati management discontinued Babe Herman's employment. Luck prefers winners to needy also-rans.

August 15 at home brought another double-header. On a Saturday afternoon, the Polo Grounders' visitor was the hapless Phillies. They had lost a dozen straight. Against Hubbell, the Phillies pitted Bucky Walters who — traded to Cincinnati a couple of years later — succeeded Hubbell as the National League's finest pitcher. Though he and Hubbell performed in the same circuit for nine years, by the luck of the draw they came to grips with one another as starters only twice.

On this day, the game was fought out in "almost overpowering humidity."[3] Hubbell, from Oklahoma, proved to have the greater stamina in the heat than Walters from Pennsylvania. The Phillies' twirler held the Giants runless through five innings, but caved in the next due to the searing heat. The home team racked up four runs against him, two driven in by their pitcher. The poor Phillies absorbed their thirteenth loss in a row.

In his description of the game, Derringer offered a tidbit explaining the primitive means that teams took in that distant day to protect their hurlers from collapsing on the mound in the heat of a summer day. Between innings, interludes resembled a prize fight between rounds. Once finished with his half-inning of mound work, Hubbell would head for his corner — the Giants' dugout — where his second, the team trainer or a coach, awaited him. The exhausted combatant then would be "revived ... with a general dousing of a water-logged sponge."[4] With his energy thus presumably restored, Hubbell would trudge back to the mound for his next half-inning of pitching. Carl lasted all the way, but that day Walters could not. One might say that as much as Carl had wanted never to do the job as an adult, hoeing on hot humid days in Oklahoma as a boy had prepared him for just this type of effort as a hurler.

After three days off, on August 19, "King Carl" garnered a hard-fought 3–2 win over Brooklyn. With the Giants in Cincinnati a full week later, he picked up a shakily tossed 6–5 win over the Reds. As so often, Derringer lost to him. It was the only one of Hubbell's sixteen straight wins in which the opposition scored as many as five runs.

By this time, in late August, the Coogan's Bluff contingent had attained first place by a narrow margin. Involved in a high-stakes western trip, they reached Chicago. On Sunday, August 30, the Cub management scheduled a double-header. With the Bruins only three back, a sellout crowd of 45,401 fans bought tickets. The Giants downed the Cubs twice. In the opener, Hubbell, despite a crowd in the left to make his — and his opponent Bill Lee's — task harder, won 6–1. The Cubs could make only seven hits along with a single walk that the Giants' star surrendered. It was Hubbell's tenth straight success and his twentieth of the season. Even though it was Chicago, when Hubbell, along with Terry and Ott, left the field, "ear splitting cheers ... greeted them."[5]

By late 1936, a consensus had developed that Hubbell's pitching stood out as the best that either major league had to offer. That season the "Great One" himself, Dizzy Dean, clinched the matter when he conceded that Hubbell was the best.

Insofar as Dizzy Dean/Hubbell duels went, the one in St. Louis, September 3, only four days after the Chicago double-header, featured the rivalry at its peak. Never were the stakes higher. With the Cardinals at home and trailing by three, this game, the closer of the series, towered over the teams as a "four-twoer." That is to say that if Dean should beat Hubbell, the Cardinals would be only two back, with much to drive them onward. On the other hand, a loss meant four down for the Cards, with less than a month to go and most games on the road. For the Giants, it meant the opposite. If their "ace" lost to the Dizzy, they would be only a shaky two up and with a damaging loss to think about on their long train ride back home. On the other hand, if Hubbell could beat Dean, the resulting four-game advantage would be very helpful.

September 3 was midweek. A crowd of 23,000 fans attended. This was large for a weekday in St. Louis. For eight tingling innings, Dean and Hubbell fought to a draw at 1–1. In the Giants' ninth, their pitcher would be fourth batter up. After an out, Mancuso singled and Bartell doubled him to third. Terry had to decide whether to pinch-hit for Hubbell or let him bat.

If he decided to use a pinch hitter, opposing manager Frisch probably would have ordered a walk for him, and Terry's best pitcher would be out of the game. The Giants' manager told Carl to bat. Terry was aware that his pitcher often did come up with a helpful hit or out. As expected, Dean pitched to him. Hubbell succeeded in lifting a fly to slightly shallow right field. Whitehead, running for Mancuso, set sail for home. Pepper Martin's peg home came in high and a little to the right of the plate. Whitehead slid between Spud Davis's legs as Davis reached up and out to grab Martin's throw. The umpire called Whitehead safe.

With the Giants up 2–1, Hubbell then faced the problem of holding his one-run lead with a hostile crowd cheering on the home team in its last of the ninth. This was the same scenario he had faced eight years before that first drew national baseball attention to him. The other time a Cardinal had reached third. This time he stopped the Redbirds cold. Hubbell had beaten Dean. The Giants went home with a four-game lead.

Mostly at home, the Giants succeeded in marinating their shaky lead to the finish. The Sooner southpaw contributed five more wins to the final tally. He beat the Phillies again, 6–2; September 9, the Cardinals, 7–5, in the afore-mentioned relief service; September 14, the Dodgers and Van Lingle Mungo, 9–1; and on September 19, the Phillies one final time, 5–4, on September 23.

Of these four games, the one that had the greatest impact was his victory as a reliever over the Cardinals. In the same game, Frisch, too, used his best, Dizzy Dean, in relief. That so late in the season each manager would use his overworked best hurler in a relief stint illustrates how far field bosses at that time would go in order to try to win a pennant.

Hubbell's final in-season appearance against the Phillies took place in Baker Bowl. It had middling importance. The Polo Grounders had been stag-gering, even losing a double bill to their weak opponents. It had Terry worried as to whether his players conceivably could still blow the pennant.

Hubbell held the 54–100 W-L Phillies runless through seven. Suddenly the eighth brought Philadelphia to life with a three-run rally. The ninth started with their best player, Dolph Camilli, first baseman, swatting a homer. With the next batter, Hubbell walked the potential tying run. The manager, as he almost always did, stuck with his "Meal Ticket" and it worked. The next three batters made outs. The Giants had hung on to win, 5–4.

The Giants needed to add only one more to the win column and the pennant would be theirs. The next day Schumacher gained a hard-fought win over the Bees to close it out.

The players, of course, celebrated their pennant. However, unlike in 1933, the win was not followed with a grandiose celebration provided by fans and the city. It was only three years later and not enough time had elapsed for the citizenry to return to a New Year's Eve frame of mind. Besides, there was plenty for the Giant's fandom to worry about dead ahead: the World Series.

In the final pitching statistics for the season, what strikes any close observer, both then and in retrospect, is the extent to which Hubbell domi-nated the most significant categories. He ranked first in ERA at 2.31, about half a run less than the runner-up. He was first in winning percentage at a dazzling .813. His total wins of twenty-six were also first. Carl was second to Dizzy in complete games at twenty-five. He was third in innings pitched, 304, and fourth in strikeouts, 123. Sports writers conferred the Most Valuable

Player Award on him for the second time. Hubbell was the only National League player to win this award twice in the fifteen and a half years he was in the majors.

Though not ranked as a special achievement, at 26–6 W-L, Hubbell, in a single season, won twenty more games than he lost. Though in no sense a record, it is a pitcher's feat rare enough to earn attention. As of early in the 21st century, the last time it had happened dates back to the mid–1980s. This pitching trend might suggest that it is no longer an attainable objective.

The 1936 World Series awaited the team and its rooters. New Yorkers were blessed with another "subway series," a return to the early 1920s. Team traveling expenses were limited to the players' taxi rides to and from the Polo Grounds and Yankee Stadium; the owners thereby received their own bonus.

For fans and players alike, the series each year served as a source of anticipation and inspiration. However, the Giants' players also had much to worry about in the opponent they faced. Three years before, the team's statistics had suggested the Senators were the better team, yet the Giants had won. This time the statistical gap was even greater, diminishing the likelihood of another upset. The late 1930s New York Yankees were widely, and correctly, judged to be one of baseball's all-time great teams. Managed by Joe McCarthy, once with the Cubs, they were about to launch a stretch of four straight world championships. Their three opponents could win only three games. At World Series time in 1936, it was already obvious they would be a formidable Giants opponent.

That year, the Yankees' team batting average reached .300 to the Giants' .281. They had distanced the runner-up Detroit Tigers by a cool 19½ games. Had the Giants been in the American League and been the runner-ups instead, they still would have trailed by 10½ games. The Yankee sluggers amassed 182 home runs — a record at the time — to the Giants' 97. They also batted far more doubles and triples. Though neither team offered much speed, the junior leaguers even stole quite a few more bases than their opposites. Perhaps most impressively, the Yankees racked up 1,065 runs in their 154-game schedule. This was an amazing almost seven runs per game average. The Giants totaled 742 runs, a little fewer than five each game.

How the opponents matched up in pitching was hard to measure. That year the Americans as a league out-hit the older circuit, .289 to .278. Their pitchers showed a run higher ERA than their National League brethren. Despite appearances, the Yankees, except for being "Hubbell-less," had a solid pitching corps. Observers ranked the two as about even except for the one case.

In fielding, although the rivals had almost identical defensive percentages, opinion held that the Giants were superior, especially in the infield. They were considered slightly better in the outfield also. Catching ran about even.

Though the Giants held their own, or had a slight edge, in pitching-fielding, nevertheless the Yankees' formidable hitting array made them strong favorites. Jack Doyle quoted them at almost two to one over the Giants except for any game in which Hubbell would pitch. Then the odds switched to five — three in the Polo Grounders' favor. In the *Times*, John Drebinger quite accurately foresaw the series outcome, saying that if Hubbell should lose either of his starts, the Yankees would win quite decisively.

With the teams located in the same city, the series was to be another one of "no off-days" unless for rain. The first game was to be Wednesday, September 30. The day dawned with weather very unpropitious for play. Nevertheless, Commissioner Kenesaw Mountain Landis decreed the game should go on, since the weather prediction for the following day was also bad. The inclement weather held the crowd at the Polo Grounds down to slightly less than 40,000.

Of course, Terry opened with Hubbell as his first game starter. Against him Joe McCarthy countered with his twenty-game winner, Charley Ruffing. A questioner asked Hubbell what he foresaw as far as the Yankee hitters were concerned. He answered by saying they would come out "swinging from taw."[6] Drebinger, mindful of Hubbell's country origins, described this phrase as "quaint." What the Oklahoman obviously meant was that he expected them to come out slugging.

Actually this was not the case. The Yankee hitters did some waiting out of Hubbell. This usually was not a wise tactic. Apparently McCarthy, observing the muddy playing conditions, figured Hubbell would not have the fine-line control he usually had, and advised his hitters to string out the count. After the game, Hubbell mentioned he had worried in the early innings over his high pitch counts due to the muddy mound.

Once the game began, rain fell steadily. Playing conditions were described by old-timers as the worst since the last game of the 1925 World Series. In a box seat not far from Babe Ruth's wife Claire sat Sue Hubbell, very fashionably attired. She was pulling hard for her husband to win, and incidentally for the Giants as well.

In the *New York Herald-Tribune*, Rod Rennie described Hubbell as "the man with a rubber arm ... as unruffled as if he were in an armchair at home playing checkers with his wife."[7] After the game, he noted that while during the season the Yankees had scored over a thousand runs, when up against Hubbell in the World Series, they scored only one. Though Hubbell did remain serene throughout, actually the game was a tighter squeeze than Rennie's description suggests. In the third, the Yankees broke through for the first — and their only — run of the game. It came in the form of a George Selkirk home run to right field.

Ruffing pitched effectively until the fifth and sixth. In the fifth, Bartell got to him for a tying home run to left. In the next inning, an Ott double and Mancuso single moved the Giants up 2–1.

For the Yankees, other than Selkirk's homer, their offense consisted of an occasional hit, a single walk, and a plethora of ground balls as inning followed inning. In the seventh, neither team did anything. Then in the first of the eighth, the Yankees posed a serious threat. Crosetti, Yankee shortstop, doubled. Hubbell, in another of his fielding lapses, fumbled their third baseman Red Rolfe's bunt. Then came the break of the game. Freshman star Joe DiMaggio lashed a low liner that Whitehead stabbed, then turned into an easy double play. After a Gehrig HPB, catcher Dickey grounded out. Thus ended the Yankees' only major threat in the game.

In the Giants' half of the eighth, they broke the game open with a four-run outburst. The Yankee infielders, floundering in the mud, provided help. The Giants' offense consisted of three hits — one bunt and two walks, one of them with the bases loaded — and two throwing errors. The Yankees, now far behind, succumbed easily in the ninth for a 6–1 Giants' victory.

The Yankees' feeble offense came from their hitters making the mistake against Hubbell that many National League batters had: swinging too soon. They managed seven hits and Hubbell gave one walk. He struck out eight, exceeding his average. Most remarkable, the Giants' outfielders might just as well have stayed home out of the rain. In fly outs, there was not a one. At first base, Terry had twelve putouts: Mancuso, nine had in the infield; and Hubbell accounted for the other six. When McCarthy had been manager of the Cub team back in 1929, the same thing had happened. Did he remember it?

After the last out, Hubbell hurried to the Giants' dressing room. In a moment of exuberance and atypical self-promotion, he yelled to his teammates as they joined him, "Did I clean the bases for you in sloppy weather?" They hollered back, "You dry-cleaned them."[8]

After the Giants' opening triumph, the series, with one exception, followed the path that the betting odds foretold. The second engagement, delayed a day by rainout, ended in a crushing 18–4 loss for the Giants. The Yankee hitters pounded the Giants' pitchers for eighteen hits to match the runs. The starter, Hal Schumacher, was the chief victim of the Yankee slaughter.

The series switched to Yankee Stadium for games three through five. In the third encounter, Fred Fitzsimmons did a fine job, outpitching Bump Hadley, the Yankees' starter, but still losing 2–1. The Giants pecked away at Hadley for ten hits in eight innings, but could score only one on a Jimmy

Ripple homer. In contrast, Fitzsimmons allowed two hits: a Gehrig home run and, in the eighth, a single off his body that scored their winning run from third. Pat Malone, former Cub star, acquired a save via a scoreless ninth in relief of Hadley.

Terry, down two–one, had to return to his "ace" for game four. Unlike 1933 when Hubbell had pitched this one in a sequence with only two days' rest, this time, due to the rainout, he had the standard three days. McCarthy countered with Monte Pearson, his in-season number three starter.

The Yankees had four regular starters in 1936, giving them the advantage over the Giants in an everyday-play series. Pearson was a talented hurler, constantly plagued by arm trouble. Due to it, he lasted only ten years, winning only a hundred games, but pitching at a .621 pace. In 1936 he really was better than Gomez and Ruffing.

In this encounter with Hubbell, Pearson outpitched baseball's best pitcher, defeating him, 5–2. The fifth Yankee run came in the eighth off a Giants reliever replacing Hubbell. The Yankees took a run lead in the third, largely due to a Travis Jackson error, followed later by a Selkirk single. The fourth brought in three Yankee tallies. Crosetti doubled and Rolfe singled for one. Then Gehrig got to Hubbell for a two-run homer off what he described as the "wildest curve in the world."[9] That year Hubbell had greatly reduced his home runs, falling to only eight. Gehrig's was the first with a runner on. After the fourth, Hubbell pitched well enough, allowing only seven hits and two runs, but the Giants were incapable of a game-saving rally.

Down 3–1, Terry returned to Schumacher, who had failed badly in the 18–4 rout. This time, however, he hung on doggedly for ten innings, finally besting the Yankees, 5–4. Observers were surprised that the Giants were able to bounce back for a second win. For the Yankees, Malone, in long relief of Ruffing, took the loss.

Back to Coogan's Bluff went the series. Terry gave Fitzsimmons his second start. McCarthy's choice was Lefty Gomez. Neither starter shone. Fitzsimmons fell far short of his first start, not even lasting through four innings. The Giants hung close until the ninth. Then the Yankees broke loose for seven runs for a 13–5 clincher. On the whole, they showed why the pre-series betting odds had been so favorable to them. For the Giants, the series represented a respectable, almost a valiant loss to a team clearly their superior.

Chapter 12

"Waiting for Lefty"

Despite the World Series setback, 1936 closed on a positive note for the Polo Grounders. For management, it provided the first season in the black since 1930. For the players, it offered a salary supplement via the World Series share each received, even if only the loser's portion.

With the '36–'37 off season at hand, Terry understood that if the Giants hoped to continue as steady pennant contenders, there would need to be improvement at several lineup positions. Although Terry succeeded in making only one significant advance, the team managed to scramble to another pennant.

The players' slowness afoot continued to be an area of weakness. In this sphere, Terry accomplished no improvement. The team had as many lead-footed runners in 1937 as in 1936.

Terry, due to his own worn-out legs, had retired as a player with finality. Sam Leslie as his replacement did not suffice. Most of the time Johnny McCarthy, up from Newark, was the first baseman. He fielded well, but his hitting fell short. Leslie held on as first base fill-in and pinch hitter.

After the 1936 World Series, Travis Jackson retired. The best the manager could do for a third base replacement was Lou Chiozza, a Phillies infield-outfield reserve. By the season's second half, third base had become a serious problem.

The one defensive area in which the manager scored a notable success lay in his pitching department. Fitzsimmons and Schumacher had declined to only .500 in the 1936 season. Terry badly needed another starter. This he obtained in the person of Cliff Melton, a tall left-hander from Baltimore. Melton helped greatly in 1937, but thereafter he declined into more or less a .500 hurler. In the new season, further help came from Slick Castleman, who improved on his 1936 showing. However, he was unable to maintain it into 1938.

Once the season got started, Terry made two trades in June. Feeling that Fitzsimmons was about finished as a successful starter, the manager let him go to the Dodgers. In return, the Giants obtained Tom Baker, who did nothing for the Giants — or anyone else. Many felt Fitzsimmons deserved a better fate than banishment to the cross-town rival. Worse, in a couple of years, the trade boomeranged badly.

In center field, Leiber, who had suffered a severe spring training injury, could play only part-time. Riddle served as a helpful fill-in but more was needed. Accordingly, Terry obtained Wally Berger from the Boston Bees. In previous days when they were the Braves, Berger had been their sole power hitter. However, by 1937, he had begun to slip, so he added very little to the Giants' outfield. Gabler, a second-level pitcher, departed for him.

Spring trainings rarely are recalled. The 1937 one, however, lingered on as memorable, especially for Hubbell. He admitted that, just as in 1934, pitching in relief a number of times in 1936 had left him at season's end with a "tired" arm. A different way of putting it would have been to state simply that his arm had grown sore. However, like athletes generally, he preferred words of minimally suggestive worry. Thus, that spring the question about the extent to which his arm retained its elasticity needed clarification.

Fortunately, practice hurling soon loosened up Carl's left arm without a recurrence of soreness. Since his curve had brought such favorable returns in 1936, he mentioned that in the new season he would rely on it more than the screwball. Why would a hurler, famed for his reliance on an oddity pitch, start using another type of toss as his primary delivery? It looks as if Hubbell decided he was far enough along in pitcher years to start exercising caution in flinging his "scroogie."

There are also indications that finally Terry, too, had begun to exercise more caution in the extent to which he turned to the old "Meal Ticket." Through most of the season, he succeeded in providing Hubbell with three days off between starts. However, during the usual close August-September chase, the manager lapsed into his former habit of turning to Carl too often.

In late March, the Giants departed from their Havana base for their rendezvous with the Cleveland Indians, their annual pre-season travel companions. Two events took place en route northward that stuck in participants' memories. They applied especially to Hubbell and to a yet little-known Cleveland newcomer.

Over the winter, the Cleveland and Giants managements — urged by Terry, who had a keen head for business — had decided on a means to enhance attendance at stops along the way. Late the previous season, the Indians had used their freshman hurler several times. His strikeouts along with a commensurate wildness had created a furor. The youth was Bob Feller. Would it not be a fine idea for the Giants' master of finesse pitching and the Cleveland wunderkind with the great fast ball to face each other a time or two along the way?

On Sunday, April 4, at New Orleans, Oklahoma's most famous ex-farmer and Cleveland's recent budding acquisition from Iowa, squared off. As anticipated, 11,000 fans jammed the minor league park. Cleveland's manager was Steve O'Neill, the very person who at Toronto more than a decade before had given Hubbell encouragement. He, along with Terry, decided to restrict the pitchers to five innings. In the battle between Perspicacity and Power, each pitched five scoreless rounds. The pre-game ballyhoo had produced a huge success but for one alarming incident. A Feller blazer struck Leiber directly in the head. Batting helmets were still in the future. Most of the time throughout the season, the injury kept Leiber as only a fill-in player. The injury probably stunted his career.

On Wednesday, April 7, the teams arrived at Shawnee, Oklahoma, to play a game. Ordinarily the town was nowhere nearly large enough to induce major league clubs to play there. However, the town was only about 25 miles from a tiny village named Meeker. Everybody in Lincoln, Pottawotamie, and Oklahoma counties was expected to turn out to watch their most famous person pitch.

Unfortunately, that day a drought-induced Oklahoma dust storm blew through. This cut the attendance by half. Nevertheless, 5,000 were on hand in a little park whose seating maximum was 3,500. No one said a word about Shawnee's fire ordinance. Conspicuous in the first two rows of seats were Hubbell's parents and his in-laws. His mother, who had never before had the opportunity to see her famous son pitch, had her wish to do so realized at last.

Under dust bowl conditions, the game was a pretense. Nonetheless, the "5,000 of Hubbell's friends and neighbors, [though] choked as the dust swirled in, watched closely as he pitched."[1] The acclaimed product of the Hubbell family pitched only three innings before the home folks, allowing a run. This was a dust-blown home run off the bat of Hal Trosky, the Indians' first baseman. But "the populace had too many mouthfuls of mud to moan" when Trosky hit it.[2] Otherwise, the game was utterly forgettable. Hubbell mentioned that to him dust was nothing new.

Hubbell and Feller had a final encounter. The Giants' star figured to be the starting pitcher for the season opening game. However, Terry anticipated that, weather permitting, the opener would be a sellout no matter who pitched. Why not have Hubbell pitch in the final exhibition instead? It drew a crowd of 33,000, very large for a pre-season game. Though the Giants won it, on the whole, Feller outpitched his opponent. The latter was perhaps not feeling up to snuff, giving up a rare five walks.

Once underway, the 1937 season soon resembled its immediate predecessors. In the Giants' case, this brought moments when they ranked from second to fourth, and, rarely, fifth. As before, an August resurgence followed a July slump. By early September, they had seized a small lead that they were able to maintain to the end.

Anomalies accompanied Hubbell's relationship to the familiar pattern. For one, contrary to the estimate of the long-serving reporters on the Giants' star, Hubbell was no longer the "colorless" wonder. From late 1936 straight through to mid–1938, his appearance meant larger, sometimes immense crowds. The long winning streak primarily explained why, but his duels with Dizzy Dean, the memories of the great All-Star Game strikeout day, and the eighteen innings pitched also helped.

Though the unbeaten run continued well into 1937, Hubbell's hurling developed an unevenness that had been absent since the early thirties. Had it not been that early in the 1937 season the Giants' batters usually hit very well on most of the days Carl pitched, the streak probably would have ended a few wins earlier than it did. It is possible that the ups and especially the downs were a harbinger of what was to come.

With each new win, the fans' expectation for their favorite's next start grew. "Waiting for [their] Lefty"[3] became the order of the day. Two early wins in impressive fashion whet appetites. May 4 was the date of his third start, a home game. Hubbell had the Cincinnati Reds team as his challenger. Ordinarily, a Tuesday game so early in May drew poorly, but for this one, 20,000 were present. With the streak at eighteen, one more would enable him to tie Rube Marquard's nineteen straight back in 1912.

To the fans' pleasure, the Giants hitters pounded the Reds' hurlers early, building a large lead. Years afterwards, Hubbell remembered that never did he have better substance to his pitches than on this day. In the first five innings, he fanned ten batters.

Then suddenly the Reds fell upon him. In the fifth, sixth, and until two outs in the seventh, they tallied six runs — three unearned — on nine hits and three walks. By then they trailed the Giants only 7–6. Possibly the extra pitches so many strikeouts entailed caused Hubbell's endurance to run out. At any rate, Terry replaced him with Harry Gumbert. As a rookie the previous year, he had done quite well as a mixed reliever and starter. He pitched the remainder of the game, not allowing a single Cincinnati batter to get on base. Thus, Hubbell — thanks to Gumbert — won his nineteenth straight, tying Marquard. However, it was not a win of which Hubbell could feel proud.

In the next two that he won, May 9, 4–1 against the Cubs and Bill Lee, and May 15, 5–2 against the Pirates, he pitched much better. On May 19, the date of his next start against the Cardinals, the game turned into a famous one.

It was a Wednesday in St. Louis, ordinarily far from a large crowd day. This time 26,000 bought tickets. The reason was that Dizzy Dean was to take on Carl Hubbell. With the streak at twenty-one by then, who was better fit to throw the visitor a loss at last than the Dizzy pitching at home?

Rarely could the opposite hurler be better suited, but this time it was insufficient. Hubbell had one of his great days. He defeated the Cardinals, 4–1, needing only 93 pitches, 70 of them strikes. In the ninth, Johnny Mize and Joe Medwick, the Redbirds' two best swingers, went down swinging. Yet something else involving Dean made the game even more memorable.

Dean came out determined to stop his opposite at twenty-one. He liked to pitch batters not only inside, but high. To start the game, he threw one to leadoff batter Bartell that cleared his cranium by only an inch or two. From then until the sixth, he shook up a Giants hitter periodically. At that stage, he led Hubbell by a run. But Dizzy's own penchant for defying the rules, plus his teammates' miscues, then did him in.

The National League had a rule that with a runner on base, the pitcher had to pause in his delivery for a second while pitching to the next batter. The umpires tended to enforce it only intermittently. With a Giant runner on, Dean pitched to the next batter without a trace of a slow-up. The home plate umpire called a balk, allowing the runner a free advance to second as penalty. From there the inning fell apart for the home team, with three Giants runs scoring.

In his wrath, Dean proceeded to throw at one Giant hitter after another until the ninth. At that point, Jimmy Ripple had to dive for the ground as a pitch approached his head. On the next pitch, he lay down a "collision" bunt and dove at Dean as he ran toward first. Nearly everybody in both of the dugouts tore out onto the diamond to engage in hand-to-hand combat against their opposites. A near riot followed.

One who stayed in the dugout was Carl Hubbell. When asked why afterwards, he replied that he was paid to pitch, not fight. So much common sense was too much for everybody else.

Finally, the game resumed. Dean was not expelled, unlike the norm in later days. All the Giants asked was that he quit throwing at them. As for Hubbell, he walked off with a well-earned twenty-second straight victory.

"King Carl's" twenty-third straight success bore some resemblance to the nineteenth, increasing doubts among close observers as to whether the string could be extended much further. With the Polo Grounders in Pittsburgh, the game was played on Monday, May 24. Again, on a normally weak draw day, 17,000 Pittsburghers showed up. Due to poor Pittsburgh defense, plus a Mel Ott home run, the visitors led by 4–1 into the home eighth. Suddenly the Pirates rallied for two runs on three hard hits. In the ninth, Pittsburgh batters made two more hits. Only an out remained for the Pirates, but Terry decided to replace his ace. In this situation in earlier years, he would not have done so. Cliff Melton then walked a batter and the bases were loaded. Dick Coffman came in and retired Johnny Dickshot, Pittsburgh outfielder, to enable the starter to chalk up his twenty-third straight win, 4–3.

Oddly, the twenty-fourth — and last — of Hubbell's great winning streak came without opportunity to draw a large crowd. In Cincinnati three days later, Hubbell came in as a reliever for Coffman in the seventh. The Giants rallied to win, 3–2, giving Hubbell the victory for two innings of work in which he retired all six of the batters he faced. Though not an admirable victory, it was not without some measure of respectability.

The winning streaker's opportunity to go for his twenty-fifth came just after Memorial Day, Monday, May 31, 1937, at the Polo Grounds. The usual double-header stood ready and Hubbell was scheduled to go in the opener. His opponents were the Giants' cross-town Flatbush enemies. In honor of what Hubbell would be trying to do, 61,756 fans sat and stood waiting for "Lefty."

When Carl was ready and set to work, on this of all days, the "King" had absolutely nothing. In 3⅓ innings, he allowed seven hits and three walks, gave up a wild pitch, and hit a batter for a total of five runs. This turned into a mammoth 10–3 loss for the Giants. The streak was over. And who had ended it but his evil spirits, the Brooklyn Dodgers. The dispirited centerpiece left with the "cheering of a sympathetic crowd ringing in his ears."[4]

Between games, on this, Hubbell's worst pitching day in a long time, he received his second Most Valuable Player award. There to present it to him was baseball's wistful job seeker, Babe Ruth.

Some years later, Hubbell offered his thoughts on winning streaks. He stressed that any pitcher or team enjoying a long winning run could be sure that when it ran out, its exact opposite would set in. In the 1937 season, this was exactly what struck him.

From early in June to about mid-month, Hubbell made five appearances, one in relief, losing three straight. In 23⅔ innings, he gave up a worrisome 20 runs, 15 of them earned, for about a 6.45 ERA during this slump. The losses were to the Cardinals, Pirates and Reds. The primary reason for the defeats lay in Hubbell's inferior hurling. Nonetheless, his teammates' defensive lapses also hurt. Rollers barely scooted by infielders; outfielders missed catching line drives by half a step; and foul balls drifted into the stands just barely beyond reach.

The setback at the hands of the Cardinals grew the largest crowd. Played at the Polo Grounds on June 9, it featured Dizzy Dean versus Hubbell again. This time the Redbird star kept his temper. He won easily, 8–1. In the *Times*,

John Drebinger observed that the "hitherto matchless Hubbell ... again offered little. His screwball lacked 'snap.'"[5]

After the Pittsburgh and Cincinnati setbacks, the Meeker favorite partly regained his footing on June 23 by defeating Chicago, 8–4. Shaky, he gave up a dozen hits along with the four runs. Still, it seemed to put him on the right track for his next effort.

On June 27, a Sunday, the Giants reached St. Louis. The usual double-header waited. In the first clash, Dean and Hubbell met for the third time. A huge crowd waited. Fans from nine Midwestern states had come to see the battle. Because of Sportsman's Park's limited capacity, only 38,719 could squeeze in.

Hubbell defeated Dean easily, 8–1. The Oklahoman gave up no bases on balls and only a scanty six hits. In an echo of earlier days, it took the Cardinal batters until the ninth to hit a fly to the outfield. By contrast, Dean got raked for six runs and ten hits, two of the latter circuit clouts.

In the seventh inning, Frisch removed Dean. From the field came the announcement that he had been withdrawn due to a sore shoulder. Unrealized at the time, this game, unfortunately, proved to be the last Dean/Hubbell battle.

On July 2, Hubbell pitched effectively again, this time against the Boston Bees, winning 6–2. On the Fourth of July, Terry used him for a runless one-inning relief duty against the Dodgers in a 6–5 win.

On July 7, 1937, the fifth All-Star Game gook place in the nation's capital. Fans from the American League wanted to see the hurler with the twenty-four-straight streak. This almost compelled Terry to use Hubbell for the third time in only six days.

For the Nationals, Dizzy Dean pitched the first three innings, surrendering two runs on a Gehrig home run. Hit in the toe by a line drive, Dean tried to resume pitching too soon. Thereby, Dizzy inflicted permanent injury to his already tender arm.

Hubbell succeeded Dean, but could not finish the fourth inning. After an out, Bill Dickey singled. Then Sam West, St. Louis Browns outfielder, drew a walk. This was followed by the pitcher's striking out, but Yankee third baseman, Red Rolfe, tripled. Then Charlie Gehringer singled home Rolfe. Terry withdrew Hubbell. The American Leaguers won, 8–3.

Once the regular season returned, Terry's best hurler continued his in-and-out performances. When he won, he usually pitched well. However, the opposite was equally true. Twice he was spared losses thanks to the Giants' batters continuing to hit well for him.

The Cubs were a team that belabored Carl. In Hubbell's last four appearances against them that season, July 23 and 31, August 25, and September

23, they hammered him for 23 runs — 21 earned — and 38 hits, in only 26 innings. Carl easily could have suffered all four games as defeats, but escaped with only two. One defeat was avoided via a Giant rally and another game was won despite Carl's pitching poorly in relief.

The immediate aftermath of the celebrity game found the screwball specialist offering his best pitching of the season. On July 10, Hubbell defeated the Dodgers, 4–0, allowing only three hits while having to face only thirty batters. The loser was Hubbell's long-time Giants teammate, Fred Fitzsimmons. Next on July 14, Carl defeated Pittsburgh, 4–2. This was followed on July 18 with a 6–5 win over the Cardinals. The Cardinal win brought to a close a six-game victory streak, three on each side of the All-Star contest.

Another bad stretch followed immediately. On July 23, before a Ladies' Day crowd of 25,000, the Cubs crushed Carl, 11–3. Even though Hubbell allowed seven runs and thirteen hits, Terry probably kept him in until the eighth because of the female attendees.

Another western excursion followed immediately. During it, the manager arranged a position realignment that helped. Terry convinced Mel Ott to move to third base to replace the ineffective Lou Chiozza. Hank Leiber, somewhat recovered from his spring training head injury, was able to resume playing part of the time. This created an outfield of Moore, Jimmy Riddle, and sometimes Leiber, or sometimes another to fill in.

The Giants soon began to narrow the gap between themselves and the first-place Cubs. The Bruins were hit by injury to Rip Collins, obtained from the Cardinals, and by pitcher Curt Davis's off-and-on sore arm.

Despite the team's rally, Hubbell stayed in the doldrums. Against the Cardinals on July 27, he lasted only 3½ innings while giving up eight runs on ten hits. Due to a Giants rally that tied the game for a while, Carl was able to avoid a defeat.

July 31 placed the Giants and Hubbell in Chicago for a Sunday game. Wrigley Field was in the early stage of a renovation; the crowd comprised 25,00. His foe was Tex Carleton, by then with the Cubs. Texas trounced Oklahoma thoroughly in this one, 8–1. Hubbell hurled the entire game for his side, as did his long-time rival. In mid-game, the Cubs racked up four runs, with Hubbell leaving the mound "crestfallen" at inning's end.[6]

Suddenly the portsider's pitching improved. On August 6, 13, and 18, he pitched successive solid wins over Pittsburgh (6–3), Philadelphia (5–0), and Boston (9–1).

Returning to the Polo Grounds, the Giants awaited the westerners. Before their arrival, on August 20, in a 13–6 loss to the Phillies, Terry seemed to waste Hubbell. The manager used Carl in a 3½ innings relief.

Then, with the western clubs before them and the team turning red-hot, Hubbell went through another off-skill interlude. On August 25, a Thursday double-header, Hubbell started the opener against the Cubs. The Bruins pounded him for six counters — five earned — in seven rounds. Nine out of ten times he would have lost this one, but a five-run game-tying Giants ninth, capped by a Jimmy Ripple homer, spared him. They won in the eleventh, and the second game as well.

Again in a two-days-off situation, the Giants' workhorse started against Pittsburgh on August 28. Lasting only 6⅓ innings, Carl gave up four runs on a dozen hits, his second highest of the year. The Giants did win, 9–4, but Hubbell was not the winner.

Hubbell's only solid contribution during this rallying period came in a valuable 2⅓ innings of closer relief. The game was against the Reds on August 30. Carl allowed only a single hit. The Giants won, 4–3.

By this time, depending on the day, the Cubs and the Giants were in a virtual tie. In the first week of September, completed by Labor Day, the Polo Grounders grabbed the lead by two. In September's race to the finish line, Hubbell contributed five successes to only two setbacks. Pitching much more in the mold expected of an ace, Carl disposed of his old Dodger opponents on September 4, 3–0. He permitted just six hits and gave up no walks. It helped the Giants to grasp a two-game lead. He also helped on September 14 with an easy 12–2 win over third-place Pittsburgh.

Nonetheless, inconsistency still beset Carl. Trying to do the Dodgers in again on September 9, he lost, 5–1. The Giants' feeble bats hurt, as did fielders' mishaps, but mainly Hubbell's so-so hurling hurt the most. On September 18 he lost to the mediocre Reds, 4–3, lasting only five innings. During those five innings, the Reds nicked Hubbell for seven hits and three runs.

Of the five wins, two were as reliever. On September 20 in St. Louis, Hubbell pitched seven innings. He gave up only four hits and a run in an easy 10–3 win.

His other relief win came in a game of major importance in Chicago on Thursday, September 23. Almost 30,000 made up the crowd. At game time, the Giants led by 2½. If they should lose, the Cubs would draw very close.

Terry's starting pitcher was Hal Schumacher. By the fourth inning, he had fallen behind with the bases loaded and none out. The manager replaced Hal with Hubbell. Only two days had elapsed since the Cardinal contest in which he had pitched seven innings. Perhaps for this reason he was no improvement on Schumacher. On a three-two count to the first batter, Carl gave up a walk, forcing in a run. After that there were a couple of force-outs with no runs scoring. Up came Billy Herman, Hubbell's leading batting threat. Bill smashed a drive to deep center field that looked like a sure triple. The

Giants' center fielder captured it to end the inning. The next round, Hubbell managed to stagger through again. In two innings, he allowed three runs on as many hits.

Fortunately, the Giants in their at-bats scored runs. In their fifth, they got one run and in the sixth, four. At that point, Hubbell's service ended. However, the Giants had taken the lead over the Cubs. They held it, finally winning, 8–7. Since his teammates went ahead while he was the moundsman, he received credit for a win despite pitching poorly.

Four days later on September 27, Hubbell was back as a starting pitcher. He pitched seven innings of a game against the Boston Bees that the Giants won, 5–4. This time he did not get credit for the win, despite pitching quite well. The Giants scored the decisive run after he had departed. In a pitcher's record, over time, wins, losses, and "no decisions" tend to even out as to the relative merits of accreditation.

Near the end of the season, the New Yorkers managed to win as often as the Chicogoans. By the last day of September, this put the Giants in the position of clinching the pennant should they win and the Bruins lose. Fortunately, their foes were the Phillies. Though again Hubbell had only two days off, the manager dispatched him to flatten the Phils. Year after year, the low-level also-rans rarely had much chance against the "Sooner Slickster," and this day was no exception. Carl beat them, 2–1, with the Phillies' one run coming with two outs in the ninth. Again, as in 1936, it was a homer by Dolph Camilli. Hubbell whiffed nine and gave up only five hits and a walk. If Carl had possibly been feeling some arm tenderness on his puzzling "off" days, he clearly had overcome it by season's end.

The season statistics showed Hubbell taking the three firsts:

- Winning percentage, .733
- Total wins, 22
- Strikeouts, 159 (a surprise).

The figures were a little misleading. His first in strikeouts was only because Dean and Mungo, usually the leaders, lost time due to arm trouble.

Significantly, for the first time since 1930, the Sooner Southpaw did not finish among the ERA leaders nor complete at least twenty games. The wear and tear on his arm was beginning to show. On the Yankees — against whom the Giants were to be matched again — the three leading starters, Lefty Gomez, Charles Ruffing, and Monte Pearson, all had lower ERAs than Carl's. In 1937, Hubbell, although still very good, definitely did not rank as the year's best.

Viewed in a broader light, during the five-year span from 1933 to 1937, Hubbell was indisputably baseball's greatest hurler. He won 115 games, tying Dizzy Dean in this category. In winning percentage, he outdid Dean, .697

to .660. His 2.55 ERA during this stretch made Carl the only one among the major league's five best to finish lower than 3.00. It was nearly half a run lower than Dean and Gomez, the next lowest.

How indispensable Hubbell was to the Giants is evident from his winning percentage compared to that of his team's. The team's winning percentage stood at about .600, while Carl's was nearly ten percentage points higher. Instead of winning three pennants with him, had the Giants been without him, they probably would not have won any. Next at hand was the 1937 World Series.

The opponents in the 1937 World Series were the same as in 1936: Giants vs. Yankees. However, the statistics for each from the regular season were noticeably different. The Yankees' lead over Detroit, the repeat second placers, shrank to only thirteen ahead at season's end, contrasted to the Giants' mere two over their second-place finisher, Chicago. Again the Yankees led in home runs, 174; in runs scored, 979; and in pitching, a 3.65 ERA. The last was in spite of being in a harder-hitting league. In batting average, they ranked second, .283. In fielding, they stood at a mediocre third, .972.

The Giants led in homers in their league, but only with 103. In runs scored, they totaled 732, 247 runs fewer than the Yankees. In hitting, the Giants were third at .278. For fielding, they reached second, .974. Their 143 double plays slightly outnumbered the Yankees' 134. In pitching, their 3.43 ERA placed them in second and was also lower than the Yankees.' However, this was misleading. Only in fielding did observers give them the edge.

The Yankees fielded the same team as in '36 except for the outfield. Because George Selkirk missed many games due to injury, in the World Series their outfield included Myril Hoag — previously only a substitute — in left. In center field it was once again Joe DiMaggio; Jake Powell and Hoag shared left and right fields.

The Giants' instability had brought player shuffling at several positions: third base, right and center field, as well as catching. In the latter spot, Gus Mancuso and Harry Danning shared duties. The several changes suggested unsteadiness.

With the teams much the same, and the statistics giving the Yankees a wide edge, the oddsmakers favored the American Leaguers almost two-one, as they had in 1936. Rather surprisingly, John Drebinger in The *New York Times* thought the Giants might have a chance simply because they had held up well in September. He was to learn otherwise very quickly.

Since, like the year before, this was to be another "subway" series, it meant playing every day, barring rain. With 60,000 on hand, the opener took place Wednesday, October 6, at Yankee Stadium. To nobody's surprise, Terry and McCarthy opened with their aces, Hubbell and Gomez.

Hubbell and Gomez had ample rest and therefore pretty much squelched each pitcher's opponent in the first half of the game. Hubbell in particular seemed to be in fine form, retiring fourteen straight hitters from the first through the fifth. In the fourth, for instance, Gehrig swung mightily at a Hubbell twister, missing by a foot. Gomez did almost as well. The Giants did eke out a run, scoring from third on an infield double play in the fifth.

Hubbell had been benefiting the most from breaks in luck for some time. In what followed, the demon of ill luck seemed to be aroused by a double blunder that he committed.

Suddenly in the Yankees' sixth, the Oklahoman's world collapsed. It began with an inexplicable double lapse on his part. The initial one consisted of surrendering a walk to the weak-hitting Lefty Gomez. Worse, this provided an opening to the Yankees by permitting the first batter of their half of the inning to get on. The usual rule was never to give a base-on-balls to as weak a hitter as Gomez, so Hubbell had twice slipped up in a serious way.

With the blessing of his pitcher on first free, Yankee manager McCarthy signaled for leadoff batter Frankie Crosetti to sacrifice. Twice Crosetti muffed the bunt. Having failed, he then did better than if he had succeeded by hitting a single. Instead of one out, there were runners on first and second with no outs.

Red Rolfe was up next. Gus Mancuso noticed that Gomez, in expectation of another bunt, had strayed too far off second. The catcher fired a pickoff to Dick Bartell. Gomez could have been an easy out, but Bartell dropped the ball. Afterwards, Terry labeled this error as the turning point of the game.

Rolfe did try to bunt, but like Crosetti, failed twice. Next his dinky hit to short left landed among infielders and outfielders for a bases-loading single. Up came DiMaggio. He singled sharply to left center, scoring Gomez, while Crosetti stopped at third and Rolfe made second on the throw home. With Lou Gehrig up, Terry had Hubbell give him an intentional walk.

Still no outs. With Bill Dickey up, Terry did the opposite of what he had done at the decisive moment in the fourth game of the 1933 World Series. Instead of playing the infield back, he moved them in for a hoped-for force-out at the plate on a grounder. Dickey's sharply hit grounder would have been ideal double play fodder had the fielders been back. Instead, Burgess Whitehead, at second, could only slow up, but could not throw the ball, resulting in a single and another run.

At last the first out came when Hoag's roller forced DiMaggio at home. However, Selkirk then singled, scoring Gehrig and Dickey. Terry removed Hubbell. In the rest of the inning, another Giants' fielding fumble and a bases-loaded walk scored two more. Altogether, the Yankees tallied seven. Later another came in on a Tony Lazzeri home run, enabling the Yankees to win, 8–1.

Down one, the Giants' position quickly sank from bad to worse. Cliff Melton, Terry's twenty-games-winning first-year pitcher, received the second game starting assignment. McCarthy countered with Red Ruffing. At just 58,000, the crowd had declined mildly. Melton melted in the fourth. The Yankees won easily, matching the 8–1 score of the first engagement.

With the Giants deep in trouble, the series moved over to the Polo Grounds for games three through five — if the series made that figure. The Giants' fans were fast losing confidence. Attendance shrank to 37,000. Since Schumacher had won a game in a hard struggle in 1936, Terry chose him as his starter for game three. Monte Pearson did the Yankee hurling. Again the Polo Grounders showed little. Schumacher lasted longer than Melton, but gave up five runs in six innings. Though needing last-out help, Pearson handled the Giants easily for the second straight year, winning 5–1. At this stage, the Yankees had scored twenty-one runs, the Giants, three.

Up three games to none, and needing only another one to win the World Series, McCarthy was in an ideal position. He could use Gomez again, trying to win immediately in four. Or he could give his ace more rest, use another pitcher, and perhaps win four straight anyway. Since Bump Hadley, though pitching quite poorly during the season, had beaten the Giants the year before, McCarthy chose him again.

Terry did the unavoidable and selected Hubbell. Perhaps as a morale booster, he announced that no team in the world could beat Hubbell back-to-back. This was an exaggeration, as twice during the season it had happened.

In this instance, Terry was right. Not even the Yankees could flatten his best twice in a row. The Giants' 7–3 win spared them the ignominy of a four-straight sweep. In the second inning, the home team sank Hadley under a barrage of singles and a walk for six counters. In the seventh, they tallied another on a walk, single and double.

Hubbell hurled not a spectacular but a sound, steady game. Carl allowed six hits and a walk. The three Yankee runs should have been one. Two officially were earned runs. In the first, Leiber incautiously tried for a catch on a Rolfe short fly, letting it get away from him for a triple. DiMaggio's fly scored him. In the third, two more Bartell errors, plus one by Ott, led to another Yankee score.

Only in the ninth did the visitors make a potential threat. Gehrig got to Hubbell for a homer to right. With two outs, Hoag singled. Then Selkirk, who usually could hit Hubbell, swatted a fly to very deep center field. Leiber, playing him back, succeeded in collaring it for the last out.

The next day, Sunday, the attendance had dropped to 38,000. Gomez defeated Melton, 4–2, making the latter a two-time loser. The World Series was over.

In 1936, the Giants, thanks especially to Hubbell's brilliant season, had presented themselves as respectable challengers of the powerful Yankees. By winning twice, they had demonstrated their respectability.

However, in 1937, they exposed themselves as feeble World Series challengers. Had it not been for Hubbell rescuing them with one win, a four-straight wipe-out probably would have been their fate. In the three World Series in which the Giants participated in the middle thirties, they won seven games altogether. Hubbell won four of them. By 1938, their days as a serious pennant contender had run out.

Chapter 13

Arm Rebellion

The narrowness of the margin by which the Giants had won the pennant, as well as the comparative ease of the Yankees' World Series triumph, made it evident that over the winter the team needed improvement. However, at the major league off-season meetings, Terry could not find another club with whom to trade players with the expectation that the Giants would be improved by the exchange. As a result, the pennant defenders entered 1938 spring training with important question unanswered.

A major problem concerned second base. Overcome by crises of nerves, Whitehead missed the 1938 season entirely. No helpful trade having been completed, the manager moved Chiozza, who had not helped at third the year before, over to second as Whitehead's replacement. Before long, it was clear that he did not do any better there. In June, Terry, trying to solve the problem, traded Wally Berger to the Reds in exchange for Alex Kampouris, recently superseded as their second baseman. With the Giants, Kampouris' fielding barely passed muster. His hitting was inadequate.

Ott continued as third baseman. In the outfield, Riddle proved satisfactory as a right fielder. Leiber, as middle outfielder, barely passed muster. To fill in for him some of the time, the Giants obtained "Suitcase" Seeds, a thirty-year-old part major/part minor leaguer from Newark. In left field, Moore continued. However, he missed quite a few games due to injuries. Behind the plate, Harry Danning showed himself to be a better hitter than Mancuso, replacing him as first-string backstop.

Privately, Terry must have worried about the team's pitching. In appearance, there were four regular starters: Hubbell, Schumacher, Gumbert and Melton. The latter two were recent additions. This younger pair seemed sufficiently reliable, but as to Hubbell and Schumacher, there were doubts. Hubbell reached age thirty-five in June. Further, his 1937 hurling had been noticeably uneven. Also, prior to the most recent year, he had had spells of arm soreness. As for Schumacher, in 1936 and 1937, he had been a one-under-.500 moundsman. Fortunately, in 1938, he took up some slack created by

Hubbell's troubles. Relief needs continued to be well served by Dick Coffman; ex–Yankee Jumbo Brown also assisted with relief.

In spring training exhibition engagements, Hubbell's hurling created mild concerns. At the beginning of April, Indians and Giants set forth on their annual northward journey. When they reached Houston, a crowd of 11,000 greeted them on April 3. The reason was that Hubbell and Feller resumed their 1937 exhibition rivalry. Feller got the better of the Giants' premier moundsman. On April 11, at Memphis, in anticipation of the approaching regular season, Hubbell ventured upon his first full game of pitching. He and the Giants won, 8–7, but the Cleveland run total was worrisome. In Drebinger's opinion, his hurling left "rather much to be desired."[1] However, on April 17, just before the regular season was to begin, worries diminished when Carl pitched quite well against Cleveland for seven innings. The Giants won, 5–3. Thus began a two year up-and-down roller coaster ride for Hubbell and his pitching.

In retrospect, looking at the National League on a broader scale, the circuit was passing through an interval in which the best it could produce was two or three fairly good teams, but no really first-rate ones. The Giants' shakiness mirrored that of the league. The Cubs were the eventual pennant winner, but did so with the second-lowest winning percentage of the century.

In the case of the Cardinals, their season went nowhere due to a rebuilding program. They sank into sixth place. Just before the season started, they traded Dizzy Dean, with his sore arm, to the Cubs. The Cardinals were replaced as contenders by the Pittsburgh Pirates. By the end of the season, the Pirates barely trailed the Cubs.

Suggestive of the changing times, the Cincinnati Reds showed significant signs of emerging from among the also-rans. Two or three of their young players showed signs of developing into high-quality performers. Also, their general manager, Warren Giles, convinced Bill McKechnie to leave the management of Boston in favor of leading the Reds. The Cardinals temporarily dropped into the second division. Chicago, New York and Pittsburgh were only marginally successful clubs. The 1928–38 three-team monopoly on the National League pennant ran out this season.

To return to the start of the season, the Giants, despite their question marks, got off to a fine start. Their early momentum lasted half the season. On Memorial Day, they occupied first place. They maintained the top spot until mid–July, when they slipped down a peg or two. They were not able to regain first for the rest of the season.

An important feature of the early success was Hubbell's high-quality pitching. He won six out of seven games. In 62 innings of pitching, his ERA came to only 0.94. On May 28, for example, Carl defeated the forlorn Phillies,

11–0. He allowed them only one hit. However, one must admit that it did not say a great deal, as there was not a team that could not route the Quakers. Over the season, the Phillies won only 45 of 153 games. In mid-season the year before, the Phillies had moved out of Baker Bowl as their home grounds into Shibe Park. In so doing, they deprived themselves of their only weapon, their hitting. The Phillies were in constant need to trade off their few good players to the prosperous teams and became, in effect, a major league "farm team" for the well-to-do.

After the great start, a definite up, Hubbell's pitching steadily deteriorated from early June until mid–August, a down section on the roller coaster. During the slide, he won only seven and dropped nine. In sixteen appearances, Carl surrendered 49 runs and 131 hits in 112 innings. This gave him an ERA of 4.19 for this time period.

Hubbell's arm was giving him increasing difficulty. The wear and tear is evident from the downward slope of his pitching. Eventually the day would come when he could no longer continue. With hindsight, it is possible to backtrack and spot the indicators in the performance of hitters against him. There were occasional days when the pain may have been minimal, enabling Carl, through acute pitching, to come through with capable performances. More often, however, he was hit hard by many batters. The proportion of extra base hits increased. Home runs especially showed up as a recurring bugaboo. At times, his teammates must have wondered, and surely their manager worried, about what they were witnessing. Wishful thinking is a handy means of putting off unpleasant truths.

On June 4, in a game at Cincinnati, Hubbell's opposing batters battered him for five runs — four earned — on seven hits in just three innings. One was a 400-foot home run swatted by Ival Goodman, Cincinnati's up-and-coming right fielder. It was the first obvious sign that Carl's arm was seriously bothering him. Nothing was said, because no one wanted to say anything. It was almost as if to say anything would make the problem not only real, but worse.

From Cincinnati, the Giants entrained for Chicago. In the Windy City, the park renovation at Wrigley Field, started the previous summer, was completed. On June 8, a midweek day, the clubs came to grips in a two-for-one. A large crowd gathered. On-field standees no longer were permitted. As a result, several thousand fans had to depart dejectedly.

Though the month was only June, the teams played as if it were September. It was while the Polo Grounders still led, but the Cubs, Pirates and Reds were close behind. In Hubbell's own situation, he had by this date won 198 games. A personal milestone was not far ahead.

This season Terry often used his ace for the second game of a double bill. Hubbell won it for the Giants, 4–1. This made Carl's 199th victory. A faint cause for concern was that the Cubs nibbled away at him for ten hits, though they could turn them into but a single run. Hubbell's pitches, though slender in substance, were strong in savvy. One of his (dwindling) skillful days, this game typified how he could finesse the opposition into submission.

After leaving Chicago, the fading ace suffered three straight setbacks. They were 4–1 to St. Louis on June 12, 10–2 to Pittsburgh on June 16, and 6–2 to Cincinnati on June 21. In each encounter, he lasted seven innings. The hit total of twenty-one was respectable, but the fourteen earned runs meant an ERA of 6.00 per nine innings for this stretch. This was definitely one of the low dips of the roller coaster.

The loss to St. Louis was routine, but the manner in which the swingers hammered him in the other two offered further signs that Hubbell's arm was giving him trouble. In the Pittsburgh loss, one of the home runs came off the bat of an undersized Lloyd Waner. Previously the younger Waner brother had not hit any four-baggers. Another hitter, Al Todd, the catcher, slashed a triple that he was able to hit much harder than Lloyd Waner's home run.

In the Cincinnati loss, played at the Polo Grounds, Hubbell gave up two more circuit blows. Ival Goodman got another off him. The second one came off the bat of Ernie Lombardi. The Cincinnati catcher, Lombardi was large, strong and all muscle. A line drive hitter, he had the league pitchers, who were close to him when they pitched, silently praying he would not decapitate one of them with one of his savage liners. He drove a Hubbell pitch that hit the balustrade between the upper and lower decks in deepest left center for a titanic home run.

Hubbell was seeking his 200th win. On Sunday, June 26, the Giants faced the Cubs at home. Because of a steady, slow rain, only 13,000 attended. Pitching much the way he had against the Bruins in Chicago, Carl got his 200th via a 5–1 win. The Cubs "hit Hubbell hard enough..., but made outs just when they needed hits."[2] In the later innings, from the sixth to the end, they collected eight hits. There was also a Giants error. Nonetheless, the Cubs could score only their one run. Their total of eleven safeties usually would bring three, often even four, runs.

It had taken the Giants' ace a month less than ten years to reach 200 wins. In only a decade, he had averaged twenty victories a season. In the "lively ball age," this was a phenomenal achievement. In the American League, Grove, too, had managed to pitch his 200th win in ten years. No other pitching star of the late '20s and '30s came close to equaling the two great left-handers' achievements.

In July, the tenderness in Hubbell's arm may have receded temporarily. The roller coaster went up with only minor dips down. He succeeded in pitching quite well throughout the month, winning four and losing two. The wins included an 8–1 triumph over Brooklyn and Fred Fitzsimmons on July 2. Carl also had a momentarily valuable success against Pittsburgh, 2–1 on July 17. This was followed by a pair over the Cardinals, 5–2 on July 21, and 2–1 on July 28.

In a loss to the Boston Bees, 7–0 on July 9, Carl hurled ineffectively. In three innings the usually stingless "Stingers" got to him for six runs on eight hits. In the action, three consecutive Boston batters connected for home runs. They were second baseman Tony Cuccinello, left fielder Max West, and first baseman Elbie Fletcher. Up to this time, there had only been seven times that three home runs in succession had been done, and none against Hubbell. Drebinger lamented, "No club has ever taken such liberties with the screwball maestro."[3]

The second setback in July, at Chicago on the 24th, offered high-level excitement. Gabby Hartnett had just replaced Charley Grimm as Cub manager. In addition, the day before, Dizzy Dean, another sore arm sufferer, had defeated the New Yorkers 2–1, with cleverly aimed slow pitches. The combination of the manager shift with Dean's clever pitching had Cub fans in a dither.

The day was Sunday; 35,000 "crazed" local fans crowded into Wrigley Field.[4] With Pittsburgh in first and Chicago a close second, the visitors sorely needed a win in order to stay close to the two in front of them. Nor was fourth-place Cincinnati much behind the Giants. Once the game got underway, the Giants led by 4–2 in the seventh. The Cubs loaded the bases. Though only three days before Hubbell had defeated the Cardinals, the manager called him in to pitch. He might have gotten the travelers through unscathed, but an error by Ott enabled the Cubs to score a run. In the ninth, they tied the score, 4–4, on a pair of singles. The game went for six more innings, lasting four hours. Terry kept Hubbell in to do the pitching to the end. At last, in the home team's half of the fifteenth, the Cubs, despite what Drebinger described as the Oklahoman's "heroic"[5] hurling, won the game, 5–4. This was accomplished through a run-scoring double following a single. Cub fans went home in ecstasy.

On the Giants' side, Hubbell's having to pitch eight relief innings, so soon after his win over the Redbirds, likely imposed further strain on his throwing arm. Nonetheless, four days later, July 28, back at the Polo Grounds, Carl succeeded in defeating St. Louis again, 2–1.

Chicago followed St. Louis. On August 2, the one-time Terry "Meal Ticket" took on the Windy City aggregation another time. The Cub hitters "hammered him to cover in the seventh inning under the most blistering attack the Giants' Ace had experienced since July 9."[6] The opponents' offensive featured seven runs on ten hits. Chicago shortstop Bill Jurges hit one home run, and third baseman Stan Hack, another. Neither had previously struck a home run in the 1938 season. Frank Demaree, the center fielder, slammed a triple further than their home runs.

Pittsburgh, temporarily leading, arrived next. On Sunday, August 7, the Giants played the Corsairs a double-header before a large crowd. The Pirates knifed the Giants in both contests, 5–1 and 13–3. Hubbell tried to halt them in the second one. The Pittsburgh hitters pummeled him until his removal in the seventh inning. Pittsburgh batters had tallied five runs on ten hits. In addition, the control maestro handed out three walks. Catcher Al Todd, second baseman Pep Young, and third base incumbent Lee Handley all struck home runs. None was known as a home run hitter.

The manager left his battered star unused for almost a week. Fortunately, the league's last-place Phillies arrived. Used against them on August 13, Hubbell won, but so did almost everybody else against the cellar dwellers. Hubbell's teammates provided him with eleven runs while he gave up only four hits.

The upswing was only momentary. His next start, August 18, finished him. As fate would have it yet again, the team that did him in was the Brooklyn Dodgers. They won what would have been looked upon in ordinary circumstances as an easily forgettable game, 5–3. Hubbell gave up all of the runs in five innings, together with five hits. While the Giants were at bat in their half of the fifth, Hubbell informed Terry that his arm was finished. It felt as if "knives were cutting through it."[7] It hurt so much he could not hold it straight out. At last, the arm had rebelled against the owner. His season obviously having ended, he had won 205 games in ten years and a couple of months. No other pitcher of the day could say as much, except Lefty Grove with the Boston Red Sox.

Considering all that had been happening to him, his statistics at the season's end were respectable. Through August 18, he had appeared in twenty-four contests. This was fewer than would have been the case in mid–August during his great years. Yet it was up to the average of most starters. His innings pitched reached only 179. He won 13 and lost 10, a thoroughly respectable total for some starters. His 3.07 ERA likewise was far from a disgrace. On the other hand, for the first time since his half-season debut in 1928, his name did not appear among the league's five best hurlers in any category.

In the *New York Times*, Drebinger voiced the opinion that Terry knew nothing about Hubbell's arm pain until Hubbell informed him that day. This seems very unlikely. Surely observing his star pitcher pummeled repeatedly made him wonder. How hard a batter hits a hurler's pitch is often an indicator of whether the pitcher may be having arm trouble.

Moreover, in the years immediately preceding 1938, Hubbell had been bothered by arm soreness, not only in spring training, but a couple of times during seasons. On three occasionsfrom 1934 to 1936, management had had his arm X-rayed. They showed nothing structurally wrong. Though this probably was reassuring, the fact that X-rays had been taken should have served as a warning. Hubbell's "cure" was not to rest his arm entirely for a while, but to use it to work out the soreness. This time was once too often. Had Hubbell lived most of a century later, he probably would have been placed immediately on the disabled list. But in his own time, Terry displayed, at most, only moderate concern. Other teams carried on in about the same manner, as the Dizzy Dean example shows. A pitcher pitched until he pitched out. This was how the hard-crusted baseball of the 1930s was played.

Reflecting on the subject years afterward, Hubbell felt sure that excessive reliance on his trademark pitch was what had done him in. Actually, the excessive number of innings pitched, along with such a large total of mound appearances, had as much to do with it as the screwball. Four straight years of 300 or more innings hurled was too much. Dean and Mungo, also 300+ hurlers, likewise had arm trouble, and before Hubbell did.

Once the furor over Hubbell's incapacitation had cooled down some, Terry urged his injured ace to consult Dr. J. Spencer Speed. He was a bone specialist in Memphis whom Terry and others had consulted. Once Carl met with Speed, it became obvious that he suffered from bone chips in his left elbow. The doctor urged an immediate operation. Hubbell complied. At the time, operational methods and procedures, though not primitive, fell far short of modern techniques. The "Tommy John" highly developed technique for arm surgery still was quite far into the future.

For several years prior to his surgery, Hubbell's arm had been developing a gradually increasing inward bent. After the surgery, the lower arm almost became the upper and vice versa. At a later time, specialists surely would have insisted that he refrain from trying to pitch again for at least a year. However, largely based on only his own judgment, Hubbell — as desirous of pitching as ever — determined to return for the 1939 season. To that end, over the winter he treated his arm three times every day. Carl would bathe the six-inch scar in 135° heat. Then he would rub paraffin on it to retain the warmth.

While Hubbell was treating his arm, Terry, though concerned, was looking at the team from a broader perspective. Over the winter break, the manager was able to consummate an important trade with the Chicago Cubs. Both he and Gabby Hartnett, his Chicago equivalent, acted as if they had given up on the regulars they traded, but had a great deal of confidence in the players the other manager was willing to let go. Shortstop Dick Bartell, outfielder

Hank Leiber, and catcher Gus Mancuso found themselves playing for the Cubs in 1939. In return, former Cubs shortstop Bill Jurges, center fielder Frank Demaree, and reserve catcher Ken O'Dea of the Cubs found themselves playing for the Giants in the new season.

First base had been a problem since the manager's own retirement from active play. Terry obtained Zeke Bonura from the Washington Senators. Unfortunately, all too soon Terry learned that Bonura's good hitting did not offset his extreme immobility around first base.

The times were still changing. Over the course of the 1939 season, the Giants as well as their rivals in the National League moved places. The '38 winners slipped to fourth. The Giants dropped to fifth from third, barely an over-.500 club. The Cardinals, however, aided by their farm system graduates, jumped from sixth to second. Among the "Big Three" of the outgoing decade, they alone played a major part in the early years of the decade just dawning. While the Cubs and Giants were slipping, the Reds and Dodgers replaced them. Cincinnati won the pennant, with Brooklyn coming in third.

Hot Springs, Arkansas, became the Giants' training center in 1939. Present with the veterans and the neophytes was Carl Hubbell. The question of how he would do in the wake of the operation hung in the air. By this time, since he could partly bend his arm, the principal himself felt quite encouraged. Only time would tell how the roller coaster ride would go — more ups or downs? Would the rebellion of the arm be quelled?

In the training games, Hubbell was able to hurl, but the results were inconclusive. On one occasion he held the Cleveland Indians runless for several innings because his slow tosses threw them off stride. Dizzy Dean had had some success with slow pitches in response to his own sore arm.

In an intra-squad game a little later during training, his batting teammates tattooed his offerings all over the field. Terry decided he needed to size up Hubbell's work close up. The manager stationed himself directly behind the aspirant on the mound. Terry offered a bleak assessment: Hubbell "just hasn't got it and he simply can't pitch the way he is."[8] All of spring training the hope that Carl would be a "come backer" had been questioned by ongoing arm soreness. Therefore, Terry sent Carl back to Dr. Speed for further treatment.

Back in Memphis, heat applications were resumed as a remedy. The discomfort in his shoulder disappeared fairly quickly. Since his trouble was in the upper arm rather than the elbow, Dr. Speed informed the Giants that the ailment was not serious.

As usual, the season opened in the third week of April. As a precaution, the Giants refrained from using their erstwhile ace until May 8. By this time the weather was a little warmer. With the team at home, Terry used Hubbell for the first time in a short relief task against the Cubs. The Chicagoans led 4–2. When the 8,000 fans present recognized Carl, the small crowd "spontaneously leaped to its feet in loud voiced acclaim."[9] The three batters he faced went out on four pitches. In the ninth, two of the outs were strikeouts. The Cubs' win seemed insignificant compared to the expectations immediately ignited by Hubbell's appearance.

On Sunday, May 14, six days later, with 23,485 fans present, Hubbell made his first start. That Philadelphia was the opponent was no accident. The Phillies' pitcher was Max Butcher, a passable moundsman who was always handicapped by the poor teams for which he pitched. The game lasted ten innings. In typical fashion, the Phillies could score only one run, even though they pecked at Hubbell for eleven hits.

Hubbell was due to bat in the home half of the tenth. Terry removed Carl in favor of pinch hitter Ken O'Dea. Fortunately, O'Dea hit a short home run into the right field lower deck, winning the game for the Giants and for Hubbell, 2–1. The crowd rejoiced. Was the ride going up? Was the arm rebellion finally quelled?

Unfortunately an abrupt drop came next. In terms of ultimate morale questions, it might have been better for the team — but especially for Carl — had not the returnee been so successful in his first starting try. Four straight setbacks struck him. With Hubbell pitching, the Giants lost to Pittsburgh, 4–1 on May 21; to Cincinnati, 6–1 on May 25; to Brooklyn, 3–1 on Memorial Day; and the Reds again, but at home, 4–1 on June 4. The last was a double-header day and Carl started the second clash by giving up a walk and three singles. Terry immediately withdrew him. The despondent ex-ace departed "a dejected figure ... the cheers still ringing in his ears." Though only singles, the hits off the "fading hero" were "savagely hit."[10] One indication of how well a hurler is doing lies in the strength with which the batters can hit his tosses.

In each of these losses, the Giants' batters provided Hubbell with only one run. Thus it could be seen that his troubles were not exclusively self-inflicted. Nevertheless, Carl's ineffectiveness was reason for alarm. In only 16⅓ innings, he had given up 14 runs — eight unearned — and 21 hits.

Hubbell was still using his screwball occasionally. Long after retirement, he said that he could throw it again, but it had lost the "bite" it had in his great days. Soon Carl all but abandoned the screwball, but in this early period of his return, it took him a little while to realize the hitters were bashing it. Also, his arm was still on the mend.

After what the Reds had done to him, Hubbell was sidelined by the manager for two weeks. Then, in a contest with the Cardinals on June 18, the Giants having fallen behind early, Terry inserted Carl as a middle-innings reliever. His new "comeback effort" did not go well. In only two innings, the Cardinals chalked up three runs on five hits.

Three days later, Terry once again tried Hubbell in a relief capacity. This time he did better, allowing no runs. However, this was in only 1⅓ innings. Terry sidelined him. This time it was for nine days. Presumably, judging by what followed, the time off, plus perhaps more treatment, helped. Restricted again to relief hurling, he had a run of six appearances for a total of nine innings. The results were a turn for the better: eight hits, two runs and two walks.

˙The improvement earned Hubbell another start. It came July 18 against the Cardinals. The Redbirds won, 5–3. Carl allowed four runs on nine hits and three walks in seven innings. Demoted to his relief duty again, Carl did an inning of runless service on July 22 against the Cubs.

On July 25 came the day that restored him as a regular starter with flying colors. Mostly on the road, the Giants had fallen into a nine-game losing streak. It pretty much did them in for '39. The travelers reached St. Louis. Though it was only three days since his brief Chicago relief appearance, the manager risked Hubbell as a starter in spite of the disarray in his pitching. His pitching might be questionable, but Carl's desire to pitch and do the best for the team was not.

In the game, the Giants, both hitters and fielders, were at their worst. The batters hit into four twin killings. Nevertheless, they could have won a regular length game had not Burgess Whitehead — back playing again — made three errors. But Hubbell "unruffled, undismayed [by] the amazing helplessness that surrounded him," toiled on.[11] The game went into the thirteenth. The Giants finally broke through when Frank Demaree and Mel Ott contributed home runs. The 6–3 win broke the losing streak. Even though Hubbell had had surgery barely a year before, Terry permitted him to pitch for the entire thirteen-inning struggle.

On July 30, with his starting position regained, the veteran southpaw defeated the Cubs in another complete game, 3–1. The ride had started up and stayed there mostly for the remainder of the season. From the date of the win over the Cardinals to the season's end, Hubbell won nine, lost four, and had an ERA of 2.82. Only once did Terry turn to Carl in a relief role. It was in a rain-slowed game against Boston, August 9. Terry replaced Harry Gumbert with Hubbell in the eighth. Hubbell provided 3⅔ scoreless innings. When the Giants scored a run in the eleventh for a 6–5 win, Hubbell received the credit. With the help of the relief win, he ran off a five-game winning streak in this interlude.

The other two preceded and succeeded the relief appearance. One was a win over Pittsburgh, August 4, 4–2, and the other over the Philly tail-

enders, August 13, 6–2. Against the last-placers again, August 20, Hubbell
lost 3–2, ending the brief streak. Hugh Mulcahy defeated him. He had the
nickname L.P. (Losing Pitcher) Mulcahy. A much later age, stressing sensi-
tivity, would not have tolerated so dismissive a moniker. Mulcahy, however,
seemed able to live with his psyche undamaged.

In Hubbell's last seven appearances of 1939, he won four and lost three.
Two of the wins were against the Dodgers: 7–1 on September 5, and his season
ender, 9–5 on September 26. The others came against the Cardinals, 2–1 on
September 17, and over the Cubs, 4–2 on September 20. With only two days
between these starts, they represented a rare return to his heavy-duty days.

Of the three losses, the Boston Bees buzzed him for one, 4–3 on September 7. The other two were against the pennant-bound Cincinnati Reds
and Paul Derringer, 7–2 on August 27, and 8–5 on September 14. That year
Derringer defeated Hubbell four times. It was the reverse of their meetings
during the Reds' downtrodden days. With a poor team, a good pitcher can
look nowhere nearly as good as he actually is.

In Hubbell's time, a rule in force for many years specified that a pitcher
must complete ten games as a minimum to be considered a regular starter.
Hubbell's win over the Dodgers provided him with his tenth full game. It
was also his eleventh and final win in 1939.

The modern contrast in seasonal complete games offers a further illustration of how much the old game has changed in its pitching dimension. By
the 2000s, no National League hurler has reached ten complete games, not
as a low but as a high, since 1994.

As far as the Oklahoman was concerned, his eleven wins contrasted
sharply with the twenty-six he had obtained only three years earlier. The other
Giants starters all won more games in 1939 than Hubbell did. However, in
ERA, he finished lower than they did.

His comeback, considering the seriousness of his operation, had worked
out fairly well. That he had won more than he had lost indicated that he
could still pitch in the major leagues. On the other hand, his low win total
suggested that he was at most a limited-service pitcher. On the whole, however, although Carl's stamina and longevity were doubtful, the positive
exceeded the negative in his return. His arm rebellion had at least been partly
contained, although not quelled.

An encouraging note appeared in the season statistics regarding the
league's best pitchers. Hubbell made it to second best in ERA. By this time,
Bucky Walters had succeeded him as the premier hurler. Walters had a 2.29
ERA, with Hubbell's 2.75 ranking next. Never again did the southpaw from
the Southwest finish among the first five in any category.

In a sidebar to that year's field actions, back in August, Hubbell had been a participant in a series of interviews on a topic causing increasing concern in baseball's establishment circles. The subject had to do with the absolute exclusion of black Americans from white organized professional baseball. On a larger scale, it was but a specific example of the discrimination against blacks that permeated American life more generally at the time. In the years after World War II, the problem reached the level of a major social concern.

The *Pittsburgh Courier* employed Wendell Smith as a reporter. He arranged interviews with various National League players and their managers. Smith's theme bore on white players' receptivity or resistance to blacks' admission to white professional baseball. In addition to asking about the fundamental problem, Smith also asked whether his white interviewees felt that black players were equal in ability to themselves.

When Smith queried Hubbell, the Oklahoman agreed that some blacks — naming the two most familiar stars, Josh Gibson and Satchel Paige — were up to major league caliber. However, he gave a somewhat ambiguous answer to the other question. He seemed to be saying that admission to major league status was their due, but via establishment of a third league comprised of the blacks. Presumably Hubbell meant that ones who had major league potential but were not as yet that skillful, could, through infusion of funds, be advanced to that level. At any rate, there would be no intermingling on the same teams. Instead there would be three separate leagues, two white and one black.

This man-on-the-street version of the Supreme Court's "separate but equal" doctrine looks like an evasion of Smith's central questions. During the Court's long *Plessy vs. Ferguson* period — still operating in 1939 — the result had produced definite separation, but no equality in professional baseball — nor in many other aspects of American life.

Hubbell was Meeker's lone familiar public figure of the time. Carl probably expressed reasonably well the social views of mid-state Oklahomans. In the northernmost sections, there might have been a few not averse to racial equality. By contrast, in the southeast — "Little Dixie" — the population strongly opposed ending segregation. Living between, the midland Sooners held middle views reflective of their location.

The full integration of the blacks into baseball fabric following World War II took a decade or more to complete. Often, time and circumstances determine a person's reaction to a changing condition. For Hubbell, the position he expressed after his pitching days was very conducive to acceptance of integration. The years passed, and by the time baseball was integrated, he had no trouble accepting the new social order without a murmur.

Chapter 14

Pitched Out, 1940–1943

The winter of 1939-40 brought Hubbell into a very positive frame of mind. By then his operation was more than a year in the past. Judging by his late 1939 pitching, his arm appeared to have regained much of its resiliency.

At the time, Carl lived in Fort Worth, Texas. His oil firm maintained offices there. He spent the off-season working there half the time. In the afternoons, he arranged time off so that, weather permitting, he was able to play golf three times a week. His golfing companion usually was Pete Donahue, a pitching teammate from his early Giants years.

How Carl's living in Fort Worth affected his relationship with his wife Sue would be interesting to know. Presumably she was busy raising their two boys, one of whom was an infant. This was James, born in 1939. Since the times were largely without today's press and media scrutiny, there are no sources on the subject. The interested reader is reduced to sensible speculation, at best.

Hubbell was interviewed in the off-season by a *Sporting News* reporter. Carl ventured a forecast astonishing for its display of self-confidence: "I believe I'll have another twenty-odd victory season in the coming race."[1] Such a Dizzy Dean–like pronouncement illustrates how far he had traveled since the days of the shy, reticent young man of his early years with the Giants. Subsequent events were to make it evident that Hubbell made a mammoth overestimation of what he would be able to do.

Offering thoughts concerning the pitching craft broadly, Carl felt that the adverse conditions in which pitchers had to work explained the recent increase in sore wings. Hubbell forgot that from 1933 on — and especially in the 1933 season — pitchers' lives had been eased at least to some extent by adoption of the less dynamic baseball. Carl attributed the sore arm epidemic to constant rule changes in the batters' favor. To get the better of their foe, pitchers had to resort to more than an average arm strain by developing "off-beat" throws.

During the last years that Hubbell served, the team amounted to the second-division remnants of the one that had won pennants. Except for 1942, the Giants were lower level also-rans until 1947. In this season of 1939, they finished fifth, 18½ games behind Cincinnati, the winners. In 1940, they dropped to sixth, 27½ behind the Cincinnati repeaters. In 1941, they advanced a little, returning to fifth, but still 25½ in arrears of the winning Dodgers. Then in 1942, they reached third. Nonetheless, they were twenty back of the winning Cardinals.

What brought on the club's plunge? Probably the fundamental cause stemmed from the lack of a farm system modeled after the one St. Louis had developed. An alternative that might have improved results which the Giants could have used, and chose not to, was the employment of a dynamic office boss. Larry MacPhail, first by launching the Reds' revival in the mid-thirties, then reviving Brooklyn a little later, exemplified the type of office boss the Giants could have used.

Important, too, was the fading of the pitching stars who had helped bring the Giants their '33, '36, and '37 pennants: Hubbell, Schumacher and Fitzsimmons. Most notably, after his 1938 arm operation, the left-handed leader won at only half the pace of his salad years. Additionally, Schumacher and Fitzsimmons (until his trade to Brooklyn) likewise slipped. Their successors were considerably inferior or were full-scale disappointments.

Further, changes in position players were disappointing. In Hubbell's last five years with the Giants, the team averaged three to five position replacements per year — not conducive to stability or success. In the trade market, the club's mediocre players did not bring first-rate replacements. Also, Terry made one serious trade mistake. In 1940, Harry Gumbert had an off-season. In the 1941 season, Terry traded him to the Cardinals for Bill McGee, annually a seemingly promising hurler, but mostly a non-arrival.

Various minor leaguers were obtained. As a group, they were at best only mediocrities. The successful ones were Babe Young, who temporarily solved the first base headache, and Ace Adams, a very modern reliever in 1940s clothes. Adams pitched in as many as sixty and seventy games a season. Another who was successful in helping the Giants, but mostly after World War II, was Willard Marshall.

Otherwise the players were an odd assortment. Occasionally former discards would reappear. For instance, at different times, Dick Bartell, Hank Leiber, and Gus Mancuso played again in the Giants' uniform. None provided significant help. Sometimes, management would employ an odd fit, such as Gabby Hartnett. Released as the Cubs' manager, he served as Harry Danning's backup in 1941. Injuries also hurt. Billy Jurges' injury during the 1940 season inflicted the worst damage to the team.

Despite the sub-par personnel and other handicaps in both 1939 and

1940, the club probably should have finished at least one notch higher than it actually did. In both years, the Giants played in the first division in the first half of the season. Then in the second part, they would join hands with the lower-level strugglers.

With team conditions such as they were, Hubbell, until the 1940 campaign ran its course, had trouble admitting to himself that he was no longer destined to continue as a great "slabman." For some time fans, sportswriters, and teammates — ever hopeful of his making a complete comeback — tended to bolster him in his illusions on days he had done well. They tended to overlook his bad days. By the end of 1940, however, Hubbell had come to see that his great days were behind him. By that time, up against major league competition, Carl had settled into an eleven-win total per season as the most he could do.

With circumstances what they were, the significance of Hubbell's appearances diminished proportionately. No longer did the Giants get involved in late-inning cliffhangers. Far behind were the days that brought him the startling 1.66 ERA. After 1938, only once did he exceed 200 innings pitched in a season. This was in contrast to the 300+ years.

Now and then a brilliant performance reminiscent of his great days would be his. Occasionally, also, there would be winning streaks. Essentially deceiving, these apparent signs of revival of the Hubbell of old would have his admirers convinced each time that the "Meal Ticket" had returned. Disappointment would follow. Up and down continued the roller coaster ride of Carl's career.

The 1940 season illustrated these tendencies especially clearly. For opening day, Terry, with Hubbell's successes late in the 1939 season in mind, chose him as the inaugural hurler. Though he lost to the Phillies, 3–1, at that early stage there was no distinct feeling of disappointment since he had pitched a passable game. His opponent happened to be Kirby Higby. Higby soon became the Philadelphians' fourth good pitcher whom they had to trade. Like the others, he went on to win twenty games a season with a better club.

Immediately after the opener, Hubbell had a "no decision" then a second loss. Next a turn for the better set in. The Sooner set forth on a five-game winning streak. Excellent batting support helped. But also, Carl's pitching was solid and on one occasion, scintillating.

This came to pass on Memorial Day, 1940. The Giants were at Ebbets Field for a double-header. At last the tables had turned and it was the Dodgers, rather than the Giants, who were the team on the way up. Close to 34,000 Brooklyn fans occupied every seat. Reportedly 20,000 were turned away.

In the first game, Hubbell took on his career-long tormentors. For once, everything went his way just when the Dodgers and their manager, Leo

Durocher, wanted otherwise. In the Flatbushers' fourth inning, their second baseman, Johnny Hudson, struck their first hit, a single. It was also their last. Trying to steal second, he was immediately thrown out as part of a double play. Other than Hudson, only two other batters hit the ball out of the infield, both for easy outs. Hubbell faced the absolute minimum of batters: 27. It took him just 80 pitches in nine innings, or an average of three per batter, to finish his nemesis. The Giants won, 7–0, knocking the Dodgers out of first place. The win must have given Hubbell immense satisfaction. Revenge at last!

On June 23, the Giants played the first-place Cincinnati Reds in a memorable double-header. Over 50,000 fans crowded the Polo Grounds. Hubbell pitched the first game, once again facing Bucky Walters. This was the second and last time for this match-up. Through six innings they matched each other at two runs each. In the Giants' seventh came a dismaying event. A Walters pitch struck leadoff batter Bill Jurges in the head. It sidelined Jurges for much of the rest of the season. Disturbed, Walters lost his bearings; the Giants scored two runs to lead, 4–2. The Cincinnati ace was relieved. It looked as if Hubbell was on his way to defeating him. However, a barrage of Cincinnati hits routed Hubbell in the ninth. The Reds won after all, 7–4, and the losing pitcher was the downcast ex-ace.

Hubbell's preceding five straight wins had made an impression. When on July 10 the All-Star game was played, it enabled him to fill a minor role. The game took place in St. Louis. Due to stellar hurling, the National League won 4–0. Manager McKechnie initiated short-term starters, using four aces two innings each and winding up with a one-inning stint for Hubbell. Although Carl permitted a hit and a walk, he allowed no run to score. After this game, All-Star showpiece performances were no longer his.

As mentioned previously, after Hubbell's operation, a characteristic of his pitching was that of an up-and-down roller coaster ride. When his control was perfect, as it was in the Brooklyn one-hitter, Carl could pitch brilliantly. But if Hubbell was even slightly off the target, a poor day on the mound followed.

For example, on August 7, the Giants, with 53,997 seated in the Polo Grounds, played the Dodgers again. Mel Ott, the team's fifteen-year veteran, received a variety of presents. For his teammate/roommate and for the Giants, Hubbell strongly desired to defeat Brooklyn again. His opponent was his old teammate, Fred Fitzsimmons. Carl's control was a little off. The Giants' starter was driven to cover in 6⅓ innings. Hubbell allowed five runs, nine hits, and three walks in an 8–4 loss. Among the hits was a home run by Dodger center fielder, Dixie Walker. The ride was on the down slope.

By contrast, in his very next start, a week later in Boston, Hubbell brought off a twelve-inning semi-masterpiece with a 1–0 win. The Bees were anything but a batting powerhouse. In the dozen innings, they managed to get only five hits and two walks. Nonetheless, to keep the game scoreless, the eighth, ninth and tenth required hairline precision. That shrewdness topped substance in Hubbell's offerings is shown by only a single strikeout in a dozen rounds. The ride was up.

On August 19, Hubbell succeeded in defeating the first-place Reds, 9–2. The ride had continued up briefly. Then down it came when four days later everything fell apart in a struggle against the Pirates. The foes engaged in a score-fest, with Pittsburgh the winner, 13–10. In only one inning Hubbell got battered for four runs, five hits, and a base on balls.

Manager Terry sentenced Carl to a couple of relief tasks. They were against Pittsburgh, August 24, and Chicago, August 26. In both, the pitching veteran obtained short-service wins. But, restored to starting on August 31 against Brooklyn, Carl lasted only 4⅔ innings in a 7–6 loss. Because of his short service, he escaped without a loss.

With a month remaining, Hubbell showed an 11–7 W-L, a quite encouraging development. However, September brought on one setback after another. Only once, in a 2–0 loss to the Boston Bees, did he pitch well. Six starts in that month brought him five losses and a "no decision" against the Cubs in a 9–8 loss. Six of the Chicagoans' runs resulted from his ineffective mound work. The season came to an end for him on September 27 with a 6–0 loss to Hugh Mulcahy again. That year Mulcahy previously had lost six straight times to the Polo Grounders. At season's end, the Giants' hurling star of other days ended up at 11–12 W-L, the only time that he lost more than he won.

However, the season did not turn out as a complete loss. His 3.65 ERA was slightly better than the league's 3.85. Also, his 214 innings pitched exceeded what he was able to turn out in 1938 and 1939. Then again, the 214 innings hurled did not seem very impressive in comparison with the other regular starters. That year fifteen others exceeded Hubbell's figure, with Bucky Walters ranking first at 305. When this pitching output is placed along side that of their 21st century descendants, it is evident that season-ending pitching totals for the latter average out to a lesser total than their distant forebears. This is true even though the season has been eight games longer ever since the early 1960s.

On the positive side, this has come about due to the much greater effort to protect pitchers' arms. Salaries have advanced into the millions. Due to this, along with other reasons, team investments have increased enormously. Thus, every possible precaution is taken to protect a hurler's throwing wing. This has probably helped lengthen the careers of several famous moundsmen. Yet sore arms seem just as prevalent as back in Depression days.

On average, contemporary players are stronger and heavier than their predecessors. Hubbell today would barely be able to qualify in height and weight as a major league moundsman. The enormous increase in home runs is an expression of the size difference. The Old Game has been transformed. Today most lineups show a majority of the batters as home run threats. Runs in bunches often emerge from the increase in circuit clouts.

The long-ago hurler usually encountered singles, doubles, and triples, but home runs much less often. Hits of the lesser scale could usually be held in check without runs abruptly appearing several at a time. The starter of Hubbell's time had a much greater chance of lasting to the end when starting on the fourth day after rest than one today on the fifth.

Apparently over the 1940–41 winter break, Hubbell spent time considering his pitching future. At spring training in Miami in 1941, Carl spoke in a much more chastened tone than he had the year before. Interviewed by reporter Jack Singer, he admitted that full strength had not returned to his arm. He implied it may never do so. Hubbell used the screwball rarely and then only as a desperation pitch. The 1941 season would make or break him. "If ... I haven't got it anymore, it'll probably be the last."[2]

For both the Giants and Hubbell, the year brought mild though not significant improvement. The team advanced a notch to fifth place. Terry used his former ace as a starter 21 times out of 26 appearances. He carefully allowed Hubbell four days to a week between starts. This probably helped Hubbell to regain stature as a winning pitcher. His ERA also diminished slightly. However, the annual win total remained anchored at eleven.

Hubbell's closest approach to an achievement during this season came in the period from June through mid–July. It comprised a seven-game winning stretch. The second of the septet, June 12, brought a 2–0 victory over the Cubs and Bill Lee. This was Carl's final shut-out. Though he permitted eight hits and gave up a walk, the innings whisked by in the way they had in his early years. It took only an hour and thirty-three minutes to play.

The Dodgers, under Leo Durocher, outlasted the Cardinals that year in a close pennant race. In this connection, in August, Hubbell hurled two games against Brooklyn that were studies in anomaly. On August 6, in a night game at the Polo Grounds, 52,791 fans turned out. Among them was an easily recognizable celebrity, Babe Ruth. Under a "full, silvery moon," the "aging left arm" of Carl Hubbell went to work on the Dodgers. Despite "masterful pitching," he lost, 3–1.[3] The intensity with which he had undertaken his old pitching duels was still within him, but his stamina failed. It was a tense battle and stayed 1–1 until the ninth. In that inning, three hits brought Brooklyn two runs and the 3–1 win.

Not quite a week later, August 14, the Polo Grounders were at their next door neighbors' for a double-header. Given the size of Ebbets Field, the 39,145 fans jammed the place to the limits. Hubbell went in the first encounter. He put forth a sloppy pitching effort that usually would have brought a loss, but this time was sufficient to enable him to win, 8–5. Carl staggered through to the end. Brooklyn made 11 hits to score their 5 runs. Hubbell gave up six walks. To this he countered with nine whiffs. For a standard length game, Carl probably threw more pitches in this one than in the hundreds of others of comparable length.

By September, for second division also-rans, the season had reached the doldrums stage. While in an "obscure battle"[4] with the Cubs for fifth place, Hubbell suffered a tough 1–0 loss to St. Louis on September 14. Lon Warneke, whom the Cubs had traded to the Cardinals after the 1936 season, bested him in a game important to the Redbirds. The Oklahoman did his best pitching of the year, giving up only three hits. The Cardinals' run stemmed from a Giants miscue.

On September 22, Hubbell's final appearance, the senior Giants hurler thwarted Boston (the Braves name restored), 5–3. "Old Hubbell" thereby was "able to retire to his home in Fort Worth."[5]

How could Carl be living in his "home" in Fort Worth when seemingly his wife and sons were resident in a neighboring state most of a day's drive away? An interview he had given to a *Sporting News* reporter over the 1939-40 season had made a somewhat similar reference. More puzzling still, two years later, in December of 1943, Carl was reported as at his abode in Oklahoma City. With his spouse and sons living less than fifty miles away in Meeker and the Christmas season approaching, how could he be living at the state capital while they were not far away? Such references to living arrangements led some observers to wonder whether some sort of serious estrangement had befallen the Hubbell marriage.

Returning to Hubbell's 1941 season, it could be summed up as his being a slightly better than average mediocre hurler. His eleven wins were second only to Schumacher's twelve. His 3.59 ERA came to a little less than the league average. Pitching for a sub-.500 team, Carl's 11–9 W-L figure looked fairly good. On the other hand, his numbers of appearances and innings pitched had shrunk, indicating a servant of limited use.

By the end of 1941, Terry had grown fed up with managing. He withdrew to the front office. Stoneham chose Mel Ott as his successor. To select another team veteran was not a wise move. Hubbell, long afterward, remarked that his friend Ott was too accommodating a person to make a good manager. Leo Durocher once made a famous remark about him, saying that "nice guys" like Ott finished last as managers.

To some extent, events bore this out. In 1942, Ott's first year as manager of the Giants, he led them to a somewhat surprising third-place finish. There-after, though, he proved to be unsuccessful, finishing last twice: 1943 and 1946.

Rather than the usual off-season, baseball faced the potential for very changed playing conditions for 1942 and after. When the Japanese attacked Pearl Harbor on December 7, 1941, the nation was plunged into World War II. Commissioner Kenesaw Mountain Landis wrote President Franklin Roosevelt inquiring as to baseball's future in wartime. The president replied that the sport's popularity made its continuance valuable as a morale booster. However, its leaders and performers were to understand that playing personnel would be on call and subject to military service just as would the male citizenry at large.

In 1942 baseball got off quite lightly as to roster diminutions. As in World War I, it took some time for the greatly enlarged military establishment to be ready for full service. It did, however, take less time than it had for the previous mobilization. Nonetheless, there were wide variations as to when teams would lose important players. One example is the comparisons between the Phillies to the Cardinals and Dodgers. The former, with their long-time losers' luck, lost "Losing Pitcher" Hugh Mulcahy, their best hurler, to the military as early as the spring of 1942. Meanwhile the other two, both top runners, actually fielded stronger teams than they had in 1941. In the first year of the war, gradually call-ups caused the quality of play to diminish slightly, but on the whole major league ball held up.

Wartime baseball brought some inconveniences, such as delayed train arrivals and rescheduled games, but they did not constitute a major problem. Night games increased, "twilight" games were tried and other novelties were attempted. None of these factors seriously damaged playing conditions.

An area that probably had an effect on batting and pitching figures was the manufacture of baseballs. These were usually produced in the United States, but the war necessitated suspension of their manufacture in the U.S. Instead, balls made in Latin America were used. These balls were made of slightly spongy "balata" and their use probably caused batting and pitching statistics to show diminution. In 1941, the National League batting average came in at .258, with the teams collectively striking 597 home runs. In 1942, the figures were lower: .249 batting average and 538 home runs. The league ERA in the earlier year was 3.63; in 1942, it was 3.31. The American League statistics also showed a comparable dropoff.

Shortly after Pearl Harbor, the Giants swung an important deal with the Cardinals. The Redbirds built up their team on the basis of speed, a good defense, and top-notch pitching. Consequently, they were willing to trade incumbent stars. In the 1940 season, they traded Joe Medwick to Brooklyn. By late 1941, they had power-hitting but slow-moving John Mize on the market. The management wanted plenty of cash, as much as players, for him. For players Johnny McCarthy, pitcher Bill Lohrman, and Ken O'Dea, as well as $50,000, the Giants landed Mize.

Mize, together with Ott, gave the Polo Grounders the league's two leading power hitters. Meantime, as manager, Ott severely shook up the different defense positions. New personnel filled five spots. Previous occupants were fill-ins. The pitching remained largely the same. Lohrman, after only a few weeks with the Cardinals, returned. The hurling department offered shaky production at best. Ace Adams helped greatly as relief strongman, appearing in an astonishing 61 games.

In this short-lived 1942 rebirth, the Giants surprised rivals. Helped by Mize's and Ott's long ball hitting, the batting improved over 1941. The new position players, though far short of stars, performed adequately. Third place became their station. Slowness of foot and the mediocrity of the pitching ruled out first or second.

With regard to Hubbell, manager and long-time friend Mel Ott decided to experiment with him in a new form of service. The Cardinals and the Dodgers clearly were the league's best teams. Ott naturally wanted to let the air out of their tires. Each team relied upon two left-handed hitting outfielders as indispensable to the offense. In the Cardinals' case, they were Stan Musial and Enos Slaughter. For the Dodgers, Pete Reiser and Dixie Walker served the same function. Each team also played another left-handed swinger in the lineup some or most of the time. With this in mind, along with the delicacy of Hubbell's arm, Ott decided to remake Carl as mostly a spot performer against the league's top teams, since left-handed hurlers were more likely to dispense with left-handed hitters. In the season's first two months, Hubbell did not appear even once against any other team.

Ott, a prey sometimes to sentiment, made his one-time roommate and friend, Hubbell, his opening game starter on April 14 against Brooklyn. This turned out very badly. In a 7–5 loss, Carl lasted slightly less than four innings, giving up six runs on seven hits and three walks.

In his three later efforts against the Flatbushers, he did no better. On May 10 and 24, he started. Carl lost 5–3 in the first one and 6–0 to Larry French in the second one. In the two games together, Hubbell pitched only nine innings, coughing up nine earned runs on sixteen hits. On Memorial Day, before a large crowd at Ebbets Field, he relieved in the eighth and ninth, retiring two in the former and one the latter inning. In the ninth, a single, walk, and double beat him, 7–6. In only 13⅔ innings, the Dodgers creased him for seventeen earned runs and four losses.

Very worrisome was that Ott had given Hubbell a week or more off before each of these appearances. After the Memorial Day loss, Ott did not use Carl against Brooklyn again. Nor did he use Hubbell in 1943 against the Dodgers. Thus, Hubbell's 1942 Memorial Day appearance brought to a close his career service against the Dodgers. Altogether he defeated them 24 times, but lost to them 35. This was the only team against whom Carl had a losing record.

Hubbell did only slightly better in his 1942 meetings with the Cardinals. In a 4–3 New York win over St. Louis, April 29, he pitched acceptably, although he did not get credit for the victory. On May 17, Carl defeated them nicely, 7–1. On June 7 and 16, however, he lost, 4–1 in the first game, and 4–3 in the second. The latter loss especially hurt. The teams were tied in the Giants' ninth. It was Hubbell's turn to bat. Letting friendship be the determinant, Ott let him hit. Hubbell made an easy third out. In the tenth inning, Slaughter hit a home run.

Ott's idea of having Hubbell serve in a spot-pitching capacity against two teams turned into a complete flop. Against Brooklyn and St. Louis, Hubbell obtained a single win for his team while losing six. The new manager dropped this experiment.

Trying to get the team's second most senior member back on track, Ott returned him to middle relief for a short time. After Hubbell's mid–June Cardinal defeat, he remained on the sidelines a dozen days. Put in against Pittsburgh, June 28 in an 8–7 loss, he presented so-so work at best. Three runs on six hits in 5⅓ innings came to the Corsairs as the result of Carl's servings. After another week sans appearances, in a July 5 losing double-header to the Phillies, 3–2 and 5–3, Hubbell appeared for an inning in each game, retiring the three hitters he faced each time.

The off-interludes seemed to have helped Hubbell this time. When next he returned to starting, either through his own request or Ott's decision, he did much better. Carl set forth on what became a surprising eight-game winning streak. It revived highly complimentary references to his hurling which had been used infrequently since his great days.

Actually, what he managed to do was to hurl solid, substantial, but unspectacular ball maintained over an extended interval. One feature was a return to his complete-game days. In seven of the eight wins, he went all the way. In the other, Carl went for 8⅓ innings.

An important boost to the longevity of the streak came from the Giants' hitting. Only in his best single-game effort, a four-hit 3–1 win over the Pirates on July 16, did his teammates score fewer than five runs. In most of these games, Hubbell enjoyed the privilege of early Giants scoring, making him a front runner.

Typical of this type was the first game of a Giants/Cubs double-header at the Polo Grounds, July 28. The home club exploded for six runs in the initial inning. This enabled Hubbell to coast all the way in a 9–5 win. An example of the less than spectacular nature of Carl's hurling is that he allowed a dozen hits and a walk. In addition, Cub outfielder Don Dallessandro, a borderline major leaguer, nicked him for two homers, Stan Hack for one. Neither of these players hit homers very often.

Hubbell's propensity for giving up home runs, particularly after his arm injury, was his only serious shortcoming. Because the number of circuit smashes in the 1930s was much fewer than in later years, less attention was drawn to this failing than would have been the case at a later time.

As early as 1932, at which time Carl's arm was at its strongest, he gave up twenty homers. It was a high total for the period. In his peak years, 1933 and 1936, perhaps cognizant of the problem, Hubbell may have made a conscious effort to diminish their numbers. In each of these years the number of homers hit off him was far down from the preceding year.

During 1938 when Hubbell's arm was giving him increasing pain, reporters did notice the number of home runs that opposing teams were hitting off him. In proportion to his innings pitched, the total continued to be high in the last five years of his career.

Hubbell did not ever happen to mention this subject in interviews. Therefore, his view of the cause of his vulnerability is not known. Two possible reasons seem plausible. First, from the beginning, Hubbell lacked a truly strong fast ball. Because pitchers have to throw their fast one frequently, a hurler with only an average "swifty" is easier for the batter to solve for a long wallop. Second, when Carl's reliance on the screwball diminished, and eventually had to be abandoned, hitters were able to get to him for long blows because his other pitches were only of average quality, or less. In Hubbell's post-operation period, the limited success that he managed came in large measure from experience, hitter familiarity and pitch control.

With Carl's teammates continuing to hit very well, his streak lasted through four more wins for eight in all. The streak ended on August 25 with a loss to Cincinnati, 3–1. From then until the season ended, Hubbell's hurling deteriorated. It was as if his arm were telling him that the combat had been a month too long.

A loss Hubbell underwent in St. Louis on September 3 has interest as an illustration of his standing among fans, in spite of the fact that any hope Carl could do better than he had in his last four years had faded away. It was a game in which the Giants fell behind early, and ended up being shut out 7–0. Hubbell started and lasted until the sixth, the inning when the number of St. Louis runs caused Ott to remove him. As Hubbell left the field, "old Hub's exit was made to a mighty cheer from a group of soldiers who yelled their admiration of their idol."[6] Perhaps they were from the New York area headed for service in the Pacific theater, stopping to see the game en route.

At the Polo Grounds, on the last weekend of the season, the Giants played a double-header against Boston. It was a Friday afternoon and Ott put forth Hubbell in the opener. He bested the Braves 6–4 on eight hits. These included a home run each for Tommy Holmes and Ernie Lombardi.

Boston's pitcher in the wind-up was an unknown newcomer named Warren Spahn. Of course, that day no one imagined that Hubbell's successor as the greatest reigning left-hander had taken the mound. It was one of Spahn's earliest major league appearances. On this day the past preceded the future.

In statistical terms, the 1942 campaign brought Hubbell his usual eleven wins to go with eight losses. However, his 3.95 ERA stood at the highest it had ever been.

By the winter and spring of 1943, it became evident that baseball, which had gotten off lightly in 1942, was about to be hit hard through draft call-ups. These occurred both before and during the new season. The Giants' roster was decimated. Except for Manager Ott and Hubbell, most of the team's 1942 regulars had to leave for the military either before the season started, or not far into it. These included Babe Young, Willard Marshall, Johnny Mize, Harry Danning and Hal Schumacher.

A further handicap arose from the limited nature of spring training. Wartime travel being restricted, the various teams had to give up their spring excursions southward for pre-season training. In the Giants' situation, they settled for limited training quarters at Lockwood, New Jersey. Since in the east, the 1943 spring was rainy and chilly, the team had to carry on some of the practice indoors. A miserable season unfolded in consequence.

Personnel changes constantly disturbed the lineup. Intermittently, positions were held by players of advanced playing age. Other times, players who had mostly minor league credentials tried to make do. On yet other times, players with promise but little experience offered their best. The only prominent player obtainable was Ernie Lombardi, whose acquisition gave relief to Hubbell.

Hubbell was a veteran whose return to the team could be largely relied upon. Carl was 39, approaching 40, and responsible for two sons still in childhood; therefore, it was unlikely that he would be called up for military service. Early in January, Hubbell indicated receptivity to a new contract. When the hodgepodge of players showed up at Lockwood, he was among them.

Overreach best describes the team's longest-serving hurler's 1943 expectations. Although rather lucky in 1942 to end up 11–8 W-L, in the spring of 1943, Hubbell felt that he might be useful for two or three years more. Training in the north could work out to the pitchers' advantage. Hitters would numb their hands trying to hit in the chilly outdoors. Old players, like himself, would benefit from so many first-ranking players departing for service, thereby diminishing overall quality. Hubbell had 249 wins at that time. With Ted Lyons at 259 wins, and Red Ruffing at 258 wins, both heading for service, Hubbell thought that he might overtake one or both in total wins. He achieved neither.

After the close of the 1943 season, Harold Parrott, in the *Sporting News*, described what befell Hubbell. Although capable of a major league performance every now and then, on the whole he faded into a "walking but weakened shadow of the man who had been Bill Terry's 'meal ticket.'"[7]

April 21 was the date of the 1943 season opener and cold weather prevented Ott from using Hubbell until three weeks into the competition. From May until late August, Hubbell appeared in only a dozen games, this in itself an indication that the end was near. To reporters, Hubbell had become the team's "forgotten man."[8] His recording during his four months of service showed 4–4 W-L, three complete games, and a 4.91 ERA. Of the dozen appearances, only three have "resurrective" merit. Two of these were against Pittsburgh, the other against Chicago.

In Hubbell's first two starts, May 13 and 23, against the Cubs and Cardinals, he was decidedly unsuccessful, though he avoided being listed as the loser in either. After two weeks unused, on June 5 he pitched against Pittsburgh. Suddenly he produced a sterling performance his last. With the Giants winning 5–1, the Pirates' only hit consisted of an Elbie Fletcher home run. It was Hubbell's 250th win.

Had Hubbell been willing to admit to himself that he was at the end of the trail, then and there, he would have had an announcement made that he was retiring. He could have left holding his head up high amidst applause.

But, encouraged, Hubbell went on to defeat Philadelphia on June 13 and Boston on June 19. Then his pitching fell precipitously below even wartime major league standards. In five more appearances, he lost four, and had a "no decision." Hubbell permitted 20 earned runs in 23 innings, or an ERA of well over 8.00.

After ten days of inaction, on August 18, friend Ott used Carl as the starter in the second contest of a double-header against Pittsburgh at the Polo Grounds. Hubbell managed a final momentary revival. He defeated the visitors, 3–2, his 253rd win. Obviously working hard all the way, he managed to last through to the end while giving up nine hits and granting three walks. Once again at the conclusion of the game he had an ideal opportunity for an announcement that he had just thrown his last pitch, but once again, Hubbell passed it up.

Consequently, the end came August 24 in a rather humiliating and momentary pitching appearance. Manager Ott was absent that day due to illness. Adolfo Luque, back this season as the Giants' coach, filled in for Ott as interim manager for the games. In the second game of a double-header, this time against the Cubs at home, Hubbell unexpectedly stepped onto the mound as middle innings reliever. Previously his eleven appearances had all been as starter. This seems to suggest that Hubbell, perhaps worried about his arm after the strenuous effort against Pittsburgh, asked Luque to insert him briefly to see if he had anything left.

It took only a minute or two for the answer to be provided in the form of a resounding "No!" The two batters he faced were Bill Nicholson and Ival Goodman, the latter over recently to the Cubs from Cincinnati. Each batter swung at Hubbell's first pitch and singled sharply. Carl thereupon left the engagement, the pitch to Goodman the last one he ever threw in his major and minor league career. In this ignominious fashion his pitching days drew to a close. Hubbell deserved a celebratory departure commensurate with his greatness as a hurler. Wartime conditions, of course, precluded it. As it actually ended, he departed as unheralded as he had come.

Carl Hubbell's reputation as one of the two greatest hurlers of his era is incontestable. To the baseball addict, what strikes home is that his career ERA stands at 2.97. When the identical statistic is examined for the eleven other Hall of Fame recipients whose careers overlapped with his, directly or indirectly, every one exceeded 3.00.

To the average fan familiar in some degree with the game's history, Hubbell's name is chiefly associated with one or more of his three memorable accomplishments. These are as follows:

- Hubbell once pitched two full games in one, the great 1–0 eighteen-inning shutout in 1933.
- Hubbell performed the spectacular feat of striking out consecutively the five straight Hall of Fame batters in the 1934 All-Star Game.
- Hubbell succeeded in winning twenty-four games in succession in 1936–37.

Obviously the other great moundmaster of Hubbell's day was Lefty Grove in the American League. As high a level as the former's attainments reached, the latter's soared higher still. While Hubbell finished first in ERA three times, Grove did it in his league an incredible nine times. To Hubbell's five 20-game seasons, Grove posted eight. One season, the Oklahoman captured 26 wins. But his counterpart holds the first and third highest for left-handers at 31 and 28. Hubbell won 253 games in total, but Grove notched 300. The Giants' ace's winning percentage was an impressive .622. Grove's soared to .682, the highest of all among the highly regarded pitchers with 300 or more wins.

In World Series performances, Hubbell and Grove had very similar records. Each appeared in three series. Each won four and lost two. Their innings-pitched totals varied by only one inning. Each had a dazzling ERA in the 1.60s. The single significant difference is observable only in home runs given up. In six starts, Hubbell was touched for three. In five starts and three relief appearances, no batter ever hit a home run off Lefty Grove in a World Series.

It can be reasonably argued, nevertheless, that the Oklahoman's gift for the spectacular surpassed the Marylander. The latter decidedly lacked his contemporary's agreeable personality. Though Grove was slightly the greater hurler, Hubbell's is the more familiar name.

Comparisons are sometimes drawn of great stars from one era to another. Would it not be worthwhile to compare Hubbell's record to those of other pitching Hall of Famers who preceded or followed him? This is not feasible because playing conditions have differed from one era to another on so large a scale that the differences preclude valid comparisons. It is better to leave baseball's greatest hurlers to the Valhalla appropriate to their time.

Chapter 15

Farming a Different Crop

Retired athletes sometimes have trouble adjusting to everyman life. To have a rewarding career draw to a close with more than half of the person's life still in the forefront can easily foster aimlessness. Replacement activities or suitable employment may take time to find. The headlines, once so gratifying to the ego, have faded away. In some, the transition is not successful. The later life becomes a tale of turmoil and embarrassment.

It took only a few months after retirement for Hubbell to escape the pitfalls of idleness and drift. He obtained a position within the framework of baseball and held it for more than twice the years that had comprised his hurling days.

However, in the last twenty years of his long life, the frailties of the flesh, and the frustrations attendant upon them, did overtake him. A health breakdown contributed to the closeout of his second position. A domestic decease beset him. Yet overall, Carl Hubbell passed through the several non-playing decades unencumbered by idleness, notoriety or turmoil.

At the time, the Hubbells' financial status probably provided them with a cushion that spared him the need for immediate reemployment. At the same time, the pitching retiree naturally desired to continue to be active on the baseball scene if he possibly could. An opportunity arose to become a minor league manager. However, feeling that supervising youthful players was not his forte, he passed up that job. Hubbell preferred the more important farm directorship. Biding his time, he attained it.

The job that came Hubbell's way was as farm director, the head of the Giants' expected postwar player development program. That Horace Stoneham offered it to him obviously came in some measure as a reward for Carl's years as the team's pitching ace, for his steadfastness as the club loyalist, and for his never having created a fuss in the form of a salary holdout.

The position became vacant because Bill Terry in the front office, after his retirement as a manager, decided in 1943 to depart completely from the baseball world and return to the South to pursue his own business interests.

While he was serving as a high-ranking official, Terry had kept an eye on the very small farming organization that the team had. He also kept tabs on their few minor league players.

By the war years, Stoneham realized that the farm system would need to be greatly expanded. The Cardinals were enjoying great success with theirs, and other high-value competitors were showing signs of emulating them. If the Giants were to regain their stature as a strong team, a training process clearly had become an essential ingredient. Thus, when Terry had enough, the selection of his successor, who would be expected to have far more expanded duties, became an important decision.

Hubbell, aware in his last pitching days of what was simmering in the front office, lobbied actively to land the position of farm director. There are no indications that at any time he hesitated to seek the position due to possible domestic complications. Carl, living in Oklahoma City in December when he received a call from Horace Stoneham offering him the position, could not have been greatly surprised. He accepted it with alacrity.

How Sue Hubbell reacted to this would be interesting to know, but it is not known. Common sense would suggest that with two small boys to rear, she would want her husband at home on a daily basis as much as possible. Yet his new position kept him at a distance a considerable part of each year. As mentioned previously, the combination of limited journalist inquiry into the personal life of sports and other stars during this era, plus the lack of comment by either principal upon their private lives, leads us with nothing but conjecture.

At the time that Hubbell stepped into his new duties, the Giants had only two farm teams: Jersey City in the International League, and Bristol in the Appalachian. The club employed only a handful of scouts. It was the new farm director's task to build the miniature organization into a large efficient one. Whatever Carl had done in his position with the oil company is not clear, but assuredly he had some business experience and expertise as a result of that association. Hubbell tackled the assignment with the same energy and zest that had struck observers back at the beginning of his pitching career. It took him considerable time to improve the structure sufficiently to make the Giants a pennant threat once more, but this was not unlike his early years pitching with the Giants.

In piecing together a successful farm system, Hubbell benefited from having a valuable front office partner. This was Jack Schwarz, who had been Bill Terry's assistant as long as the latter had been the Giants' overseer. Though at the beginning Schwarz knew from experience in management more about the farm operation than did his new superior, it was Hubbell who landed the top job. Stoneham probably gave it to Carl rather than Schwarz because he felt that a former pitching star would be more likely to attract youthful prospects than would a front-office unknown. Hubbell and Schwarz went on as an amicable partnership in the approximately thirty-four years of the former's tenure. Schwarz deserved some of the credit for his superior's successes.

In the early years of this new position, travel took up a great deal of Hubbell's time. For example, in the early 1950s, he was averaging about 20,000 miles annually, most of it by air. His conference sessions were on a scale proportionate to his travel. Carl spent much of his time and energy in fitting together a "coordinated" set of farm club managers and an experienced scouting cast. By the '50s he had expanded the initial five scouts into twenty-six full timers along with over 100 field sleuths.

Once, Hubbell explained that a successful farm organization consisted of a combination of capable minor league managers and an alert scouting force. Carl added that an efficient office manager like Jack Schwarz could provide essential help.

What are the criteria that determine a farm director's success? From the perspective of a player, statistics plus management's assessment of his value are the determinants. For a farm supervisor, other criteria enter in. However, in the final analysis, the team's level of success decides. In Hubbell's case, he benefited from a special advantage. Almost to the end of his farm directorship, the owner continued to be Horace Stoneham. With a superior who knew him well, he could count on him to show maximum patience.

The farm overseer has little time for scouting on his own part or involving himself in the elaborate training required in the development of skills in a prospect. Thus, considerable credit belongs to the scouts who locate the prospects and the minor league managers who supervise their training. The most ambitious and best trained ones eventually emerge as major league players, or eventually, outright stars. It is the farm director who puts together the organization and supervises its development. In this responsibility, Hubbell demonstrated that he could carry out his duties very well, though never quite on the scale of his success as a pitcher.

In Carl's years at the helm of the farm system, the Giants captured three pennants — in 1951, 1954, and 1962 — and one World Series, 1954. In 1969, the National League adopted the division playoff arrangement and the Giants were the West Division winners in 1971. However, they lost the pennant in the playoff against Pittsburgh. In other years, they finished second six times. These results indicate success at the farm organization level. However, in the first instance, 1951, most of the leading players who helped win the pennant were only partly or slightly products of the farm organization under Hubbell. (The one exception that year was Willie Mays.) Also in the last decade at his post, Hubbell's success ran out.

As for the players who reached the majors, the majority displayed average skills and longevity. The ones who reached stardom or Hall of Fame levels of attainment were as numerous as on other leading teams. Among the famous Giants names were Bobby Thomson, Willie Mays, Hoyt Wilhelm, Orlando Cepeda, the Alous brothers Felipe and Matty, Jim Davenport, Mike McCormick, Bobby Bonds, and Juan Marichal. Marichal fell only a little short of Hubbell's level of attainment as a pitcher.

Of course, the farm organization did not claim that skillful construction in itself ensured success. A farm program needed not only careful supervision, but occasional good luck. Hubbell described how the Giants obtained Willie Mays as an illustration of how good fortune could mean much.

A consideration that worked in the New Yorkers' favor was that Mays's availability came early enough in the process of major league teams' searching for black players so that the competition was not as severe as it became later. One of the Giants' minor league coordinators badly needed a first sacker. Hubbell had learned that the Birmingham Black Barons had such a commodity. He sent one of the scouts to size up the youngster. The scout reported back that Mays's future did not lie in the infield, but that he had great potential as an outfielder. Since this was not what the minor league affiliate needed, the scout wondered whether he should try to sign him. Hubbell urged him to induce Mays to sign a contract as soon as possible. For $15,000 ($5,000 of it a bonus to Mays), the Giants landed a youth who rose to stardom in short order. Had others seen the potential in Mays at the time, the price would have skyrocketed, and the Giants might not have obtained him.

An aspect of the minor league training process in which, in his earlier years, Hubbell did participate directly had to do with the hurling aspirants. In this sphere, his credentials were unassailable and his name an attraction. He would gather groups of a dozen or so and dispense advice. Very decidedly, he did not urge his pupils to start experimenting with the screwball. If a candidate exhibited a good fast ball, he should concentrate upon establishing control of it — as soon as possible — and his curve and change-up, too. Carl further advised that later in his career a moundsman could experiment with a seldom-used delivery, if he chose.

To his surprise and annoyance, Hubbell encountered a certain amount of resistance to his counsel. He noticed a tendency in the younger generation to be impatient, to expect too much too soon. A few, if they had a poor year, felt like giving up the game then and there. Others, after a successful year at about the Class A level of play, felt they ought to be able to pitch in the major leagues immediately.

Hubbell stressed the importance of sufficient time spent in the minors. "Instruction without experience" would not be enough.[1] Sounding a little like

John McGraw, Carl's mentor of so long before, he emphasized that to succeed in the majors a pitcher had to be able to stay ahead of the hitters. Time spent in the minors would help achieve this essential.

In 1957, the Dodgers, and with them, the Giants, abandoned New York City in favor of the West Coast. The Dodgers went to Los Angeles and the Giants to San Francisco. Out on the trail as much as he was, this did not make as great a difference to Hubbell as it did to others, but thenceforth his official headquarters were in the Bay City.

Not everything in the traveler's life consisted of farm director labors. The varying nature of his day-to-day functions, along with occasional Giants front office generosity, enabled him to engage in offbeat activities now and then. For example, in 1953, Hubbell played himself in a Hollywood baseball movie entitled *Big Leaguer*, with Edward G. Robinson as its star. Robinson had nothing to worry about the newcomer as a scene stealer.

A different form of enjoyment came his way in 1968. For years Carl had been an avid golfer. During the Christmas season that year, Hubbell succeeded in winning the annual Celebrities' golf title.

Surely back in small-town Oklahoma, life in the 1950s and 1960s did not provide Sue Hubbell with the variety available to her husband in his more cosmopolitan surroundings. In the early years of their marriage, prior to the birth of their first child, she had appeared to enjoy life in New York City. After the Hubbells' sons reached adulthood, married and departed to pursue their own lives, Sue lived in their Shawnee home as the single occupant rather than joining Carl. One of Sue's sisters and her husband also resided in Shawnee. They probably provided family support, companionship, and some entertainment for Sue — but not on the level Carl was enjoying.

In their childhood, youth and young manhood, the Hubbell boys' lives were managed by Sue. That she did well is evident from an interview that Carl gave to a reportorial admirer in 1953. Carl described Sue as "running their comfortable home" and "supervising bringing up their boys."[2] The pattern of the husband and father being the provider while the wife and mother managed the home and nurtured the children was prevalent in America at the time Carl and Sue married.

The elder son, the second Carl, advanced to adulthood in the later 1950s and James, the younger son, in the early '60s. Like most others, they soon settled into the broad middle-class mainstream. Neither attempted baseball as a career. Both married and had children. Carl Jr. rose to the rank of major in the Marines and then settled in the vicinity of Los Angeles. James entered the trucking business and lived in Nebraska.

The elder Carl, perhaps encouraged by his years of mound success, in his second career aired his opinions much more freely to interested observers.

In light of his noteworthy hurling career, his remarks on the moundsmen of later generations naturally drew writers' attention.

Predictably, as a former moundsman, Hubbell was a strong supporter of hurlers with regard to batter/pitcher relationships. Carl emphasized that only in the "dead ball" times had pitchers held the advantage. They were permitted to throw any sort of doctored ball, which had led to a reaction. Restraints were imposed on what a hurler could do to a baseball. Prior to the imposition of these restrictions, reliance on scuffed baseballs and "loaded" spheres eased the strain on the pitcher's arm. This in turn had enabled the great moundsmen of that day to accumulate high win totals.

From Hubbell's perspective, the arrival of the "lively ball" forced pitchers to put much greater strain on their arms, especially since artificial deliveries were forbidden. Their jobs were made still harder by the increase in home runs. In the 1980s, by the time of his old age, Hubbell believed that the tightness with which the ball was wound made it carry even farther than in his time.

While granting that it was the hitters who drew fans' excitement, a better hitter/pitcher balance needed to be instituted. Hubbell suggested a supervised 5 to 10 percent reduction in the velocity of the ball. The improved balance would benefit the sport. Needless to say, Carl's ideas were not adopted.

With regard to the hurlers who succeeded Carl as stars, his views did not differ significantly from other experienced observers. For example, in the case of Tom Seaver, who was then drawing headlines, Carl thought that his great stuff — along with a fine frame of mind — might enable Seaver to reach 300 wins. At the time of this comment, Seaver had already had several fine seasons, although he had not yet reached 100 wins. By the end of Seaver's career, his total reached 311.

Sometimes Hubbell offered fairly shrewd observations concerning a pitcher's frame of mind. If two stars in a game were matched, the likely winner, according to Carl, would be the one whose team scored first. Obviously any lead helped. The one whose team tallied first would feel he was in the driver's seat.

In the 1955 Yankee-Dodgers World Series, Hubbell attended the finale. In mid-game, the Dodgers obtained a two-run lead. Carl observed how Brooklyn pitcher Johnny Podres seemed to exude greater confidence after that. He felt that Podres would emerge the winner. He did, 2–0.

In the first engagement of the 1957 World Series between the Milwaukee Braves and the Yankees, Whitey Ford defeated Warren Spahn, 3–1. The Yankees were the ones who scored first. Hubbell felt that Spahn just as easily might have been the winner had the Braves seized the lead first. In the 1958 World Series, casting the same teams as competitors, the fourth game brought the two pitchers as opponents a second time. This time the Braves scored first. With this advantage, it was Spahn who won, 2–0, while allowing only three hits.

On one occasion Hubbell described his own frame of mind at the start of an important game — the second All-Star Game. This was the day of his great strikeout feat. With the American league's formidable array of hitters to face, "I had the feeling I was fighting for my own underdog league against a superior lineup. My pride was at stake."[3]

Discussing the reason that pitchers usually were such inferior batsmen, Hubbell explained that there was an important one in addition to the usual reasons offered. For example, not batting often enough in training so that when they did rush around the bases in games, they would tire sooner than other players. Most importantly, Carl said that a good moundsman concentrated so completely on the hitters from the first to the last that even when he himself was at bat, his mind was on the opposing batsmen.

When Hubbell observed pitcher carelessness, it bothered him. In 1986 the American League won the All-Star Game, 3–2. One reason was that both Dwight Gooden and Mike Scott of the Nationals allowed home runs on 0–2 counts in their favor. Probably recalling his own pitching days, Carl expressed impatience at the thought that any good pitcher would throw an 0–2 pitch within the strike area. Among the American League hurlers, he did express admiration for Roger Clemens' pitching.

A different aspect of that year's struggle bothered Carl. The Dodgers' Fernando Valenzuela starred by striking out five hitters — Hubbell's own feat repeated fifty-two years later. This did not bother him: "You don't expect records to go on forever, especially in baseball."[4] What did irritate him was the media's response. Hubbell felt that the hitters he had struck out — Ruth, Gehrig, Foxx, Simmons and Cronin — were by several light years better hitters than Valenzuela's victims: Don Mattingly, Cal Ripken, Jesse Barfield, Lou Whitaker, and Ted Higuera, a pitcher. Yet television and the press "wouldn't care if all five were pitchers."[5] Whatever the reason, the tying of a famous record brought headlines. That was all that mattered to the media.

Another time Hubbell complained that any player who broke "some kind of little old record that doesn't mean a thing, [the media] would go hog wild. Back then [in his day] you couldn't get a rise out of anybody."[6] The reader can detect a note of jealousy in this remark.

As might be expected, Meeker's most famous citizen oozed baseball traditionalism. That some day baseball could be eclipsed in popularity by any rival sport he could not imagine. This frame of mind led Carl, in 1970, to make a huge miscalculation of the future of football: "That's what I mean about football. It's all right as a sideshow, but it doesn't bring out the whole man. How can you really identify with a sport that has specialists for the hand, the foot and the shoulder? Baseball is the only game that calls for every skill from normal sized people. Fans identify with baseball and they'll continue to do so when other meteoric sports have had their innings."[7] The author of these words missed entirely the direction that professional sports would take. Not only did the day come when football and basketball would outdo baseball in popularity, but Hubbell's own sport would head increasingly toward specialization. In addition, baseball also started to lean toward players of greater size.

The caustic remarks that Hubbell often made in his later years probably were in some degree an expression of internal discontent. Like many people in the later decades of their lives, Hubbell found himself beset by physical and personal problems.

Chapter 16

"Remembrance of Things Past"[1]

April 1, 1967: a severe personal loss struck Carl Hubbell. Sue Hubbell, his wife of 37 years, died at a Shawnee hospital. For Carl, the news surely must have brought back poignant remembrances of who and what they were when they were young together.

The simple, unadorned announcement of Sue Hubbell's death appeared in the daily *Shawnee News-Star* on Sunday, April 2. The newspaper provided further, but brief, information on Tuesday, April 4. In Meeker, the weekly *Herald* carried the initial news item in almost identical form on Thursday, April 6. The announcement briefly sketched the deceased's life: her birth in Meeker, and life there until her middle years when she moved to Shawnee. Relatives and their addresses were listed, with Carl named first. Also included were the sons' names, a granddaughter and two sisters. In-laws were not listed. The preparer of the announcement did not choose to include a one-sentence depiction of her personality nor offer a reason she died. As for the latter, it was caused by a "cerebral vascular accident."[2]

The departed was a member of St. Benedict's Catholic Church. The memorial services took place on Monday, April 3. Father George McClendon officiated. Burial took place at Resthaven Memorial Park. Three of the pall-bearers were younger generation Hubbells.

Whether Carl in Casa Grande, Arizona — where the Giants held spring training — made it to Shawnee in time for the funeral is not clear. Since the death occurred in midafternoon on a Saturday and the memorial service was on Monday morning, it is possible he did not. Some years later, one of his sisters-in-law mentioned that Carl had been in Meeker "around the time his wife died."[3] If he did not make it to the services, he probably visited the cemetery and the grave as soon as he could.

Judging by his exterior frame of mind in the ensuing years, her loss did not have a lasting injurious effect. Like many athletes, Hubbell was not the meditative sort. Perhaps inwardly it disturbed him at times. However, usually in public discourse the topic did not arise nor did he bring it up. In his later life, when Carl was called upon to speak, his remarks were devoid of references to her. This is congruent with the little that either Carl or Sue ever said about their private lives in earlier years.

It is possible, perhaps probable, that a while after Sue Hubbell's death, Carl remarried. The chief source for this assertion is an article of reporter Bob Broeg's "King Carl" printed in *The Sporting News*, May 2, 1970, p. 3, but mostly written in 1969. Some years later, two other writers said the same, but the signs suggest that Broeg's article was their source.

At any rate, the marriage, if a reality, took place between Carl and Julie Stanfield of Casa Grande, Arizona. The tone of Broeg's piece suggests or implies that his source was Carl himself. Yet the reporter provided no date and no place. Moreover, the very sentence in which he declared the marriage, he erred by more than two years in mentioning Sue Hubbell's decease as occurring in 1964.

After Hubbell retired as farm director, he lived another fourteen years. That allowed sufficient time for numerous reporters to interview him. In none of the interviews did Julie Stanfield's name appear. Thus, the actuality of the marriage remains an uncertainty. Since the subject appears not to have been raised in his last years, it does not seem to be much of a loss to leave this loose end untied.

In his later farm director years, remembrances of great moments in his pitching career would be brought to his attention. As recounted earlier, the interviewer Jack McDonald brought up the subject of his great strikeout day thirty years after the event. On that occasion, Hubbell's recollection fit in quite well with what was known about the surrounding circumstances at the time. Incidentally, Carl added that as far as he knew, his confrontations that day with Babe Ruth and Lou Gehrig were his first. The other two thought the same of batting against him. All three were wrong. The 1926 exhibition game in Toronto, where they first met each other on the ball field, seems to have completely slipped all of their minds.

Ten years later (1974), again in *The Sporting News*, but with Art Spander conducting the interview, Hubbell's mixed-up recollection almost completely contradicted what he had said in 1964. Confusing the years of 1933 and 1934, he transferred his frame of mind in the earlier year before he had become mildly famous, but was close to it, over to the 1934 situation. So many years afterward, Carl decided he had not been under so much pressure. "I had no reputation ... meaning that from the psychological point of view I had the advantage."[4] Had his 1974 version been accurate, then the one he had offered in 1964 would have been completely incorrect, but the opposite was true. Such are the vagaries of the human memory in old age, especially when one has had some illness.

It was in 1974 that the afflictions of later life first appeared. A mild stroke slowed Hubbell down briefly. Two years later he was back in the hospital for a hernia operation. Far worse, in the fall of 1977, a severe stroke felled him. Carl was in a coma for many days. Gradually he struggled to a semi-recovery. Doctors urged him to use a wheelchair for mobility. However, Hubbell managed to regain the ability to walk, but only with the aid of a cane and at a very slow pace. Golfing ended as his outdoor sport. Carl also lost some digital flexibility.

In the aftermath of the stroke, Hubbell lost his post as farm director. A retirement-minded Horace Stoneham had disposed of the Giants a couple of years earlier. Bob Lurie succeeded him as the team's owner. He employed Specs Richardson as his general manager. The latter felt that it would be desirable for Hubbell to be retired. In view of the Oklahoman's close to fifty years in the Giants' service, his withdrawal was carried out as gently as possible. Lurie provided him with a small yearly pension. In return, Hubbell was to do occasional college and high school scouting on behalf of his old team.

Hubbell's doctors urged him to move to a location where his physical handicaps and his health in general could be more readily treated. Accordingly, Mesa, Arizona, the Phoenix suburb, became Carl's residence until his death. This was also the location for the Giants' spring training program.

In Mesa, Carl lived in a small apartment that seemed to some observers hardly suitable for the former pitching standout. However, he could not afford better. Somehow the prosperity that favored him at the time of his retirement as pitcher had gone its way.

At the time of the emergence of the Major League Players Association in the 1950s and 1960s, many of the 1930s–40s players, and even those from times before, had hopes they might benefit. They desired some measure of pension for themselves. With salaries of their well-organized successors booming by the 1960s, it surely was feasible. None materialized. The "ancients" were shut out.

Had Hubbell maintained his prosperity, the subject might only have been in the background of his mind. However, with his life blunted by his physical handicaps, his shrunken income, and his none-too-prosperous surroundings, the snub preyed on his mind. Speaking of his players' union successors in relation to their predecessors' needs, Carl said, "They never looked back one day."[5]

During his Mesa years, Hubbell often expressed a quite jaundiced opinion of the attitudes the contemporary players displayed. So frequently did his discontent receive voice that — to some extent — it likely stemmed from his physical hardships, his lonely life and the pension exclusion.

In 1979 Carl offered a synopsis of his feelings: "I don't blame the players.

Maybe I would have done it. But now it's the player, his agent and his lawyer. And the player will go to another team as fast as he can get a better deal. I really don't think that's fair to the fans. I feel sorry for the managers of the big league clubs. I really don't see how they can get things done with the players having so much to say about it."[6]

In another interview Hubbell complained about the players' self-centeredness: "Big league players today have three important things to concentrate on during a game. The boob tube is there and he's an actor now. He's got an agent and a million dollars or so, and he's got to give them some thought. Then if there's anything left, there's baseball."[7] On yet another occasion, Carl elaborated on the same thought: "The players are too selfish. They just have no respect for managers and no respect for owners."[8]

Carl's notion of players as actors expressed a pet peeve. He objected to the modern players' flamboyant displays of in-game successes: "All this stuff they do today, high fives and jumping up and down didn't go then"—i.e., his own time.[9]

Perhaps at the time of these remarks a majority of long-time fans and surviving ex-players of his generation shared his views. Hubbell's remark referring to fans' objections to the players' lack of team loyalty would seem to have some merit. The same might have been said of in-game histrionics that were superfluous. However, the newer fans quickly adapted to the players' moves from franchise to franchise. Players' showmanship also simply became part of the landscape. Despite several severe player strikes, by the 2000s, baseball was setting new attendance records yearly.

Hubbell was very fortunate in one respect. Unlike many of the elderly, he occasionally received a morale boost that relieved the tedium that often besets our elder citizens. In 1978 came the first opportunity to vary the sameness of everyday life in Mesa.

Back in Meeker, where he had not been in eleven years, 1978 marked the 75th year of its existence. Meeker's local leaders decided upon a celebration worthy of so momentous an event. It just happened that simultaneously, Carl reached 75 years of age. Two of the Meeker leaders, Vernon and Gail Markwell, were instrumental in convincing the Mesa retiree that it would be worth his while to undertake the trip back home. (Vernon Markwell was the president of the Chamber of Commerce, and Gail Markwell was a reporter for the *Meeker Herald*.) Gail, in particular, through correspondence and telephone calls, served as chief persuader. She promised that there would be a large turnout and a parade comparable to the one held in his honor back in 1933 to celebrate the Giants' upset victory in the World Series.

This occasion was as much a tribute to Hubbell as to Meeker's 75th year. On May 13, 1978, some 7,000 people were in attendance. At that time the population of Meeker was barely over 1,000; clearly folk came from outside the immediate area to honor Carl. Among those awaiting the honored guest were fellow Oklahoman major leaguers Lloyd Waner, Allie Reynolds, and Dale Mitchell. Not present, but sending their regards, were Oklahoman Mickey Mantle, as well as Satchel Paige and Stan Musial. Two pitchers, who in their training years had been admirers of Hubbell and could not be present but sent their regards, were Harry Brecheen and Warren Spahn.

As Gail Markwell had promised, the highlight of the day was a mile-long parade from downtown Meeker to Carl Hubbell Field, the park on which the high schoolers played. For the parade, Carl and Lloyd Waner rode together in a 1935 Rolls Royce.

At the field, after being showered with presents, the guest of honor offered a brief address. Hubbell informed his listeners that if they so desired, he would give the village custody of his baseball memorabilia. It had been solicited by the National Baseball Hall of Fame, but Carl felt that his home grounds would be a more appropriate depository. His remarks were very well received!

In some measure, the holiday served as a salute to the 1933 jamboree. Since it was saluting that era when Carl and Sue Hubbell were seen together publicly, it would have been fitting if sometime during the 1978 celebration Carl, as a gesture to his late wife's memory, could have made a reference to Sue. The time of the playing field remarks would have been an especially appropriate moment to mention memories of their glory days together. In 1933, Sue had been an active observer of all, and participant in some, of the happenings. The Meeker paper made no mention of such a remark in their reporting of the events of the day.

Like other celebrities, Hubbell must have chafed at having to go over the same ground time and again, but he retained his patience nicely. This was the same Hubbell who had been so patient with fans after games in his glory days. Several who had known him in his youth sixty years before came up to shake hands. One such was his high school catcher, Cedric Fowler.

When all was said and done, everyone agreed that the 75th anniversary had been an immense success. How the wearied featured guest managed to betake himself back to Mesa was not recorded.

During the ensuing couple of years, Hubbell kept his word and forwarded his memorabilia to Meeker. Meantime, downtown, officials hastened to complete a new layout to house City Hall and the Fire Department. An annex to the City Hall comprised the Hubbell Museum. With everything readied, a second invitation reached the retiree in Mesa. With his health somewhat improved, Carl returned for the inauguration of the new downtown center on September 16, 1980.

With ceremonies finished, a lunch awaited the prime visitor, his companions, his hosts and about 100 guests. At Carl's side was Jo-Jo Moore, who in other days had patrolled left field for the Giants most of the time when Hubbell had pitched. Allie Reynolds, who had once been an outstanding slabman for Cleveland and New York, was also there with him. A close friendship had grown up between Carl and Allie.

In his speech at the luncheon, the primary guest dwelt on how surprised he was to observe the museum completed so swiftly. Likewise, Hubbell stressed his gratitude for the many honors the Meeker citizenry had showered upon him.

Members of the audience offered reminiscences and raised familiar questions. Judging by the coverage in the *Meeker Herald*, Carl made no reference to his deceased spouse. Neither did the major Oklahoma dailies, which covered the event much more briefly. As if by tacit understanding, neither did his listeners.

In private, Carl asked Vernon Markwell to handle the obsequies whenever his own life would run out. It is interesting to note that he made this request of someone he had known only a short time, rather than one of his sons or a friend of some standing.

Meeker's favorite citizen, though fast approaching his eighties, made a final visit. It just so happened that in Dallas during the 1981 Fourth of July weekend, Hubbell received the American Academy of Achievement's Golden Plate Award. Numerous public figures had been so honored. A few had been baseball players, but Hubbell was the first former pitcher to be selected. The local paper shows pictures from that day, including one of Hubbell with the Golden Plate plaque.

From Dallas, Hubbell proceeded north to Meeker. On July 9, the Chamber of Commerce held a reception for him. Carl's companions were his son James and the latter's wife, his daughter-in-law. With them present, a passing compliment to the memory of his son's mother for all she had contributed to the raising of the sons would have been nice. Carl made no such remark. His talk had largely to do with how surprised he was to be honored by an academically connected organization a few days earlier.

Carl Hubbell undertook a final journey. In 1984 the All-Star Game's venue was Candlestick Park in San Francisco. Better yet, the game was to take place on July 10, the exact day on which, fifty years before, Carl had carried out his great strikeout wonder. Invited to attend, he dragged his eighty-one-year-old frame from his Mesa apartment to San Francisco. As the honoree in throwing out the first ball, he was asked upon arrival whether his pitch would be a screwball. Carl replied by saying that more likely he might have to tip the ball over the railing. Actually, he did better. The toss Hubbell gave the ball did bear a recognizable resemblance to a thrown baseball. Would not any human bask in the remembrance of his greatest moment?

Carl Hubbell was the recipient of one last honor. In 1986, the Oklahoma Sports Hall of Fame was launched in Oklahoma City. Hubbell wanted to attend when he was informed that he was to be one of the first chosen for inclusion in this Hall of Fame. His doctor insisted it would be too great a strain on his health. One of his brothers, John, who strongly resembled Carl, served as his replacement. Also elected at the same time were Carl's friend, Allie Reynolds, as well as Jim Thorpe. Thorpe was the famous early-twentieth-century Native American athlete from the town of Prague, just down the road from Meeker.

By his early eighties, Carl looked his age: "...withered, limbs thin, his face crinkled and dappled with brown spots."[10] Referring to himself, Carl remarked ruefully: "You're not very sharp with two strokes running through your mind. You can't hold a conversation very well."[11]

Others sought to help, but the retiree overdid his desire to be independent. Carl's landlady tried, but he resisted. He limped across to a fast food place twice a day for meals or else purchased boxed concoctions to eat at home. Hubbell would walk to a nearby bowling alley to talk sports with hangers-on there or watch major league games on television.

Some writers, apparently unaware of the honors Hubbell was receiving in his travels, felt that he deserved better than the life they saw him living. Art Spander, writing in *The Sporting News*, described seeing Carl at a spring training game, "sitting on a folding beach chair ... unrecognized, unappreciated.... Surely a king deserves better."[12] It is curious that Hubbell's honors and recognitions, especially the American Academy of Achievement's Golden Plate Award, appeared to be unknown to a reporter from *The Sporting News*.

Hubbell accepted, but did not seek, sympathy. He would make remarks indicative of how he felt about his own life in comparison with the active players he observed in his old age. Writers felt that the $22,500 peak wage that he had received was a starvation figure compared with what players were earning in the 1980s. However, Carl himself often dwelt on how hard it was even to obtain employment during the Depression. A $20,000 salary, with prices what they were then, "spent ... just like the millions the guys make today."[13]

Writing for the *Arizona Republic*, Tom Fitzpatrick believed that Hubbell had been left in the lurch. While the former great pitcher lived in his lonely little Mesa apartment, Horace Stoneham resided in a luxurious retirement abode. Except encountering Hubbell occasionally at spring training games, Stoneham never invited his once-favorite player to a luncheon or otherwise tried to make contact.

Hubbell defended Stoneham. Since their social strata differed, there was no need for other contact. Carl felt grateful to the former Giants' owner for employing him so long as farm director. Fitzpatrick wondered how Hubbell could "still [be] loyal to Mr. Stoneham sitting up there in his Scottsdale mansion and clipping his coupons and sipping his cocktails."[14] However, the writer and his subject, coming from different worlds, saw things quite differently.

Once, late in life, Carl offered a brief assessment of how he felt about his great days in relation to the world of the players he observed in his last years: "I like to remember baseball at that time.... They played because they loved it. It wasn't a business for us."[15]

Hubbell's days came to an end through an accident. One Saturday morning, November 19, 1988, apparently out early to run errands, Carl crashed his car into a metal pole. The accident having had no discernible cause, doctors thought it might have been due to a third stroke. On Monday, November 21, suffering from severe head and chest injuries, he died.

One week later, on Monday, November 28, 1988, Hubbell's funeral services were held in the Meeker High School gymnasium. About 150 people were present. As Carl had requested, Vernon Markwell handled the ceremony. He reviewed Hubbell's pitching career at some length. The late citizen's virtues of modesty, generosity, and humility received emphasis — almost to the verge of overemphasis. The speaker concluded with a religious poem and a prayer. Considering that he was performing a function usually handled by a member of the cloth, Markwell did quite well. The audience and the commentators judged it favorably.

One feature typical of funeral sermons was absent in the Markwell service. At most services, listeners expect the sermonizer to dwell upon the deceased's *whole* life. Of course, limitations or shortcomings are treated lightly or omitted entirely and emphasis is given to his or her virtues. However, since others have had some influence on the departed, their names and roles usually receive at least brief attention.

It is this last feature that is absent from the Markwell eulogy. While there is reference to the Hubbell family's move from Missouri to Oklahoma, and the names of several others are noted briefly, that is all. Surely the deceased's wife and sons, among others, were bound to have made an impact. Further, the departed spouse, just like Carl himself, probably made some impact on the sons. But no mention was made of this aspect of Hubbell's life.

Why Carl — in his instructions to Vernon Markwell concerning how to handle his funeral services — did not emphasize the need to make reference to his wife and sons, and especially to Sue, is a mystery. Though Carl and Sue Hubbell were very private people and neither gave information about their home life in interviews previously, it would seem that in this final accounting, privacy would be trumped by a desire to give recognition.

Many, if not most, married couples of Hubbell's day, realizing they were not likely to pass away simultaneously, made arrangements for the later deceased to be buried adjacent to the earlier. However, in Hubbell's case, his ashes were not placed in the Shawnee cemetery next to his wife's grave. They were deposited at the New Hope Cemetery just outside of Meeker in the Hubbell family plot. Just as in most of their married life, they resided in separate residences, so in their death, they rest in separate settings.

Such is how the quite remarkable life of Carl Owen Hubbell came and went. How could its impact on American sports history best be conveyed? In the *Washington Post*, Martin Weil wrote the obituary. Much of it provided a summary of one of the national pastime's most famous pitching star's outstanding accomplishments. In reference to his three most famous feats, Weil declared unequivocally that they "wrote [him] into the folklore of the nation."[16]

Appendix: Statistics

I. Carl Hubbell's Won–Lost Statistics Against His National League Opponents

Opponent	Won–Lost	Ratio
Philadelphia	44–14	.759
Boston	34–13	.723
Pittsburgh	49–21	.700
Cincinnati	30–16	.652
St. Louis	39–28	.582
Chicago	33–27	.550
Brooklyn	24–39	.407

II. 1933, World Series, vs. Washington Senators

Innings Pitched	20
Games Started	2
Games Completed	2
Hits	13
Strikeouts	15
Bases on Balls	6
Runs	3
Earned Runs	0
Earned Run Average	0.00

III. 1936 World Series, vs. New York Yankees

Innings Pitched	16
Games Started	2
Games Completed	1
Hits	15
Strikeouts	10
Bases on Balls	2
Runs	5
Earned Runs	4
Earned Run Average	2.25

IV. 1937 World Series, vs. New York Yankees

Innings Pitched	14⅓
Games Started	2
Games Completed	1
Hits	12
Strikeouts	7
Bases on Balls	4
Runs	10
Earned Runs	6
Earned Run Average	3.77

V. Combined 1936-37 Series

Innings Pitched	30⅓
Games Started	4
Games Completed	2
Hits	27
Strikeouts	17
Bases on Balls	6
Runs	15
Earned Runs	10
Earned Run Average	3.77

VI. 1933-36-37 Overall World Series Performance

Innings Pitched	50⅓
Games Started	6
Games Completed	4
Hits	40
Strikeouts	37
Bases on Balls	12
Runs	18
Earned Runs	10
Earned Run Average	1.79

VII. All Star-Performances

Innings Pitched	9⅔
Games Started	1
Non-Starter Participation in Games	0
Hits	8
Strikeouts	11
Bases on Balls	6
Runs	2
Earned Runs	2
Earned Run Average	2.29

Chapter Notes

Chapter 1

1. NBHF, Hubbell clipping file, an item in which the subject makes reference to his early life.
2. *Ibid.*, Keely M. Marshall, "Day the All Stars Bit the Dust," *Oklahoma Record News*, February 1984.
3. *Daily Oklahoman*, July 5, 1925.
4. *Ibid.*
5. *Ibid.*
6. *Ibid.*, August 2, 1925.
7. NBHF, Hubbell clipping file, Ed Fitzgerald, "King Carl," *The Sports Special*, May 1953, p. 6.
8. *The Sporting News*, July 15, 1926.
9. *San Antonio Express*, March 18, 1928.
10. *Dallas Morning News*, June 13, 1928.
11. *Ibid.*, June 17, 1928.
12. *Ibid.*
13. NBHF, Hubbell clipping file, Bob Broeg, "King Carl: Superb Mound Craftsman," *The Sporting News*, July 19, 1928.
14. *Ibid.*

Chapter 2

1. *New York Times*, July 19, 1928.
2. Lawrence Ritter, *The Glory of Their Times* (New York: Collier Books, Macmillan, 1966), p. 240.
3. *New York Times*, July 19, 1928.
4. NBHF, Hubbell clipping file, Bill McCullough, "The Meal Ticket," p. 7.
5. *New York Times*, July 19, 1928.
6. NBHF, Hubbell clipping file, Fitzgerald, "King Carl," p. 7.

7. *New York Herald-Tribune*, August 6, 1928.
8. *New York Times*, August 6, 1928.
9. *Ibid.*
10. A common deprecatory phrase widely used to describe the hopeless 1930s Philadelphia Phillies.
11. NBHF, Hubbell clipping file, McCullough, "The Meal Ticket," p. 7.
12. *Ibid.*, undated clipping of interview McGraw had with Frank Graham in 1928. From the context, it occurred subsequent to September 4.
13. *Los Angeles Times*, September 23, 1928.

Chapter 3

1. *New York Times*, May 9, 1929.
2. *Chicago Tribune*, June 4, 1929; *New York Times*, June 4, 1929.
3. *New York Times*, June 25, 1929; NBHF, Hubbell clipping file, a recollection.
4. NBHF, Hubbell clipping file, another rueful recollection.
5. NBHF, Hubbell clipping file, Fitzgerald, "King Carl," *Daily Oklahoman*, October 20, 1933, p. 8; *Shawnee News-Star*, April 2, 1967.
6. Charles C. Alexander, *John McGraw* (Lincoln: University of Nebraska Press, 1995), p. 296.
7. *New York Times*, August 4, 1930.
8. *Ibid.*, May 17, 1931.
9. Dick Bartell and Norman L. Macht, *Rowdy Richard: The Story of Dick Bartell* (Berkeley, CA: North Atlantic Books, 1987), pp. 152–153; *New York Times*, May 31, 1932.

10. Alexander, *McGraw*, pp. 307–308; *New York Times*, June 4, 1932.

11. *New York Times*, June 17, 1932; *Chicago Tribune*, June 17, 1932.

Chapter 4

1. NBHF, Hubbell clipping file, Bill McCullough, "The Meal Ticket," *The Saturday Evening Post*, July 7, 1937, p. 2.

2. *Ibid.*, Joe O'Day, "Screwball Had Cards Eating Out of His Hand" (no further date provided).

3. *Ibid.*, Jimmy Powers, *New York Daily News*, July 3, 1933, sports editor's column reporting the July 2 game.

4. *Ibid.*, clipping not otherwise identified.

5. *Ibid.*, McCullough, "The Meal Ticket," p. 5.

6. *Ibid.*, Joe O'Day, "Screwball."

7. *New York Times*, July 3, 1933.

8. *Ibid.*

9. *New York Herald-Tribune*, July 3, 1933.

10. *New York Times*, July 3, 1933.

11. *New York Herald-Tribune*, July 3, 1933.

12. *St. Louis Post-Dispatch*, July 3, 1933.

13. Peter Williams, *When the Giants Were Giants: Bill Terry and the Golden age of New York Baseball* (Chapel Hill, NC: Algonquin Books), p. 145.

Chapter 5

1. *New York Times*, July 23, 1933.

2. *Ibid.*, August 2, 1933.

3. *Ibid.*

4. *Ibid.*, August 27, 1933.

5. *Ibid.*, September 14, 1933.

Chapter 6

1. *New York Times*, September 30, 1933.

2. *New York Herald-Tribune*, October 4, 1933.

3. *Washington Post*, October 4, 1933.

4. *New York Times*, January 5, 1934.

5. *Ibid.*

6. Bill James and Rob Neyer, *Guide to Pitchers* (New York: Simon & Schuster, 2004), p. 249.

7. *Tulsa Tribune*, October 7, 1933. Carl's phrase expressed to catcher Mancuso, descriptive of the screwballs he intended to throw to pinch hitter Bolton.

8. *New York Times*, October 11, 1933.

9. *Ibid.*, December 18, 1933. Nationwide jury of sports editors and writers.

Chapter 7

1. *Daily Oklahoman*, October 20, 1933.

2. *Lincoln County Republican*, October 18, 1933.

3. *Ibid.*, October 4, 1933.

4. *Tulsa Tribune*, October 20, 1933.

5. *Daily Oklahoman*, October 27, 1933.

6. *Ibid.*, October 19, 1933.

7. *Ibid.*

8. *Ibid.*

9. *Ibid.*

10. A phrase of the day to label a person as unsophisticated.

11. *Daily Oklahoman*, October 21, 1933.

12. *Tulsa Tribune*, October 1, 1936.

13. *Daily Oklahoman*, October 4, 1933.

Chapter 8

1. *New York Times*, July 11, 1934.

2. *Ibid.*

3. *Ibid.*; NBHF, Hubbell clipping file, Sid Keener column, *St. Louis Star-Times*, May 20, 1937.

4. *Ibid.*

5. *Ibid.*, May 10, 1981.

6. NBHF, Hubbell clipping file, Hal Bock, AP, July 19, 1984.

7. *Ibid.*, Bob Broeg, "King Carl," p. 3.

8. *Ibid.*, McCullough, "The Meal Ticket," p. 8.

9. *Ibid.*, Quentin Reynolds, "I Can Hit Pretty Good," p. 1.

10. Donald Honig, *Baseball When the Grass Was Real* (Lincoln: University of Nebraska Press, 1993), p. 35.

11. Paul Green, *Forgotten Fields* (Waupaca, WI: Parker Publications, 1984), p. 137.

12. *Chicago Tribune*, July 18, 1934.

13. *New York Times*, July 27, 1934.

14. *Ibid.*, August 30, 1934.

15. *Chicago Tribune*, August 30, 1934.
16. *New York Times*, interview, May 10, 1981.
17. C.C. Alexander, *Breaking the Slump: Baseball in the Depression Era* (New York: Columbia University Press, 2002), pp. 88–89.

Chapter 9

1. *New York Times*, April 17, 1935.
2. *Chicago Tribune*, May 26, 1935.
3. *New York Times*, July 22, 1935.
4. *Ibid.*, September 16, 1935.
5. *Ibid.*

Chapter 10

1. NBHF, Hubbell clipping file, Broeg, "King Carl: Superb Mound Craftsman," p. 1.
2. C.M. Black, *Scribner's Magazine* (April 1939): pp. 23–28.
3. *Literary Digest*, September 26, 1936.
4. NBHF, Hubbell clipping file, Joe Duff, *Sporting Comment*, July 1969.
5. Walter M. Langford, comp., *Legends of Baseball* (South Bend IN: Diamond Comunications, 1987), p. 107.
6. B. Werber, and C.P. Rogers, *Memories of a Ballplayer* (Lincoln: University of Nebraska Press, 2001), p. 125.
7. NBHF, Hubbell clipping file, undated Carl ad with Hubbell's words, either literally or by proxy quoted.
8. Honig, *Baseball When the Grass Was Real*, p. 122.
9. *Ibid.*, p. 128.
10. *Ibid.*, p. 226.
11. Peter Golenbock, *Wrigleyville* (New York: St. Martin's Press, 1999), pp. 258–259.
12. *Ibid.*, p. 241.
13. NBHF, Hubbell clipping file, "I Won 24 Straight." In his exact words, Carl said he could throw a screwball "with ease" due to the twist his arm had developed.
14. Honig, *Baseball When the Grass Was Real*, p. 123.
15. C.M. Black, *Scribner's Magazine* (April 1938): p. 23.
16. NBHF, Hubbell clipping file, Reynolds, "I Can Hit Pretty Good," p. 3.
17. *New York Times*, May 10, 1981.

18. NBHF, Hubbell clipping file, Joe King, "Diamond Dossier Carl Hubbell," p. 1.
19. *Ibid.*, Sid Keener, "Carl Hubbell Reveals His Secrets," p. 1.
20. *Ibid.*, "I Won 24 Straight," p. 2.
21. *New York Times*, June 7, 1999.
22. *Ibid.*

Chapter 11

1. *New York Times*, July 22, 1936.
2. *Ibid.*, July 27, 1936, Debringer description.
3. *Ibid.*, August 16, 1936.
4. *Ibid.*
5. *Ibid.*, August 31, 1936.
6. *Ibid.*, October 1, 1936.
7. *New York Herald-Tribune*, October 1, 1936.
8. NBHF Hubbell clipping file, Alan Gould column, "Meeker Master." No other identification.
9. *New York Times*, October 5, 1936.

Chapter 12

1. *Daily Oklahoman*, April 8, 1937.
2. *New York Times*, April 8, 1937.
3. A borrowing from Clifford Odets's play, *Waiting for Lefty*.
4. The chapter title was borrowed from Clifford Odets's play. Clifford Odets (1906–1963) succeeded as a New York City playwright while young. He is best remembered for *Waiting for Lefty* (1935) and *Golden Boy* (1937). Later he migrated to Hollywood, serving as script writer and movie director.
5. *New York Times*, June 1, 1937.
6. *Ibid.*, June 19, 1937.
7. *Ibid.*, August 1, 1937.

Chapter 13

1. *New York Times*, April 12, 1938.
2. *Ibid.*, June 27, 1938.
3. *Ibid.*, July 10, 1938.
4. *Ibid.*, July 25, 1938.
5. *Ibid.*
6. *Ibid.*, August 3, 1938.
7. *Ibid.*, August 19, 1938.

8. *Ibid.*, April 1, 1939.
9. *Ibid.*, May 10, 1939.
10. *Ibid.*, June 5, 1939.
11. *Ibid.*, July 26, 1939.

Chapter 14

1. NBHF, Hubbell clipping file, a *Sporting News* reprint, January 18, 1940.
2. *Ibid.*, a clipping, Jack Singer column, Miami, Florida, February 17, 1941.
3. *New York Times*, August 7, 1941.
4. *Ibid.*, September 15, 1941.
5. *Ibid.*, September 23, 1941.
6. *Ibid.*, September 4, 1942.
7. *The Sporting News*, December 9, 1943.
8. *New York Times*, November 30, 1943.

Chapter 15

1. NBHF, Hubbell clipping file, San Francisco Giants news release, May 31, 1975.
2. *Ibid.*, Fitzgerald, "King Carl," p. 8.
3. *Ibid.*
4. *Ibid.*
5. *Ibid.*, Malcolm Moran column, the *New York Times*, July 17, 1986, reprint.
6. *Sports Illustrated*, Dec. 7, 1970.

Chapter 16

1. The title page quotation is the most familiar English translation of the title of Marcel Proust's famous novel, *À la recherche du temps perdu* (1913). Marcel Proust (1871–1922) was one of the most important contributors to twentieth-century French literature, writing several other well-known works in addition to the *Remembrance*.
2. Words quoted from the death certificate for Sue Hubbell as the cause of her death. Vital Records Division, P.O. Box 53551, Oklahoma City, Oklahoma 73152.
3. NBHF, Hubbell clipping file, *Meeker Herald*, May 18, 1978.
4. *Ibid.*, *The Sporting News*, July 27, 1974.
5. *Ibid.*, Tom Fitzpatrick column, *Arizona Republic*, August 6, 1955.
6. *Ibid.*, Seattle, July 17, 1979, no other identification.
7. *Ibid.*, Dick Draper column, 1985, *Times Sports Writer*, no other identification.
8. *Ibid.*, Tom Fitzpatrick, *Arizona Republic*, August 6, 1985.
9. *Ibid.*, Hal Bodley column, *USA Today*, July 9, 1984.
10. *Ibid.*, Dick Draper column, 1985.
11. *Ibid.*, Wayne Coffey, *Daily Sports News*, May 27, 1987, another identification.
12. *Ibid.*, *The Sporting News*, March 24, 1986.
13. John Ferguson, *Tulsa World*, September 27, 1980.
14. *Ibid.*, Tom Fitzpatrick, *Arizona Republic*, August 6, 1985.
15. *Ibid.*, *Tulsa World*, June 3, 1984, John Ferguson column.
16. *Ibid.*, *Washington Post*, November 28, 1988.

Chapter Sources
(Annotated)

Chapter 1

The first source is *The Archives of the National Baseball Hall of Fame*, Cooperstown, New York (hereinafter referred to as NBHF). The archives are an essential source for Hubbell study with a store of information available. The information deals primarily with Hubbell's pitching career. A portion of the available data focuses on Carl's farm directorship, and another part of the information relates to his years as a retiree. The archives' information sources are predominantly newspaper clippings. Some of these are specifically dated with author name; some are without identification. Journal articles are also a part of the archives. Scattered within the archives are Hubbell's largely anecdotal recollections of his early life.

The second source is the sports pages of newspapers from most of the cities where Hubbell served. The newspapers included the *Ardmore Ardmorite*, *Daily Oklahoman*, *Fort Worth Star-Telegram*, *Toronto Globe*, *Dallas Morning News*, and *San Antonio Express*. The most frequently relied upon were the *Daily Oklahoman* and *The Sporting News*. The sports pages provided interesting comments, observations, and reports on particular games. *The Sporting News* printed the box scores of all minor league clubs that provided the necessary data.

Two books are the third source:

Burke, Bob, Kenny A. Franks, and Royce Parr. *Glory Days of Summer*. Oklahoma City: Oklahoma Heritage Association, 1999. Covers minor league baseball in its heyday in the state of Oklahoma.

Langford, Walter M. *Legends of Baseball*. South Bend, IN: Diamond Communications, 1987. Provides a chapter on the author's interview with Hubbell.

Three particular articles are the fourth source. They are as follows:

Blaisdell, Lowell L. "The Cobb-Speaker Scandal: Exonerated, But Probably Guilty." *Nine* XV, No. 2 (Spring 2005): 57–66.

_____. "Legends as an Expression of Baseball Memory." *Journal of Sport History* XIX (Winter 1992): 227–243.

Mullins, H. "The Impact of Rural Culture on a Baseball Career: Carl Hubbell of Meeker, Oklahoma." *Nine* XII, No. 3 (Fall 2003): 102–114.

Reference publications are the fifth and final source. They are as follows:

Total Baseball, 1989 ed.

The Baseball Encyclopedia, 1979 ed.

Numerous references to these volumes on players' records appear in later sections. Other editions provide the same data, but at different pages.

Minor League Baseball Stars, Vol. 3 (SABR, Cleveland, OH, 1992), Claude (Lefty) Thomas, Western League, 1925, Des Moines, pp. 178–179.

Other than these skimpy sources, the Oklahoman's minor league career has been almost completely overlooked.

Chapter 2

The material in this chapter comes from five types of sources.

Sports pages of various newspapers from July through September, 1928, are the primary sources. For New York City, the primary newspaper consulted for this year and later was the *New York Times*. On a lesser scale, the *New York Herald-Tribune* was also used. The *St. Louis Globe-Democrat* and the *Chicago Tribune* were used in the case of particular games.

The National Baseball Hall of Fame (NBHF) was also very helpful. It contains Hubbell's pitching log that provides dates, run, hits, wins, losses, etc., for each game in which he appeared in 1928 and after. Also from this source are Hubbell's own recollections from his first days as a Giants pitcher.

Three books provided information for this chapter:

Alexander, Charles C. *John McGraw*. New York: Viking Press, 1988. This was especially useful.

Langford, *Legends of Baseball*. This has much on Hubbell's old-age thoughts on McGraw.

Ritter, Lawrence S. *The Glory of Their Times*. New York: The Macmillan Co., 1966.

The Baseball Encyclopedia, 1979 ed. References to Hubbell's 1928 pitching statistics.

The Internet source ProQuest has references complimentary to the new Giants hurler, confirming the comments of sports writers in printed newspapers.

Chapter 3

Once again, sources used fall into the categories of newspaper reports; the National Baseball Hall of Fame (NBHF), Hubbell clipping file; and books.

For newspaper reports, the most important source is the *New York Times*. The years 1929–32 are covered by this source and include descriptions of particular games in which Hubbell pitched.

NBHF, Hubbell clipping file, has the pitching logs for the years examined in this chapter. It also contains the subject's recollection of instances in which McGraw reprimanded him. Finally, from this source was an article that gave Hubbell's recall of a few of the games covered in this period.

Books that were especially helpful in providing background are as follows:

Alexander, Charles C. *Breaking the Slump: Baseball in the Depression Era*. New York: Columbia University Press, 2002.

Bartell, Dick, and Norman L. Macht. *Rowdy Richard: The Story of Dick Bartell*. Berkeley, CA: North Atlantic Books, 1987.

The Baseball Encyclopedia has Hubbell's season-long pitching categories year by year.

Stein, Fred. *Under Coogan's Bluff*. Glenshaw, PA: Automated Graphics, 1978.

Chapter 4

There are four main sources for the information in Chapter 4.

The contents of this chapter deal with Hubbell's amazing pitching feats in the first half of 1933; newspapers are the first and predominant sources. The *New York Times* is most cited. Also there are a few references to the *St. Louis Post Dispatch*, the *New York Herald-Tribune* and the *Washington Post*.

The National Baseball Hall of Fame (NBHF), Hubbell clipping file, provides Carl's remembrances of the July 2, 1933, game. Also from NBHF are Hubbell's 1933 pitching logs and selections from reportorial observers' thoughts on the game.

Books are the third primary source for this chapter. Foremost is *Under Coogan's Bluff* by Fred Stein, which provides essential data concerning the Giants' 1932-33 off-season trades, as well as important information and data about their playing personnel. Second, there are references to Peter Williams's book, *When the Giants Were Giants*.

Record books are the fourth category of references essential for this chapter because of the unique quality of Hubbell's July 2, 1933, pitched game. The two staples, *The Baseball Encyclopedia* and *Total Baseball*, are cited. *The Complete Baseball Record Book and Baseball Register*, 2002 edition, is also used.

Chapter 5

The chapter deals almost entirely with game action.

The key newspapers whose reports focused on the Giants' performance constitute the prime source. As in Chapter 4 and before, these included the *New York Times*, the *Chicago Tribune*, and the *St. Louis Globe-Democrat*.

To these should be added one reference to Stein's *Under Coogan's Bluff* and two to Jim Kaplan's *Lefty Grove* (2000). In several places, *The Baseball Encyclopedia* (1979) helped with its statistics. To this should be added the *SABR D List and Record Book* (2007), a quite useful and relatively new statistical publication.

Chapter 6

World Series information, assuming access to appropriate newspapers, is easily available for the 1933 World Series, as well as those before and after. For the 1933 Series, the two most informative dailies at that time, the *New York Times* and the *New York Herald-Tribune*, are indispensable, as is the *Washington Post*. Accounts provided by newspapers from other cities usually are not as informative because often they were from AP releases, or the reporters did not have the same sense of involvement as did the New York City and Washington, D.C., scribes. In this series, because of Hubbell's importance to the Giants, the *Tulsa Tribune* and the *Daily Oklahoman* provided useful incidental information here and there.

Likewise, very useful is *The World Series* (New York: The Dial Press, 1976) for its inclusion of all World Series box scores through 1975, along with brief game accounts. Also helpful in shedding light on one aspect of Hubbell's pitching techniques is a quotation from Bill James and Rob Meyer, *Guide to Pitchers* (New York: Simon & Schuster, 2004).

Chapter 7

The sources for this chapter consisted solely of such local newspapers as have survived. The *Daily Oklahoman*, the *Tulsa Tribune* and the *Lincoln County Republican* provided observations of Meeker's most admired citizen. Given the circumstances, they were most informative about the Lincoln County citizenry's familiarity with Hubbell. They also included odds and ends concerning his early life there.

Chapter 8

There were three main sources used for this chapter: the NBHF Hubbell clipping file, newspaper reports, and books. Since the 1934 All-Star Game is the highlight of this season, the data concerning it dominated the source gathering. The NBHF Hubbell clipping file provided a wealth of information. This source includes not only Hubbell's recollections of this feat, but also that of other individual players.

Newspapers used for the All-Star Game information were the *New York Times* and the *St. Louis Globe-Democrat*. The *Los Angeles Times* was also useful.

Books were as follows:

Alexander, C.C. *Breaking the Slump: Baseball in the Depression Era.* New York: Columbia University Press, 2002.

Honig, D. *Baseball When the Grass Was Real.* New York: Berkley Publishing Corporation, 1977.

Langford, W. *Legends of Baseball.* South Bend, IN: Diamond Communications, 1987.

Stein, F. *Under Coogan's Bluff.* Glenshaw, PA: Automated Graphics, 1978.

Needless to say, *The Baseball Encyclopedia* provided important data regarding statistics.

Chapter 9

The core essential sources for this chapter were the same as those for Chapter 8 about the 1934 season: the NBHF Hubbell clipping file, the newspapers regularly relied upon, and *The Baseball Encyclopedia. The Baseball Register* (1948) was also helpful.

The books that were most useful for the 1934 season were again helpful for the 1935 season. Three additional books helped with aspects of this season:

Brown, W. *The Chicago Cubs.* New York: G. Putnam's Sons, 1946.

Creamer, R.W. *Babe.* New York: Simon & Schuster, 1974.

Kaplan, J. *Lefty Grove: American Original.* Cleveland, OH: Society for American Baseball Research (SABR), 2000.

Chapter 10

This chapter was largely concerned with Hubbell the person and Hubbell the mound artist.

Secondary sources by reporters, fellow

players and rivals were helpful in providing observations of Carl's mound skills. Alexander's *Breaking the Slump* and Langford's *Legends of Baseball* were used as before. Also helpful were Bill Werber and C. Paul Rogers, *Memories of a Ballplayer* (Cleveland, OH: SABR, 2001), and Peter Golenbock, *Wrigleyville* (New York: St. Martin's Press, 1999).

The National Baseball Hall of Fame (NBHF) Hubbell clipping file was also helpful in this regard. It offered reporters' assessments along with the principal's recollections of batters to whom he pitched. For the references to Elroy Face (on page 225), see the *Biographical Dictionary of American Sport*, 3rd ed. (New York: Greenwood Press, 1987), p. 174.

Chapter 11

The chief sources for the following regular season games comprise the following:
The New York Times and, when the Giants were playing the Chicago Cubs or the St. Louis Cardinals, the *Chicago Tribune* and the *St. Louis Globe-Democrat*.

Occasionally helpful were:
Alexander, *Breaking the Slump*.
Stein, *Under Coogan's Bluff*.
Williams, *When the Giants Were Giants*.
Helpful in an instance or two were:
Bartell and Macht, *Rowdy Richard*.
The Baseball Reader (New York: Bonanza Books, 1986).
John Lardner, "The Unbelievable Babe Herman," p. 215.

Chapter 12

In this section on the 1937 season, the primary sources comprised the NBHF, Hubbell clipping file, for article selections and from different articles already quoted but usually on pages other than here, on his 1937 pitching log, and the appropriate newspaper dates for games played. The newspapers included the *New York Times*, the *Chicago Tribune*, and the *Daily Oklahoman*. Among secondary sources used are:
Alexander, *Breaking the Slump*.
Stein, *Under Coogan's Bluff*.
Williams, *When the Giants Were Giants*.
Scribner's Magazine (April 1938), p. 23.

Bartell and Macht, *Rowdy Richard*.
The record books cited included *The Baseball Encyclopedia* (1979 ed.), *The SABR Baseball List and Record Book* (2007 ed.); and *The World Series*, 1936 series.

Occasional NBHF, Hubbell clipping file, passages from reporters who interviewed were germane. With regard to the 1936 World Series, most information came from the *New York Times* and the *New York Herald-Tribune* accounts of games.

Chapter 13

The primary sources comprised the NBHF, Hubbell clipping file, including two or three article references, and the principal's 1938–39 pitching log. To these, *The Baseball Encyclopedia* (1979 ed.) should be added.

Newspaper use consisted only of the *New York Times* and, for a couple of games, the *Chicago Tribune*. As the Giants' team fortunes, and Hubbell's skill as a hurler, both dwindled, the importance of supplemental newspaper sources diminished.

Occasional references to book sources at the secondary level were helpful. These included:
Alexander, *Breaking the Slump*.
Bartell and Macht, *Rowdy Richard*.
James, Bill. *The New Baseball Historical Abstract*. New York: The Free Press, 2001, p. 388.
Langford, *Legends of Baseball*.
Murphy, James. *The Gabby Hartnett Story*. Smithtown, NY: New York Exposition Press, 1983, p. 37.
The Sporting News.
Stein, *Under Coogan's Bluff*.

Chapter 14

With Hubbell's pitching career drawing to a close, comparisons of his performance with others loom large. Thus, references to *The Baseball Encyclopedia* (1979 ed.), and the *SABR Lists and Record Book* (2007 ed.) are frequent. Of secondary importance are several references from the NBHF, Hubbell clipping file material. Among secondary works, for incidental information Alexander, *Breaking the Slump*, and Stein, *Under Coogan's Bluff*, were used. For basic data on World War II baseball, Charles Alexander, *Our Game: An American Baseball History* (New York: Henry Holt and Co., 1999) helped. By Hubbell's closeout year as a pitcher, the *New York Times* sufficed.

Chapter 15

Thanks to the National Baseball Hall of Fame archivists who preserved a variety of articles bearing on Carl Hubbell's later life, his second career as farm director can be pieced together. Much of the material in the chapter stems from this source.

Early in the material, there are incidental references to familiar secondary sources. Occasionally also there are newspaper references, these coming from the *New York Times*, a few Oklahoma newspapers, and *The Sporting News*. Finally, because of the references to Hubbell's pitching feats, *Total Baseball, The SABR List and Record Book,* and *The World Series* were consulted.

Chapter 16

To a very large degree, the material on Carl Hubbell's life comes from the newspaper clippings the National Baseball Hall of Fame collected in its archives.

There are a few important exceptions: the *Shawnee News-Star,* April 2 and 4, 1967, and the *Meeker Herald,* April 6, 1967, provide the information on Sue Hubbell's decease, along with the death certificate from the Department of Vital Statistics, Oklahoma City, Oklahoma. Also useful is a copy of the Vernon Markwell eulogy of Carl Hubbell from the Lincoln County Historical Society, Chandler, Oklahoma, although this is also available in the NBHF materials.

The *Daily Oklahoman,* June 9, 1986, was helpful, as well as the *Washington Post,* November 28, 1988, for its death notice on Carl Hubbell, ending with the words "into the folklore of the nation."

Bibliography

Alexander, Charles C. *Breaking the Slump: Baseball in the Depression Era.* New York: Columbia University Press, 2002.

_____. *John McGraw.* Lincoln: University of Nebraska Press, 1995.

Bartell, Dick, and Norman Macht. *Rowdy Richard.* Berkeley, CA: North Atlantic Books, 1987.

Black, C.M. *Scribner's Magazine.* (April, 1939.)

Bock, H. Associated Press. (July 19, 1984.)

Bodley, H. *USA Today.* (July 9, 1984.)

Broeg, B. "King Carl: Superb Mound Craftsman." *The Sporting News.* (July 19, 1928.)

Burke, Bob, Kenny Arthur Franks, and Royse Parr. *Glory Days of Summer.* Oklahoma City: Oklahoma Heritage Association, 1999.

Chicago Tribune. (June 4, 1929; June 17, 1932; July 18, 1934; August 30, 1934; May 26, 1935.)

Coffee, W. *Daily Sports News.* (May 27, 1987.)

Daily Oklahoman. (July 5, 1925; August 2, 1925; October 4, 1933; October 19, 1933; October 20, 1933; October 21, 1933; October 27, 1933; April 8, 1937.)

The Dallas Morning News. (June 13, 1928; June 17, 1928.)

Draper, D. *New York Times, Sports.* (1985.)

Duff, J. *Sporting Comment.* (July, 1969.)

Ferguson, J. *Tulsa World.* (September 27, 1980; June 3, 1984.)

Fitzgerald, E. "King Carl." *Daily Oklahoman,* p. 8. (October 20, 1933.)

_____. "King Carl." *The Sports Special,* pp. 6, 8. (May, 1953.)

_____. *Shawnee News-Star.* (April 2, 1967.)

Fitzpatrick, T. *The Arizona Republic.* (August 6, 1955.)

Golenbock, Peter. *Wrigleyville.* New York: St. Martin's Griffin, 1999.

Gould, A. "Meeker Master." (HOF archives)

Honig, Donald. *Baseball When the Grass Was Real: Baseball from the Twenties to the Forties Told by the Men Who Played It.* Lincoln: University of Nebraska Press, 1993.

Hubbell, C. "I Won 24 Straight." *New York Herald Tribune.* (July 11, 1937.)

James, Bill, and Rob Neyer. *Guide to Pitchers.* New York: Simon & Schuster, 2004.

Keener, S. "Carl Hubbell Reveals His Secrets." *St. Louis Star-Times.*

_____. Column. *St. Louis Star-Times.* (May 20, 1937.)

King, J. "Diamond Dossier Carl Hubbell." (HOF archives)

Langford, Walter M., comp. *Legends of Baseball.* South Bend, IN: Diamond Communications, 1987.

Lardner, John. *The Unbelievable Babe Herman.* In C. Einstein (ed.). *The Baseball Reader.* New York: Bonanza Books, 1986, p. 215.

Lincoln County Republican. (October 4, 1933; October 18, 1933.)

Literary Digest. (September 26, 1936.)

Los Angeles Times. (September 23, 1928.)

Marshall, K.M. "Day the All Stars Bit the Dust." *Oklahoma Record News.* (February, 1984.)

McCullough, B. "The Meal Ticket." *Saturday Evening Post,* p. 2. (July 3, 1937.)

Moran, M. Article. *New York Times,* reprint. (July 17, 1986.)

New York Herald-Tribune. (August 6, 1928; July 3, 1933; October 4, 1933; October 1, 1936.)

The New York Times. (July 3, 1933; July 23,

1933; August 2, 1933; August 27, 1933; September 14, 1933; September 30, 1933; October 11, 1933; December 18, 1933; January 5, 1934; July 11, 1934; July 27, 1934; August 30, 1934; April 17, 1935; July 22, 1935; September 16, 1935; July 22, 1936; July 27, 1936; August 16, 1936; August 31, 1936; October 1, 1936; October 5, 1936; April 8, 1937; June 1, 1937; June 19, 1937; August 1, 1937; April 12, 1938; June 27, 1938; July 10, 1938; July 25, 1938; August 3, 1938; August 19, 1938; April 1, 1939; May 10, 1939; June 5, 1939; July 26, 1939; May 10, 1981; June 7, 1999.)

O'Day, Joe. "Screwball Had Cards Eating Out of His Hand." *Saturday Evening Post.* (July 7, 1937.)

Odets, Clifford. *Waiting for Lefty.* An original stage production, 1-act, first performed on March 26, 1935. New York, 1935.

Powers, J. Sports Editor's Column. *New York Daily News.* (July 3, 1933.)

Proust, Marcel. *À la recherche du temps perdu*; translated, *Remembrance of Things Past.* Published in France, 1922–1931, 1913.

Reynolds, Quentin. "I Can Hit Pretty Good." *Colliers*, p. 3. (July 24, 1937.)

Ritter, Lawrence. *The Glory of Their Times.* (Collier Books.) New York: Macmillan, 1966.

St. Louis Post Dispatch. (July 3, 1933.)

San Antonio Express. (March 18, 1928.)

Shawnee News-Star. (April 2, 1967.)

Singer, J. Column, Miami, FL. *Sporting News.* (February 17, 1941.)

The Sporting News. (July 15, 1926; December 9, 1943; July 27, 1974, March 24, 1986.)

Sports Illustrated. (December 7, 1970.)

Tulsa Tribune. (October 7, 1933; October 20, 1933; October 1, 1936.)

Washington Post. (October 4, 1933; November 28, 1988.)

Werber, Bill, and C. Paul Rogers. *Memories of a Ballplayer.* Lincoln: University of Nebraska Press, 2001.

Williams, Peter. *When the Giants Were Giants: Bill Terry and the Golden Age of New York Baseball.* Chapel Hill, NC: Algonquin Books, 1994.

Index